IMAGES
of America

YARDLEY

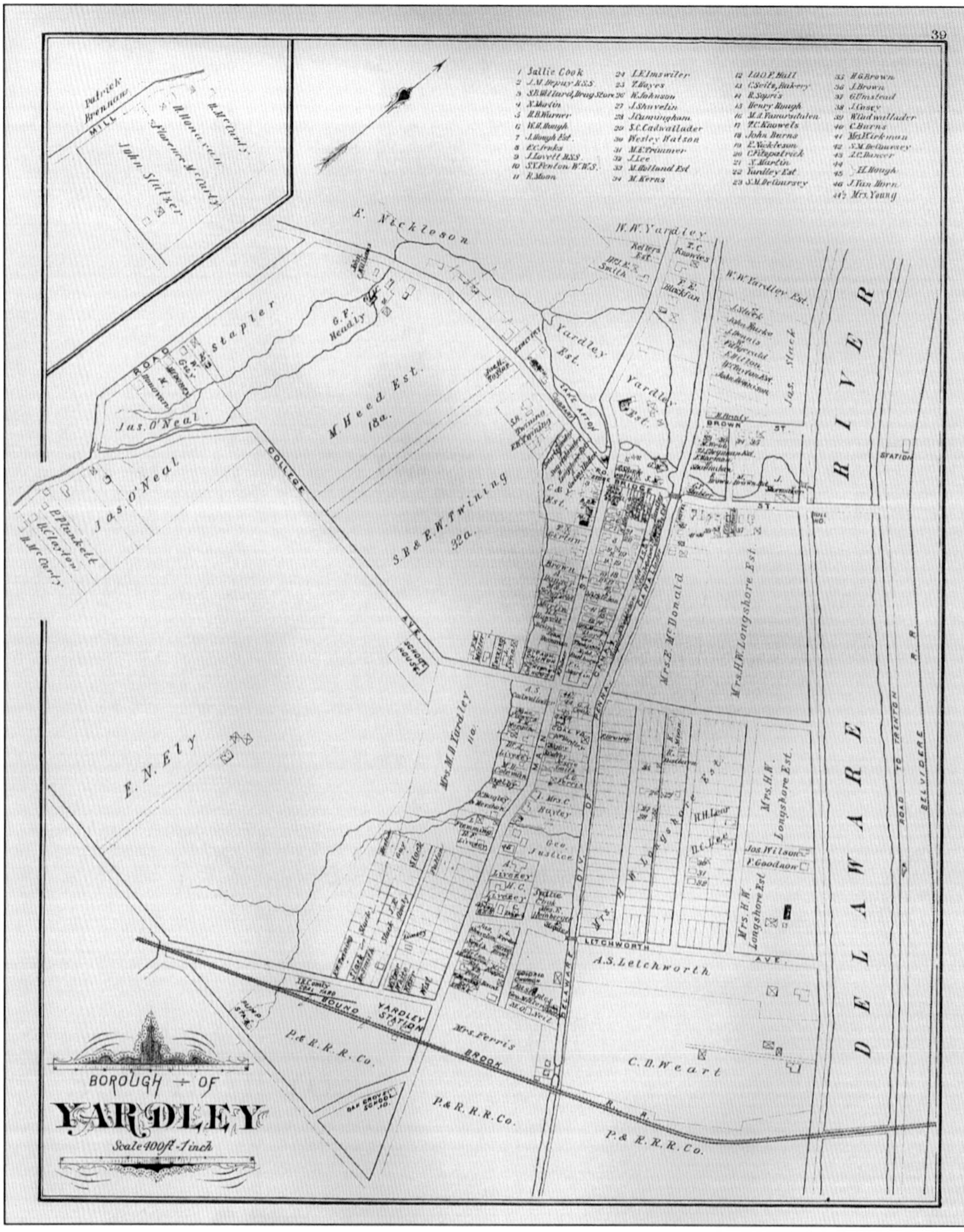

E. P. Noll's 1891 map of Yardley.

IMAGES
of America

YARDLEY

Vince Profy

ARCADIA
PUBLISHING

ISBN 978-0-7385-0072-0

Published by Arcadia Publishing
Charleston, South Carolina

Printed in the United States of America

Library of Congress Catalog Card Number: 00100308

For all general information contact Arcadia Publishing at:
Telephone 843-853-2070
Fax 843-853-0044
E-mail sales@arcadiapublishing.com
For customer service and orders:
Toll-Free 1-888-313-2665

Visit us on the Internet at www.arcadiapublishing.com

Contents

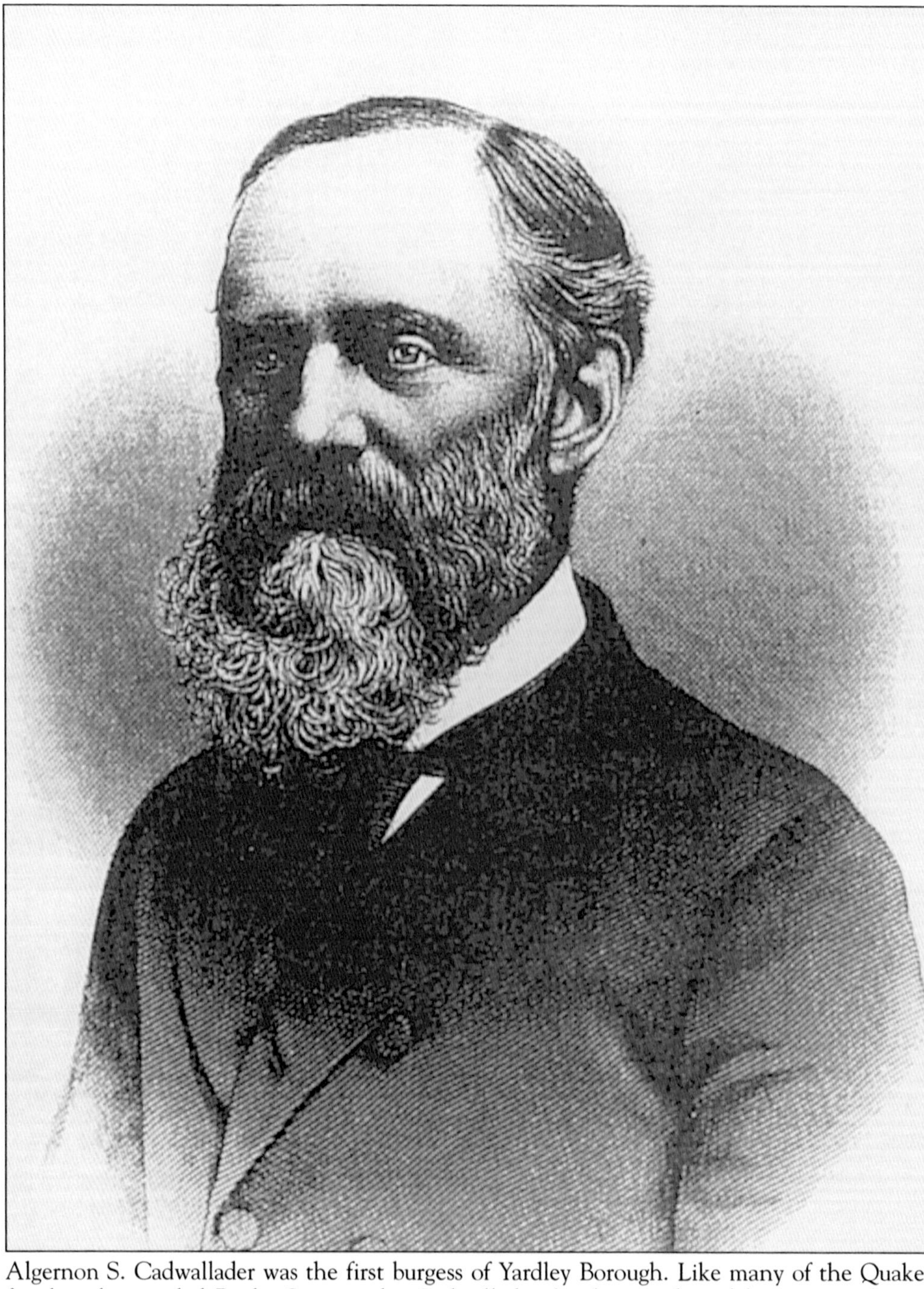

Algernon S. Cadwallader was the first burgess of Yardley Borough. Like many of the Quaker families that settled Bucks County, the Cadwallader family was shaped by meeting house, business partnerships, and marriage. When Algernon was elected burgess in 1895, he was the most influential man in the village. Through his mother, Susan Stapler, he was related to the Yardley family who settled in the area in 1682. A.S. Cadwallader was part of a close, interconnected community that was guided by family relationships, religious convictions, and economic interests. These values would play an important role in the history of Yardley.

INTRODUCTION

"In accordance with provisions of an act of incorporation," begins the first entry in a frayed, brown leather-covered minute book that records the proceedings of the first Yardley Borough Council. On March 4, 1895, at the office of Edward Twining, the newly elected officials, including six council members, were qualified by Algernon S. Cadwallader, the first burgess (today's mayor). In the next few years, officials and residents would have a full agenda as Yardley defined its new independence.

In 1995, Yardley Borough celebrated its Centennial. Throughout the year, the Yardley Historical Association solicited donations and loans of Yardley photographs. These added to a collection begun in 1982 when the town celebrated the tri-centennial of its settlement. That collection is the basis of this book and tells the unique history of Yardley. In the 18th century, a ferry and mill marked the crossroads beginnings of Yardleyville, in Makefield Township. The village was named after one of the many English Quakers who responded to William Penn's offer of land in Pennsylvania. In 1682, William Yardley and his family settled on a 500-acre plantation called "Prospect Farm," in Makefield Township. By 1703 all members of the William Yardley family had died. William's nephew Thomas arrived from England and soon purchased Prospect Farm. He obtained the right to operate a ferry on the river in 1722. Several years later he purchased a gristmill and an additional 500 acres. Thomas and his wife, Ann Biles, moved into a new home near the mill in 1728 called "Lakeside." A good businessman, Thomas expanded the gristmill, built a sawmill, and a riverside tavern. Roads were established to Four Lanes End (Langhorne,) Newtown, Kirkbride's Ferry, and Fallsington Meeting. Thomas Yardley died in 1803, but his mills, tavern, and ferry were the beginnings of the village of Yardleyville.

In about 1805, Cornelius Vansant began to buy property in what would become Yardley Borough. Along the river he constructed a large, stone, Federal-style mansion known as "Lanrick Manor." In 1832 the Delaware Division of the Pennsylvania Canal was completed. The canal transformed many of the small villages along its route. In Yardley, Aaron LaRue built a canalside store; across the street was a hotel known as the LaFarge House. Cortland Yardley built three row houses with first floor shops, known as "Quality Row." New homes and businesses were constructed on Main and Canal Streets. A coal and lumber yard was established along the canal.

By the mid-19th century, Yardleyville had grown into the largest village in Lower Makefield Township. An 1876 map shows many of the homes and businesses in the downtown area, including the Continental Hotel, druggist, butcher, blacksmith shops, wheelwright shops, harness shop, lumberyard, and several stores. The Union Meeting House was on West Afton Avenue and the Friends Meeting House was on Main Street. The Sons of Temperance had a large hall on South Main Street.

During this period, William Schively published the *Village Luminary*. Schively, originally a grocer, assumed the role of town booster. His editorials promoted business growth, heralded the coming of the railroad, and agitated for the creation of a borough. The railroad was completed in 1876, the year that Schively died and the *Luminary* ceased publication. And the railroad, as Schively predicted, stimulated business growth and led to the construction of new homes. Between 1870 and 1900, a variety of Victorian-style homes were built on South Main Street and West Afton Avenue. Other homes were enlarged and remodeled. The name of the village and railroad station, Yardleyville, was changed to Yardley to avoid confusion with Yardville, NJ. In 1897, the line had become part of the Reading system. By 1930 the Yardley yard included the 1876 station and waiting booth, a water pump, scale, freight house, switching tower, cattleshute, coal trestle, and electric substation.

A group of residents filed a petition and survey map with the Bucks County Court of Quarter Sessions in 1894. The map outlined the proposed boundaries of a new borough. The signers included most of the villagers and shopkeepers living in town. The following year, voters went to Jonathan Shoemaker's Hotel and elected a slate of local officials. Council rooms and a lock-up were constructed on Canal Street. During the next five years, borough council would pass a series of ordinances aimed at modernizing the village and moving it into the next century. Main Street was graded and paved, sidewalks and street lamps were installed, and telephone and electric lines were strung. A Fire Company was established, and in 1900 streetcar tracks were laid in town.

Yardley did not change significantly between 1900 and 1940. A new Borough Hall was constructed on Main Street and more homes were built between the canal and river. Many families continued operating the local businesses they had owned for decades. Leedom, Cadwallader, Beener, Dilliplane, Twining, and Eastburn are a few business names recognized by generations of local residents. Suburban development after WWII and the construction of Interstate 95 in 1956 accelerated changes to the small town. Shopping centers and franchise stores competed with Yardley's small "mom and pop" shopping district. The farmland that surrounded the borough filled with subdivisions.

During the 1995 Centennial, Yardley residents celebrated their past and looked forward to the future. In December, a time capsule containing historic and contemporary photographs was buried at Borough Hall. Mayor Edward Johnson spoke for the community when he expressed the hope that when the capsule is recovered, "the Borough of Yardley will still be a small community of people who work together, help each other, and love one another."

On behalf of the Yardley Historical Association, I would like to thank all the current and former residents of Yardley and Lower Makefield who shared stories and contributed photographs to this project. My personal thanks to all those who tolerated my interviews, phone calls, and requests for photographs. And finally I would like to give a special thanks to Susan Taylor, who contributed extensive research and editorial assistance, and my wife, Diane, for her constant support.

—Vince Profy
Rivermawr, Yardley, PA

One

THE EARLY VILLAGE

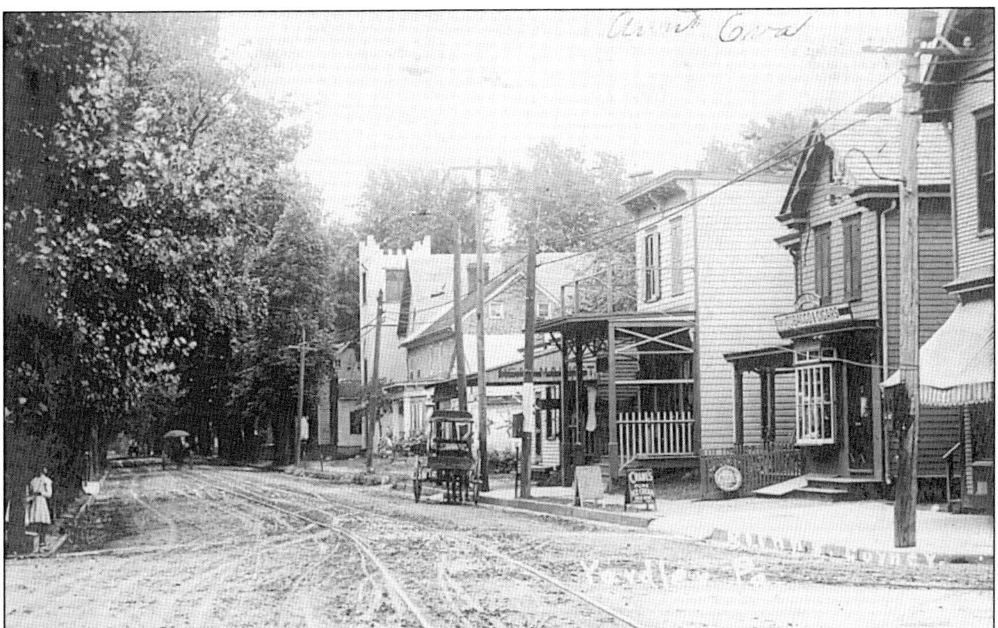

"Blinn's Corner, Yardley, Pa" is a photo postcard view of the southwest corner of Main Street from Afton Avenue taken by Doylestown photographer Linford R. Craven in the early 1900s. The photograph is rich in detail and captures Yardley in transition from a 19th century village to a modern 20th century borough. Blinn's Tobacco and Cigar store is the first full building on the right. Outside the store, a street sign advertises Crane's Pure Ice Cream. Notice the electric poles and trolley tracks, which came to Yardley in 1900. The white tower in the background is the old Methodist Church. The small child on the left and the buggy moving down the center of the street add a touch of life to the sleepy little village.

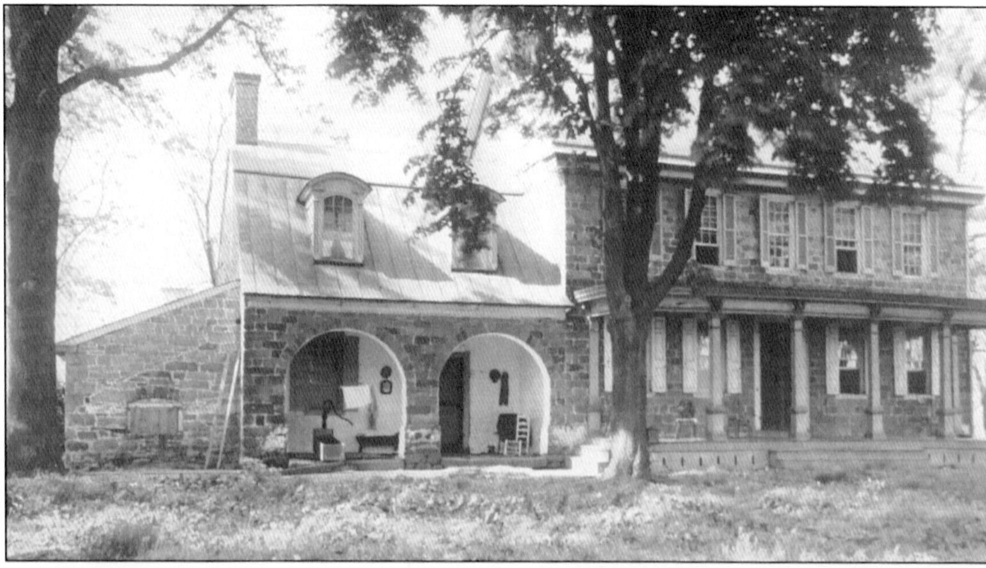

In 1682 William Yardley and his family settled on Prospect Farm, a 500-acre plantation in Lower Makefield Township. The entire family died of smallpox in the early 1700s. His nephew, Thomas, purchased the property in 1710. For generations, members of the Yardley and Cadwallader family owned the property. During the early part of the 20th century, it was the McCormick Duck Farm.

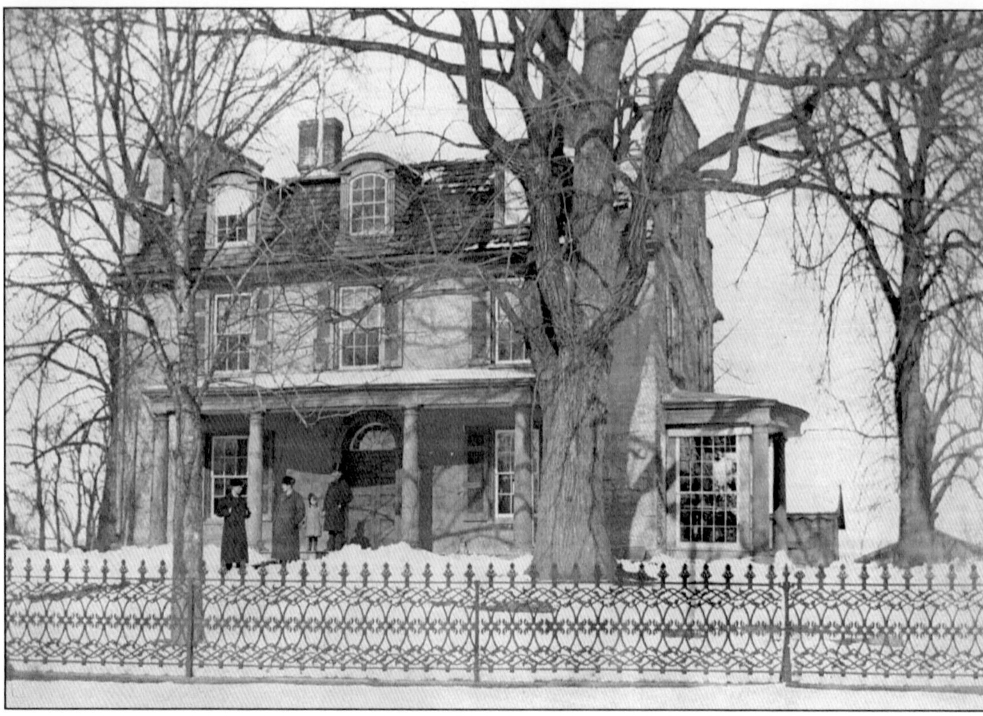

Thomas Yardley purchased land and a gristmill along Brock Creek in what became Yardley Borough. In 1728, he began to build "Lakeside," designed in the Georgian style. In 1830, his descendants added the stepped gables. Pictured in the *c.* 1885 photograph is Algernon S. Cadwallader and three of his children, Augustus, Sidney and Helen.

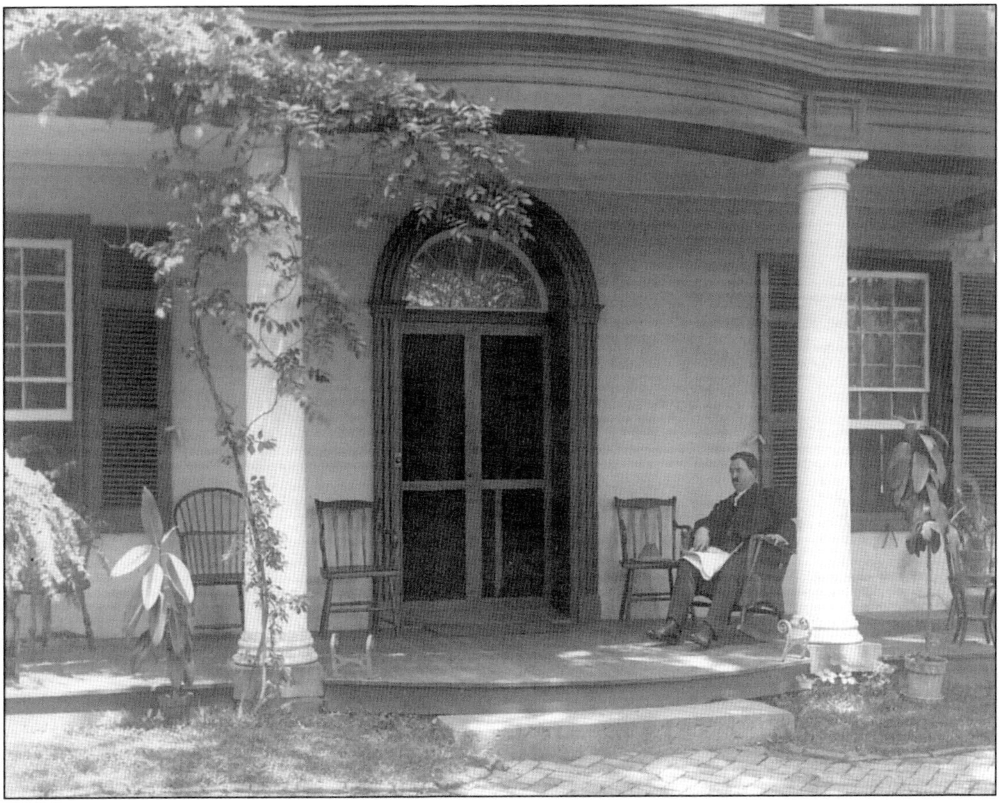

Augustus J. Cadwallader (1863–1949) relaxes on the porch of Lakeside in the early 1900s. In 1894 he married Marie Franklin; they had one daughter, Gwendolyn. Like the other members of his family, Augustus was active in the community, serving as president of Borough Council from about 1910 to 1916.

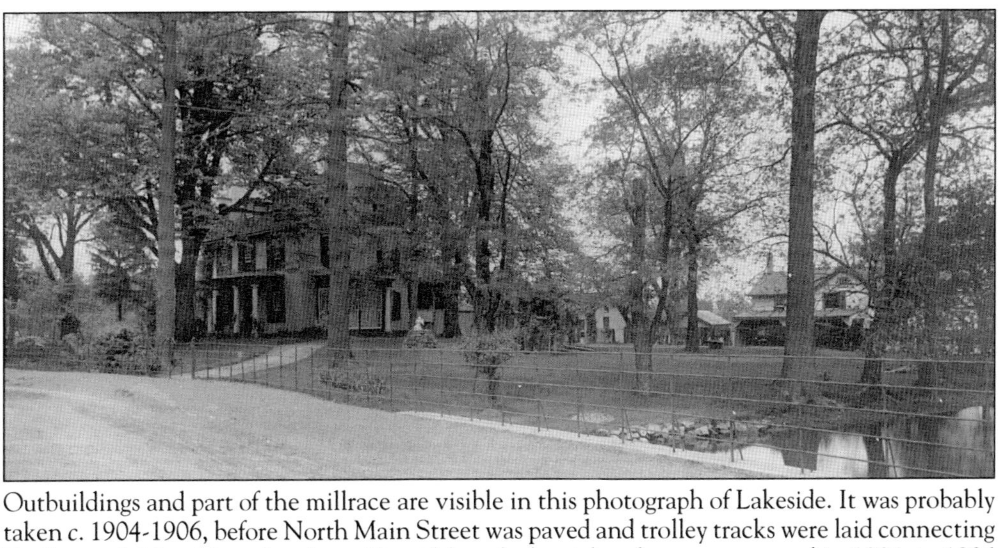

Outbuildings and part of the millrace are visible in this photograph of Lakeside. It was probably taken c. 1904-1906, before North Main Street was paved and trolley tracks were laid connecting Yardley with New Hope-Lambertville. Although the right of way was granted in 1904, in 1906 Borough Council was still negotiating with the Trenton, New Hope, & Lambertville Street Railway requesting that they complete the North Main Street extension.

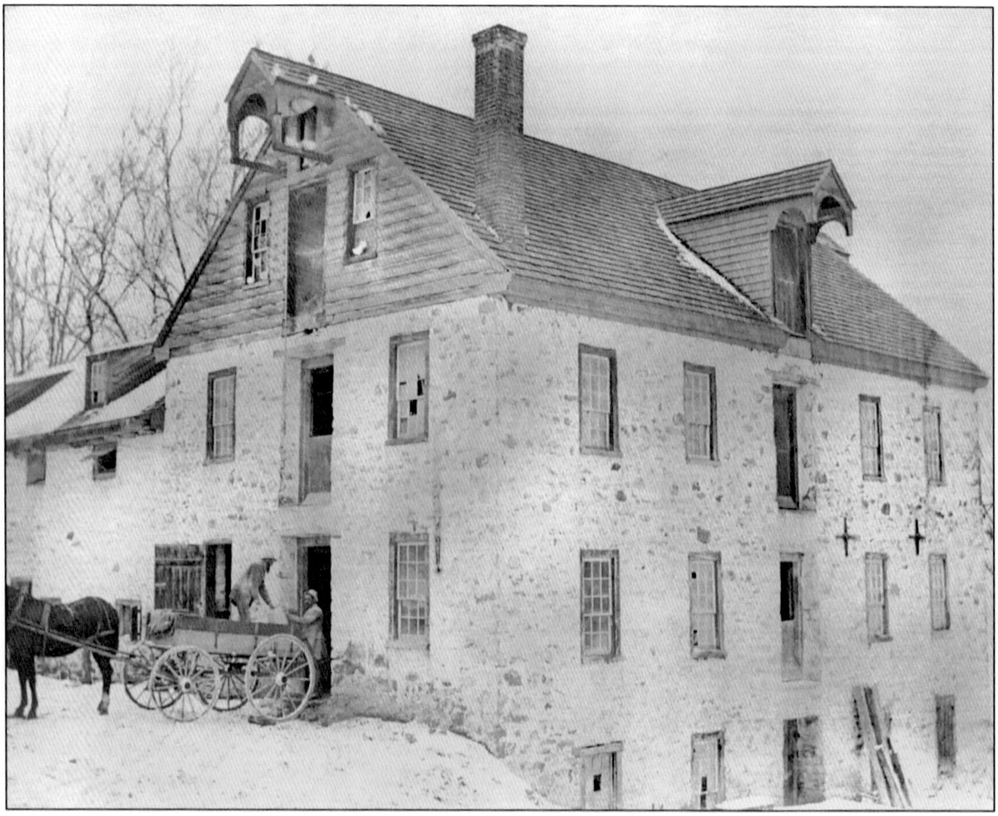

In the late 1600s, John Brock established a gristmill in Lower Makefield Township. In 1726, Thomas Yardley purchased the mill, pond, millraces, stones, and edifices. Yardley rebuilt the mill in 1769. During the Civil War it supplied tons of sorghum and meal for Union soldiers. In 1900, the mill was destroyed by fire.

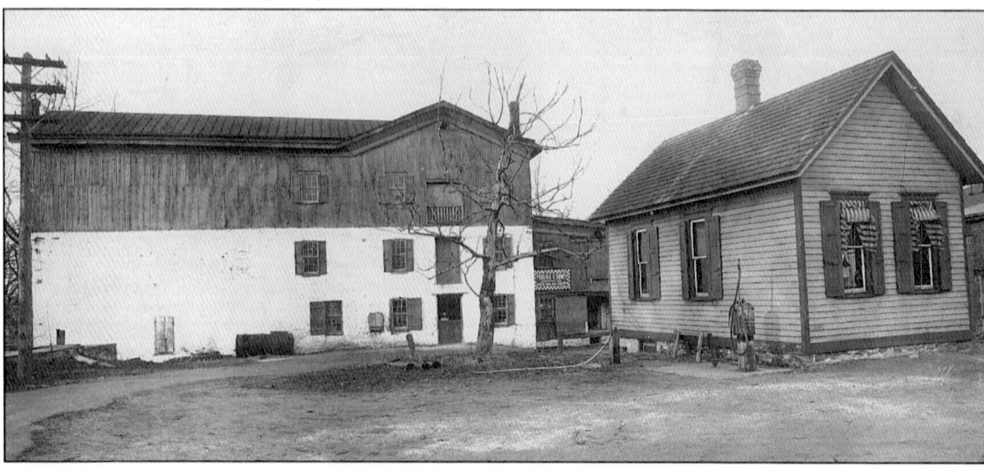

A.S. Cadwallader rebuilt the Yardley gristmill in 1901. Turbines powered by canal water replaced the water wheel that had been powered by Lake Afton. Through the 1920s, the Yardley Mill Company delivered barreled flour to Trenton in horse-drawn wagons. The mill stopped producing flour in about 1930, but continued to grind feed for livestock into the 1940s. Notice the Purina Company sign.

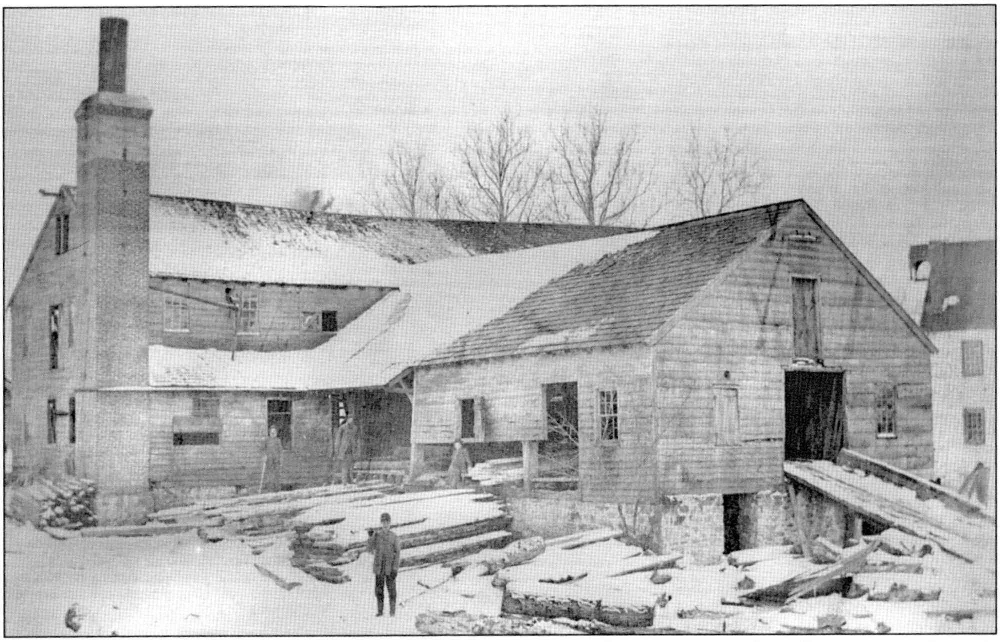

According to an 1831 deed, a sawmill was located on the 30 acre Lakeside property. Joseph Swartzlander operated the Yardley sawmill from 1848 to 1902. A barrel factory and a spoke and felloe (the circular rim of the wheel) works also may have been on the property. In the early 1900s, a power plant was built on the site.

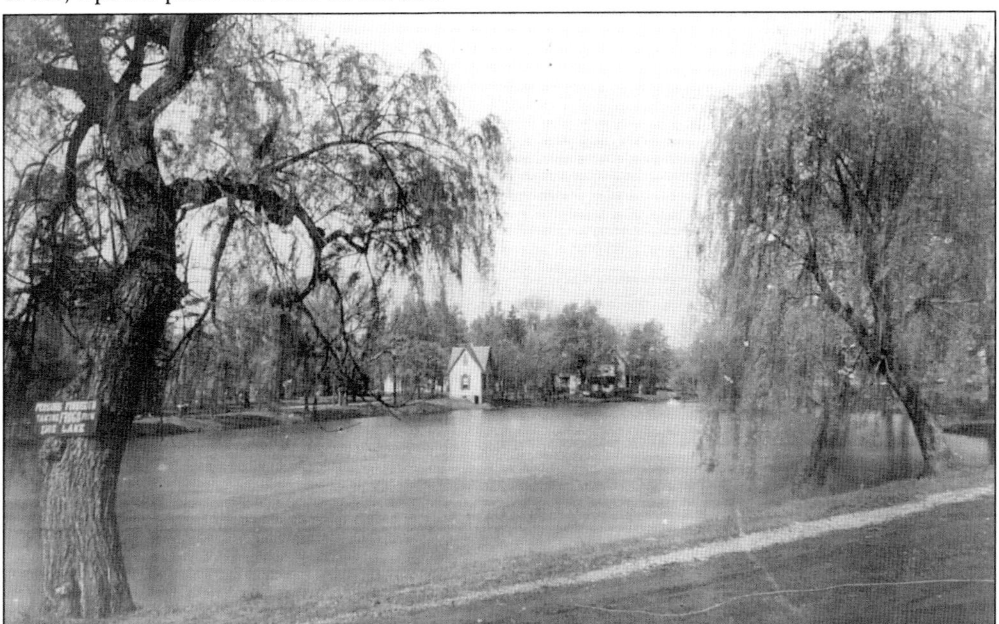

Lake Afton was a man-made millpond fed by Brock Creek. Local tradition suggests that the name Afton was taken from a line in the poem "Afton Waters" by the Scottish poet, Robert Burns — "...flow gently Sweet Afton, I'll sing thee a song." The Old Library on the lake was built in 1878. According to the sign on the left: "Persons Forbidden Taking Frogs From This Lake."

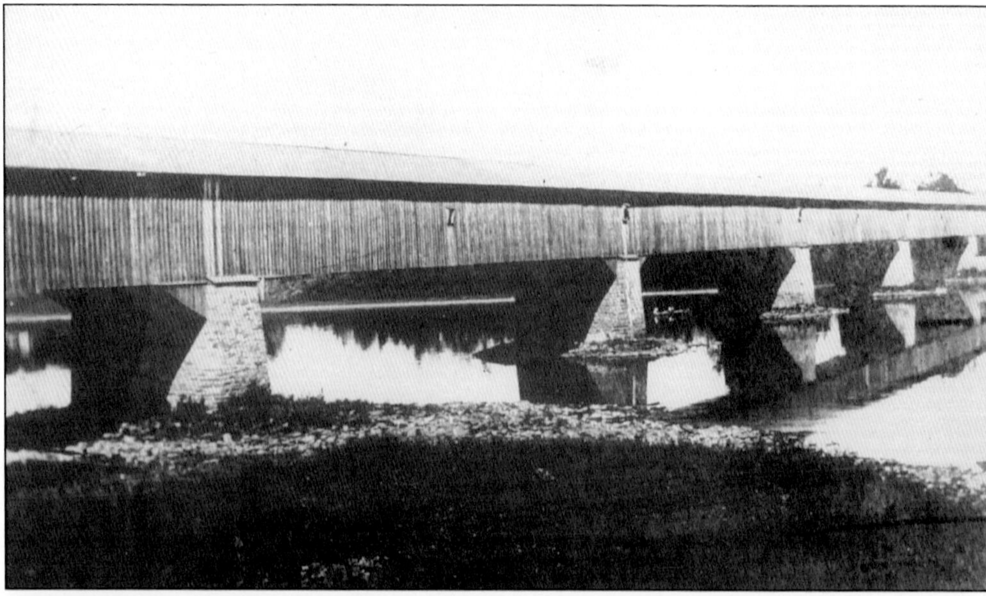

By 1710, Thomas Yardley had established a ferry in the village of Yardleyville. In 1835, the ferry was replaced by a Burr-truss covered bridge. The design incorporated a wooden arch and vertical struts that transferred the bridge's weight to stone piers. The Yardleyville Covered Bridge washed away in the flood of 1903.

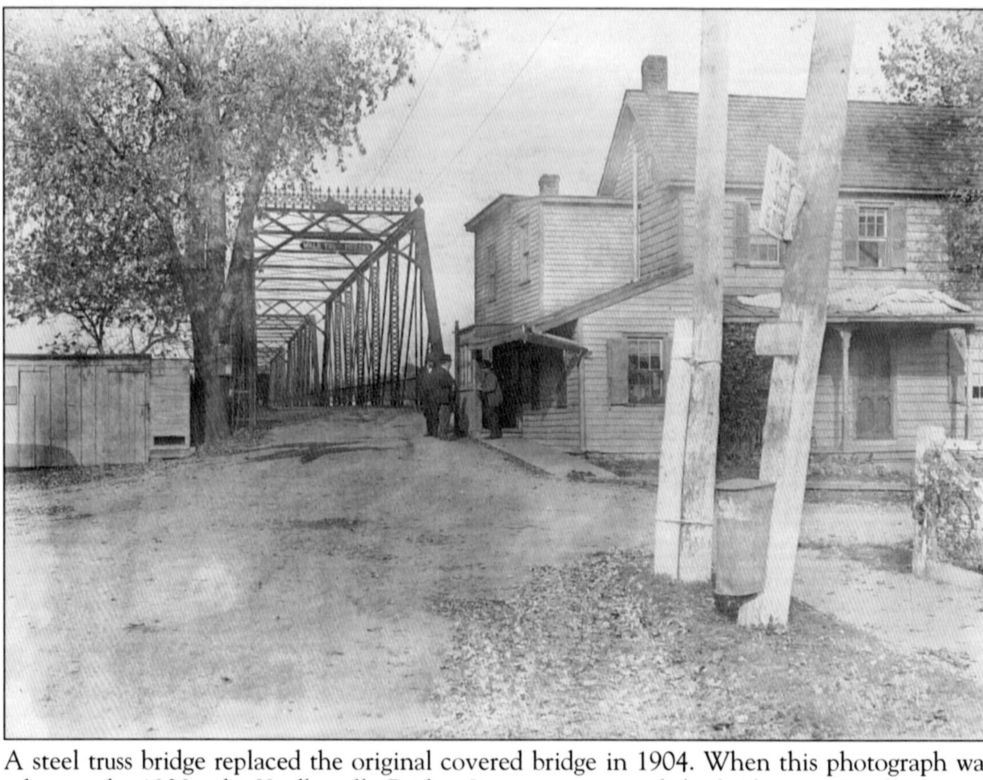

A steel truss bridge replaced the original covered bridge in 1904. When this photograph was taken in the 1930s, the Yardleyville Bridge Company operated the bridge. Notice the men at the tollhouse, and the mattresses airing on the roof of the porch.

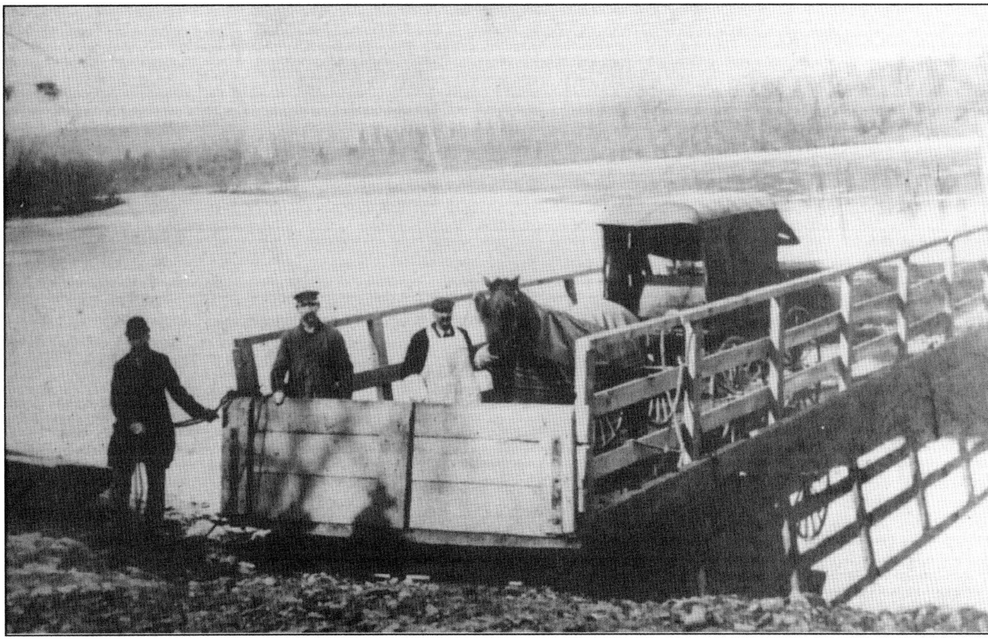

Ferry service was needed again after the 1903 flood until the new Yardleyville-Wilburtha Bridge was completed. One ferry customer was Girton's Main Street butcher shop, which made deliveries to customers in New Jersey. In this photograph, a Girton butcher in a white apron joins a ferryman ready to cross the river.

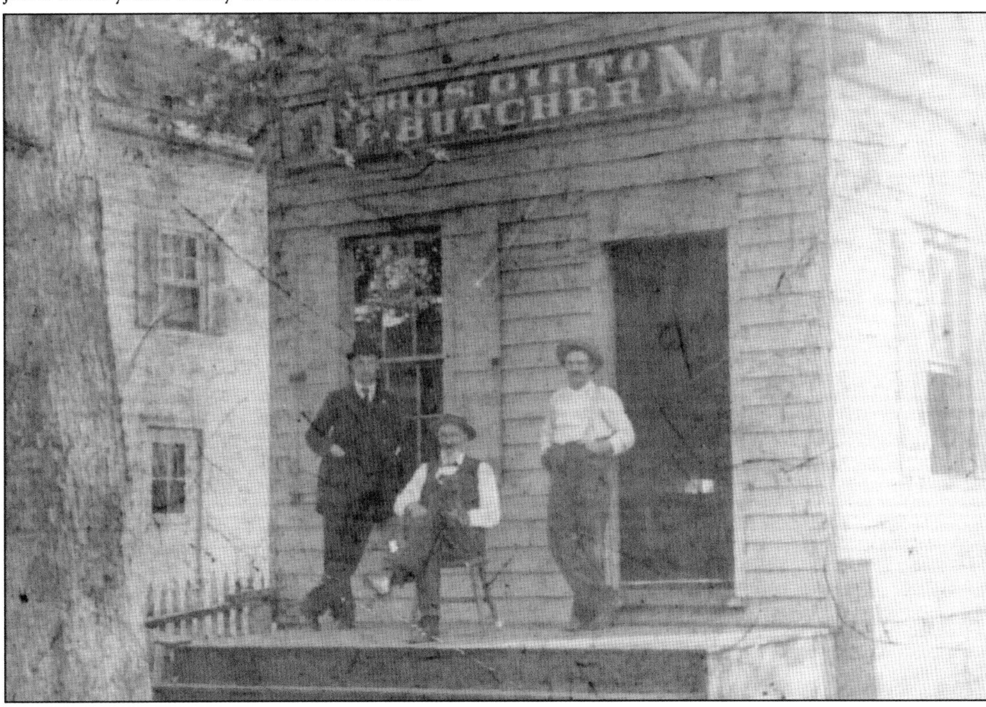

Thomas Girton, seated in front of his butcher shop (35 South Main Street) around the turn of the century, established this shop prior to 1876. On the left is his grandson Walter and on the right his son Gardner.

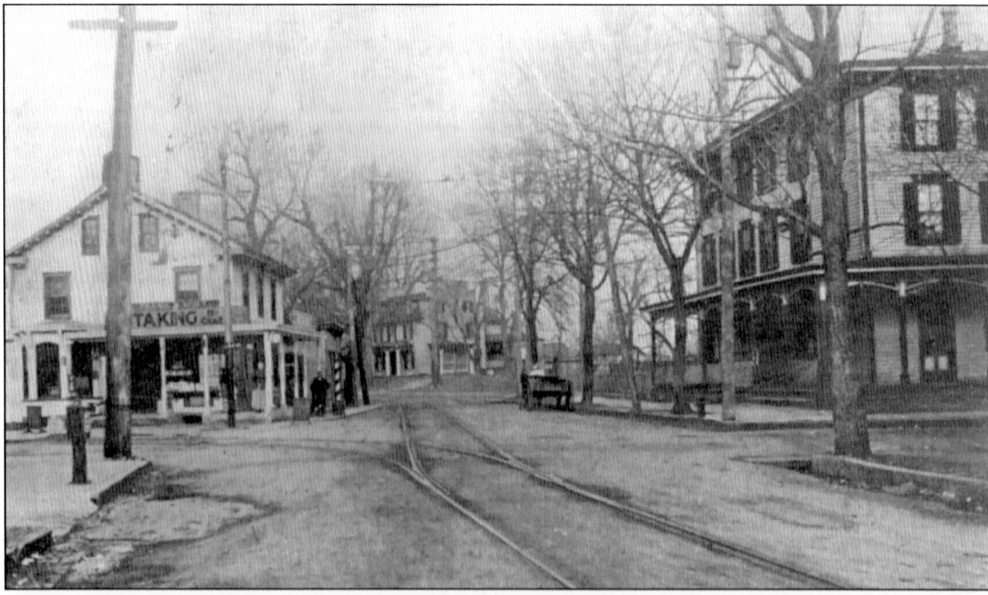

The intersection of Main Street and Afton Avenue has always been the center of Yardley. The photographer of this *c.* 1900 view stood in the intersection looking north. Lakeside is in the distance. Wist's Confectionery is on the left and the Continental Hotel on the right. Notice the horse and wagon, the streetcar tracks, the wrap-around porch on the Continental, 5¢ cigar sign, and the barber pole on the side of Wist's.

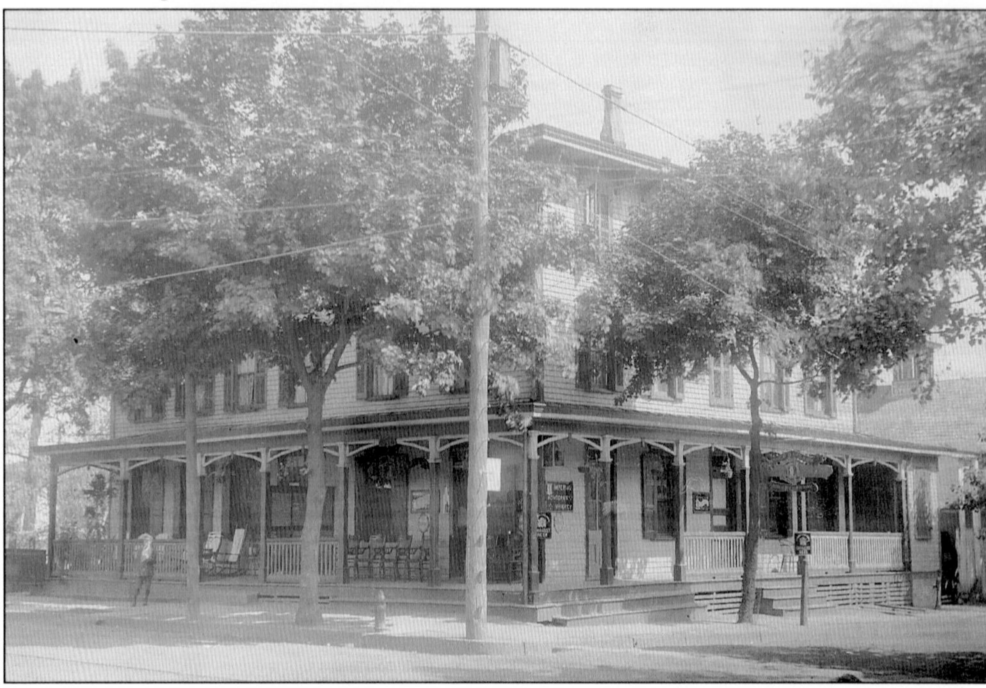

Samuel Slack operated a Temperance House and store on the corner of Main and Afton in 1845. As town librarian, he also operated a library over the store. The Continental Hotel was built on the site in 1876 after a fire destroyed the corner. This photograph was taken *c.* 1920–30.

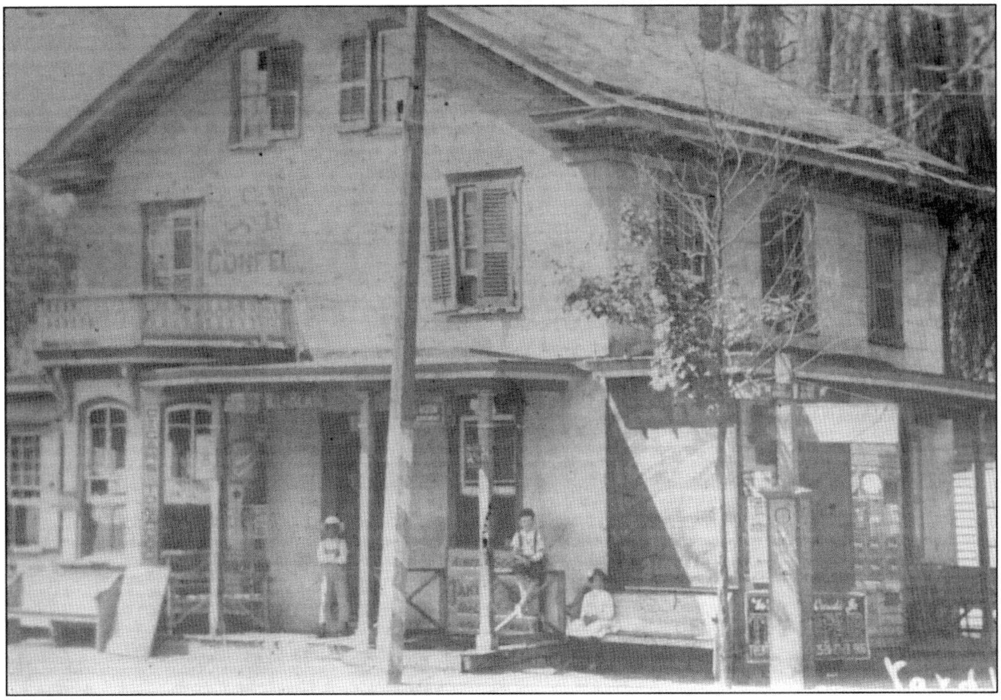

Three young children pose on the front porch of Wist's Corner, c. 1910. Inside were a confectionery shop, an ice cream parlor, telegraph office, and telephone exchange. The proprietors, Frank and Mattie Wist, were well known members of the community. In the 1940s, it was called the Orange Blossom Inn, and included a player piano, singing, and dancing.

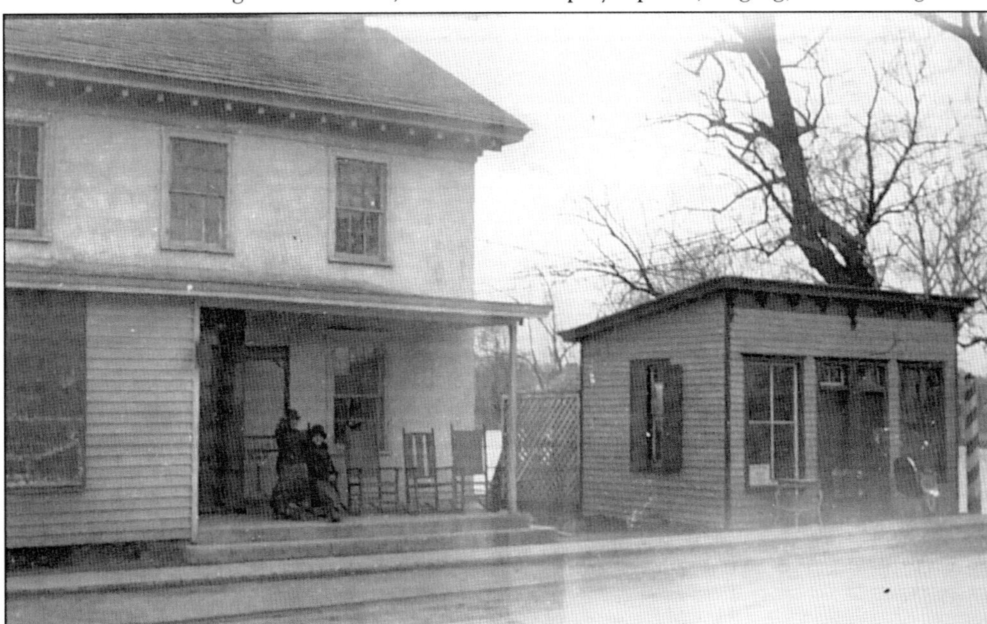

Kathryn Wist and Anna Miller pose on Wist's side porch. In 1915, Anna sent this photo postcard addressed "Miss C. Wist, Yardley, I got your number in spite of your resistance." The small building to the right was Archie Gallagher's barbershop.

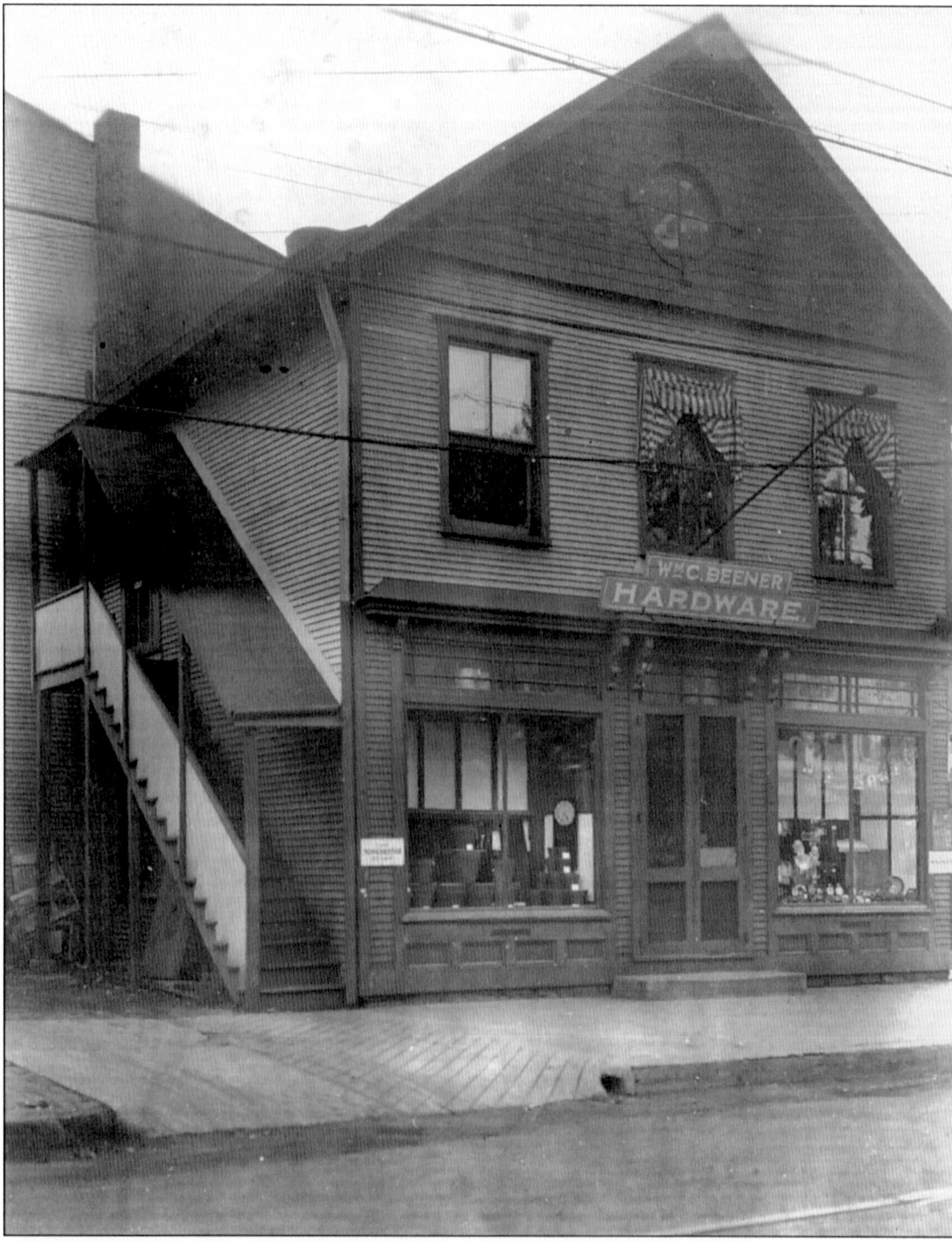

William C. Beener's Hardware Store building was constructed in 1900 after a fire destroyed a general store operated by one of Yardley's first councilmen, W. Y. Cadwallader. William and his wife Molly purchased the property in 1914 from Susan Cadwallader. In the 1920s, they renovated the building and installed an elevator on the left side. Beener's advertising slogan at the time was "Up-to-date efficiency." The hardware store carried just about everything needed for home repairs and became a Yardley institution. The business closed in 1979.

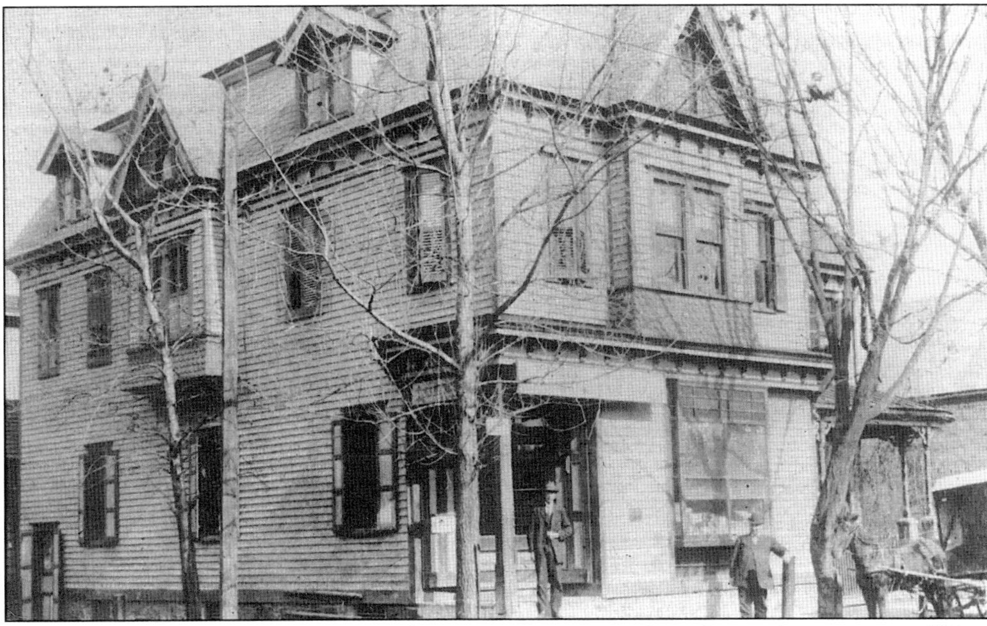

Pursell and Black's Country or General Store was constructed on the southeast corner of Main and Afton in the 1870s. The step up corner entrance led to a grocery store on the first floor; dry goods and clothing were on the second floor. The Queen Anne and Second Empire design elements in the building reflected the eclectic nature of Victorian architecture. In 1998, the building was destroyed by fire.

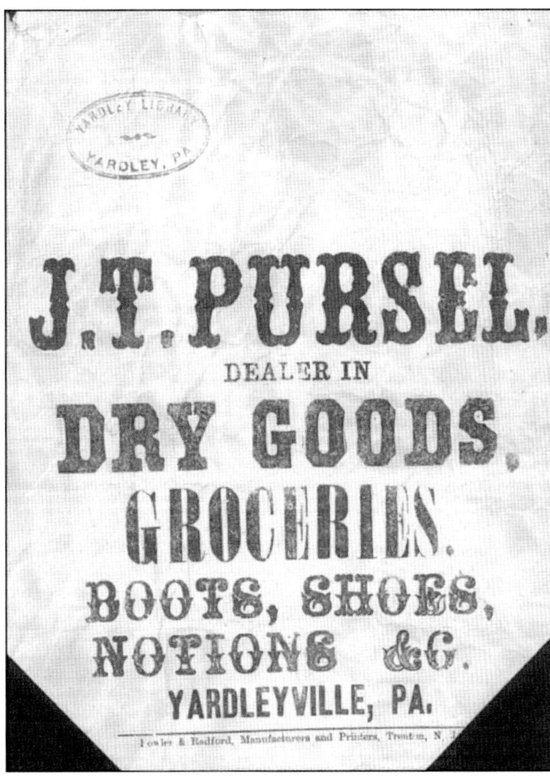

J. Thomas Pursell (1847–1923) and his wife, Sallie Iva, lived above Pursell's General Store. Notice the grocery bag uses a variant spelling, "Pursel."

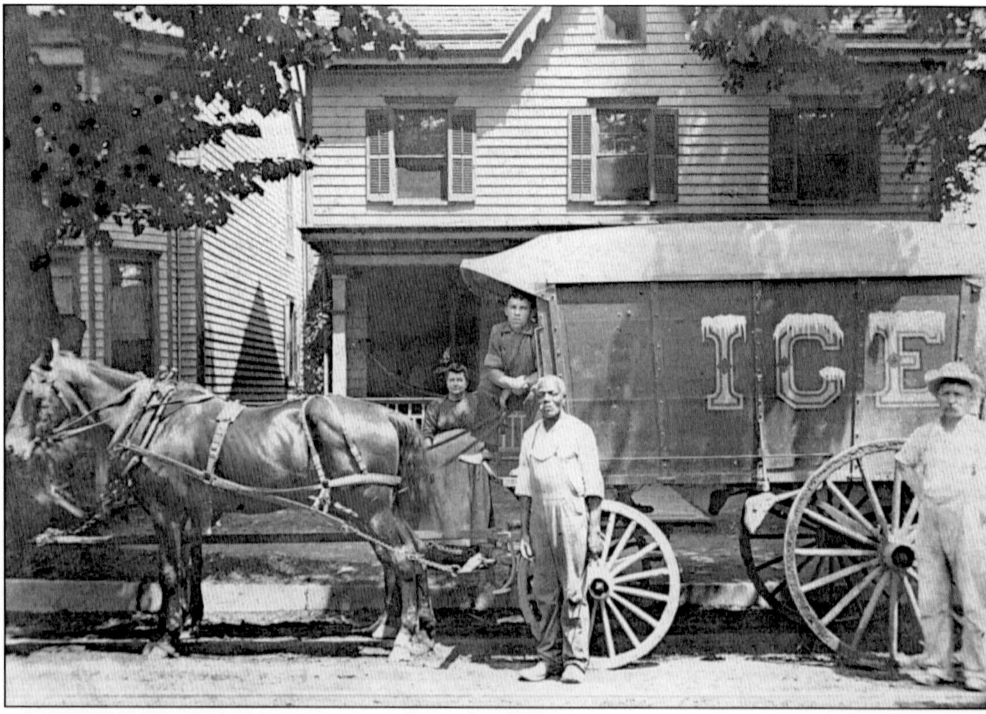

Jake Dilliplane (far right) looks on as Walter Dilliplane holds the reins. Charles Elam (center) worked in the Dilliplane Ice house, located at 170 South Main Street. It is probably Mrs. Jake Dilliplane in the background.

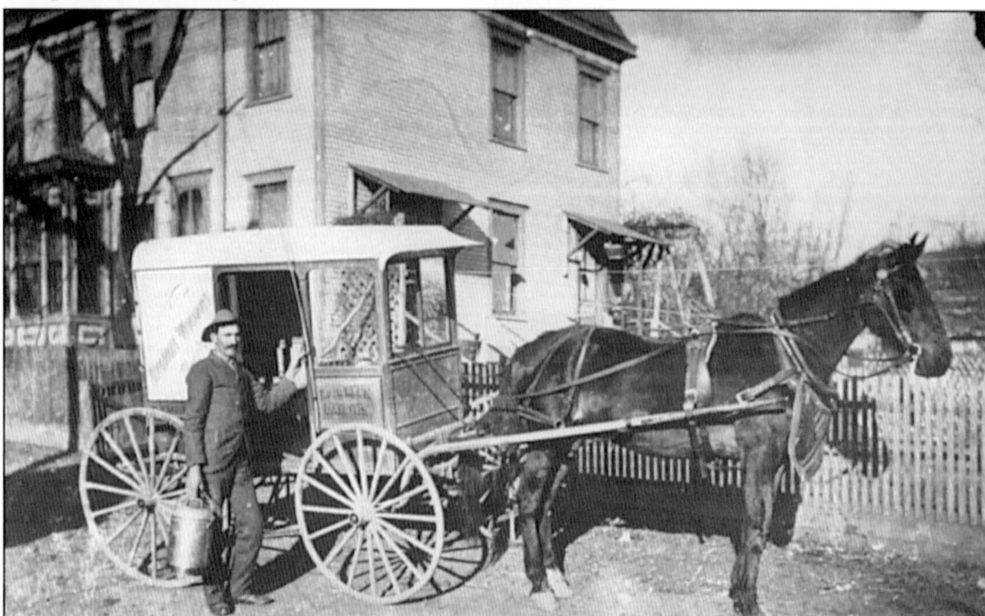

The Everett Wright farm, Rose Lawn Dairies, was located on the Edgewood Road in Lower Makefield. It was one of several dairy farms that delivered milk to the borough. Howard Lee posed next to a Wright delivery wagon in the early 1900s.

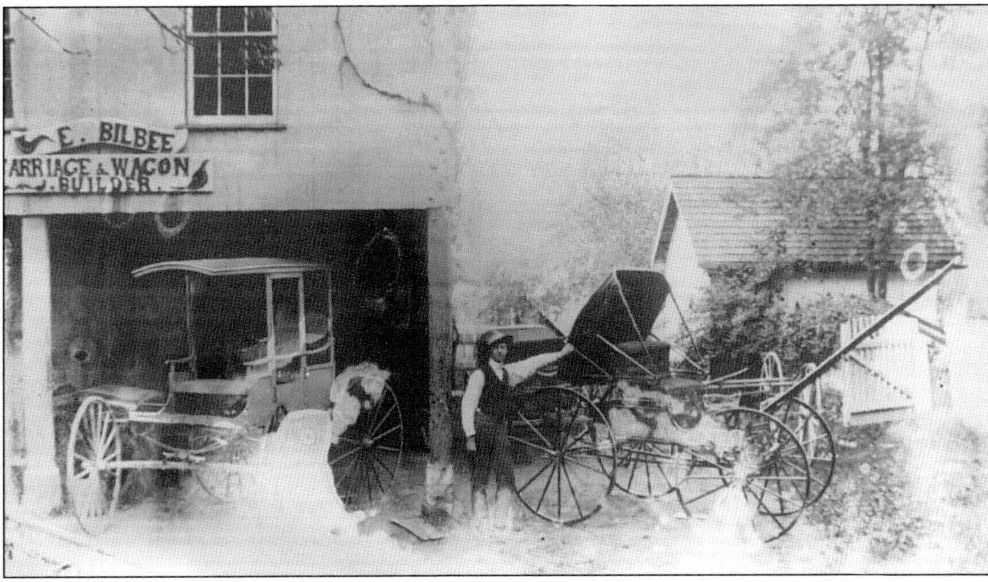

The E. Bilbee carriage and wagon works was located at 49 South Main Street. With the advent of automobiles in the 1920s and 1930s, the Bilbee works became an auto repair shop. The family eventually opened a garage in New Jersey. Their pumps were located directly in front of the River Bridge.

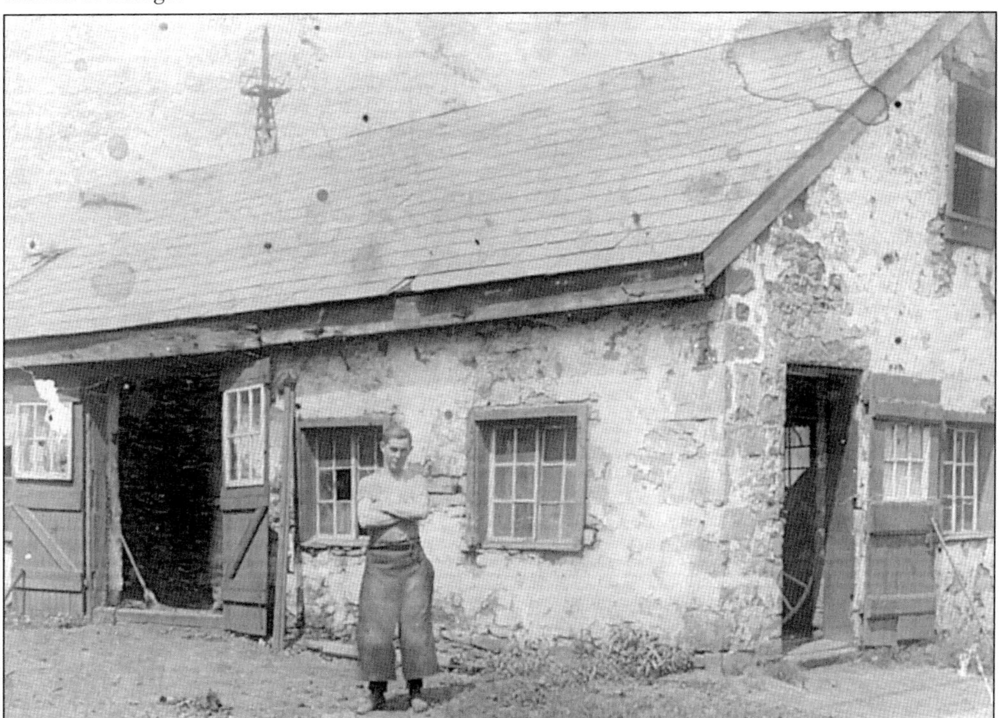

Prior to the Civil War, John Depuy built a fieldstone house at 19 South Main Street. He established a blacksmith shop near the residence. A blacksmith in leather apron, probably a Depuy, poses in front of the shop. In the 1920s, Fire Company Number 2 built a firehouse on the site, and in the 1930s the building was converted to a drug store.

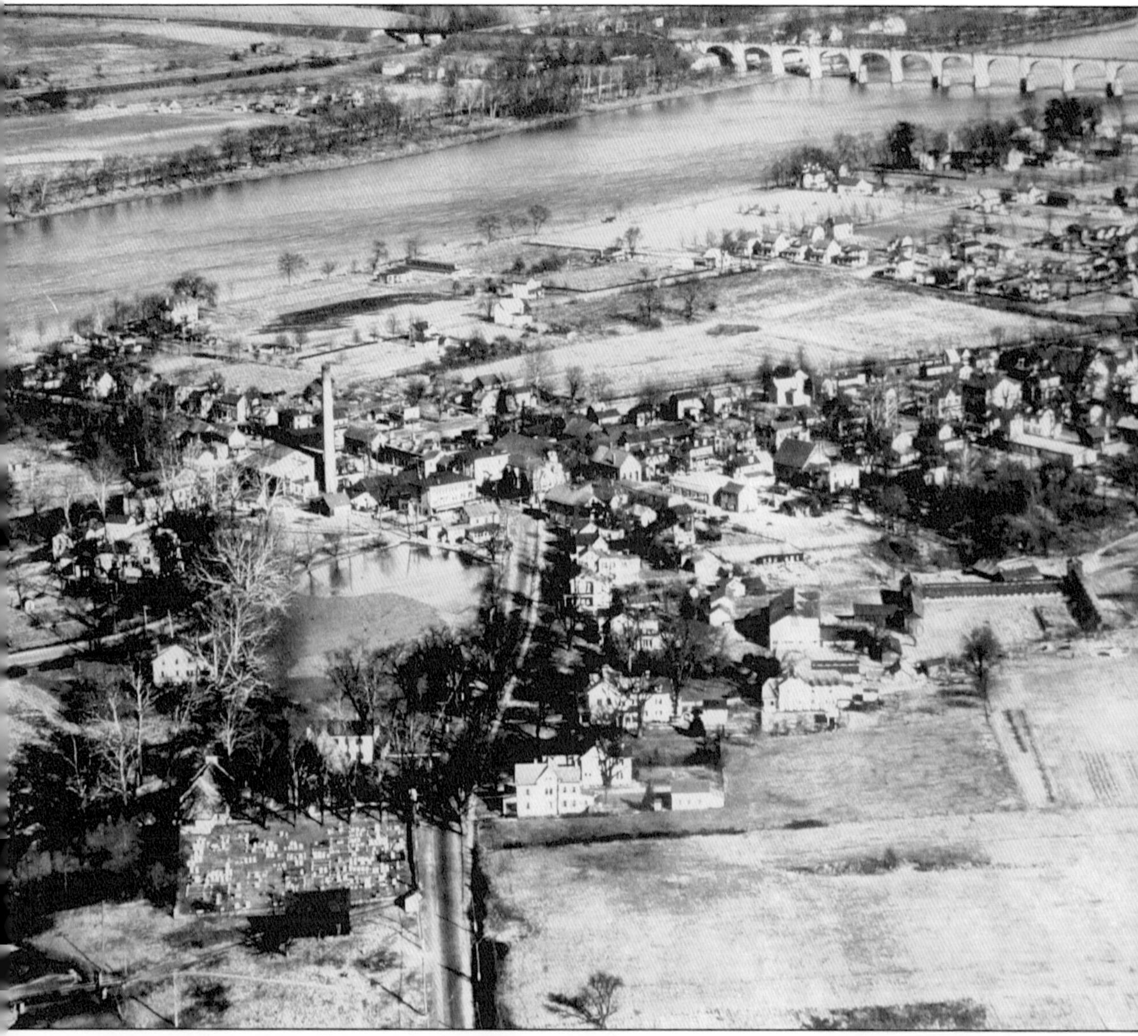

Many traces of Yardley's early history are visible in this aerial photograph taken during the 1940s. In the center of the photograph is Lake Afton, whose waters powered Yardley's gristmill. To the left of the lake, the power plant's smokestack and a line of buildings extend to the Delaware River. This leads to the site of Yardley's ferry and the bridges to New Jersey. Main Street and its business district extend to the right of the lake. The Reading Railroad Bridge is in the upper right and the cemetery of St. Andrew's is in the lower left. Yardley resident and aerial photographer Virgil Kauffman took the photograph.

Two

THE GROWTH OF A BOROUGH

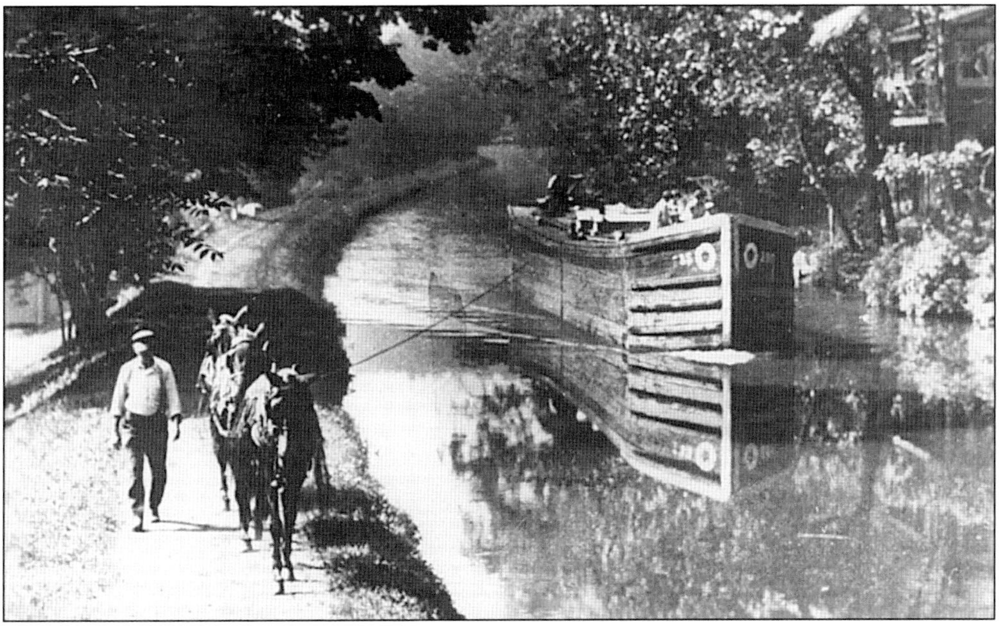

In 1832 the 60-mile long Delaware Division of the Pennsylvania Canal connected the Lehigh Canal at Easton with Bristol. The canal was built by the Commonwealth of Pennsylvania to ship anthracite coal to seaboard markets. By the 1860s, three thousand boats traveled the route moving coal, lumber, building stone, lime, cement, iron, and produce to market. Villages along the canal route boomed as coal, lumber, boat yards, and a variety of other businesses opened to serve the canal trade. Here, an empty Lehigh Coal and Navigation Company boat (notice the "bull's eye" company logo) is pulled toward Easton by a team of mules. The small village of Yardleyville grew with the canal trade.

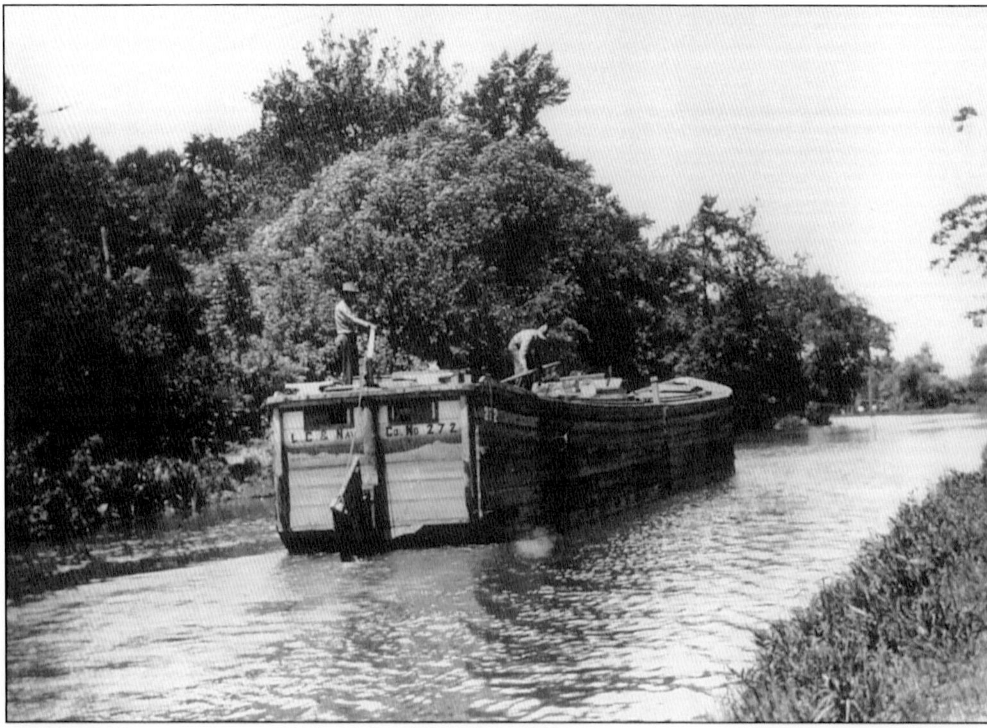

By the 1850s, competition with railroads led the Commonwealth to sell the Delaware Division. It was taken over by the Lehigh Coal and Navigation Company, whose boats moved coal to market until 1932. The run, Easton to Bristol, took about 48 hours, passing through 23 locks and nine aqueducts. In 1940, ownership of the canal returned to the state, and is now the Delaware Canal State Park.

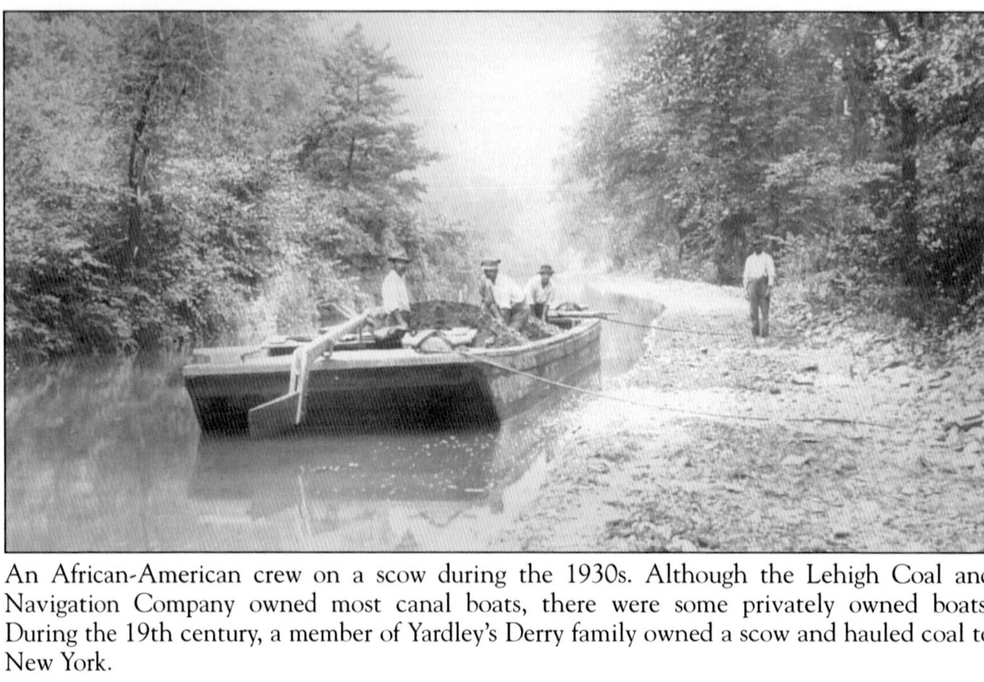

An African-American crew on a scow during the 1930s. Although the Lehigh Coal and Navigation Company owned most canal boats, there were some privately owned boats. During the 19th century, a member of Yardley's Derry family owned a scow and hauled coal to New York.

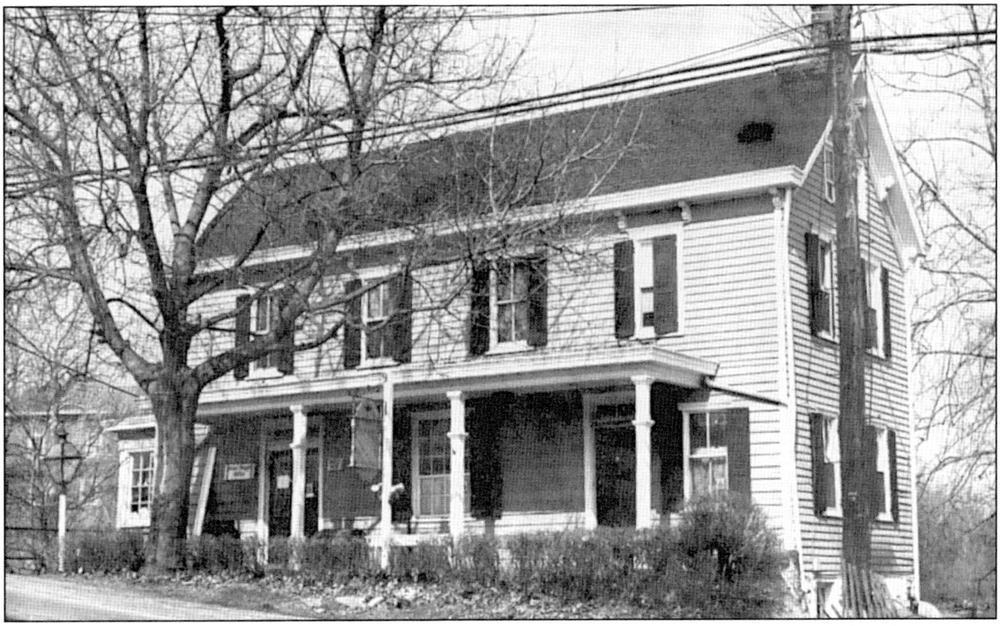

Aaron LaRue built this Canal Shop (34 East Afton Avenue) in about 1831. The shop was a general store for canal boat crews. Canal mules were kept in a barn at the back of the shop. In the years before the Civil War, the shop may have been used as a station on the Underground Railroad. A postcard *c.* 1950 shows the Canal Shoppe, coins, stamps, and antiques.

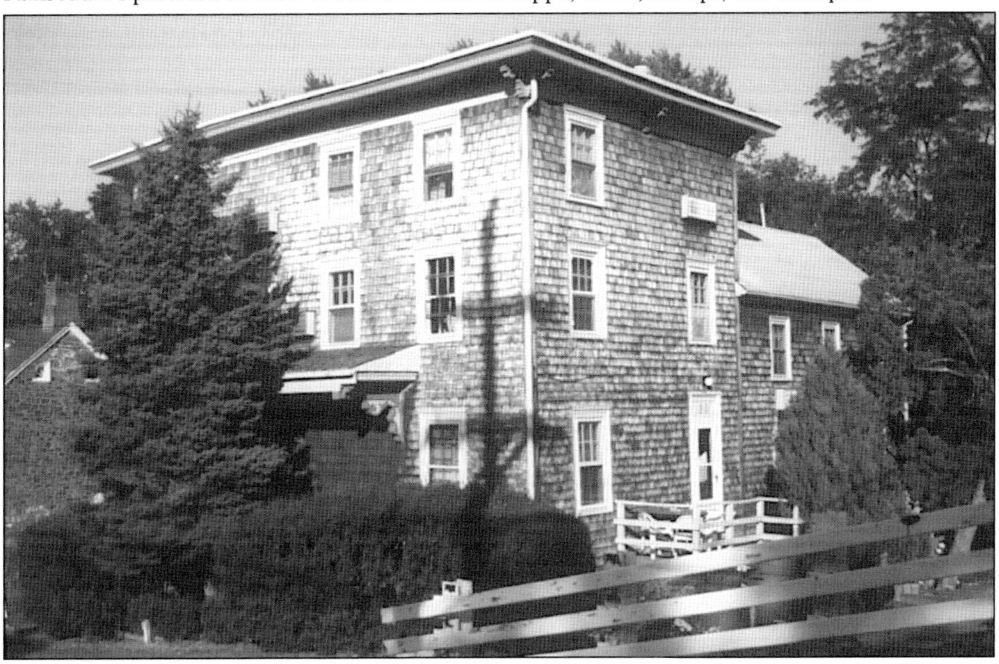

The La Farge House (33 East Afton) was built between 1810 and 1830 and served as a hotel for boatmen and other canal workers. It was also known as the Shoemaker House after one owner, Charles Shoemaker. Operators of the hotel were sometimes granted a license to sell alcohol; a situation that was frequently protested by members of the Women's Christian Temperance Union. The former hotel was converted into an apartment house.

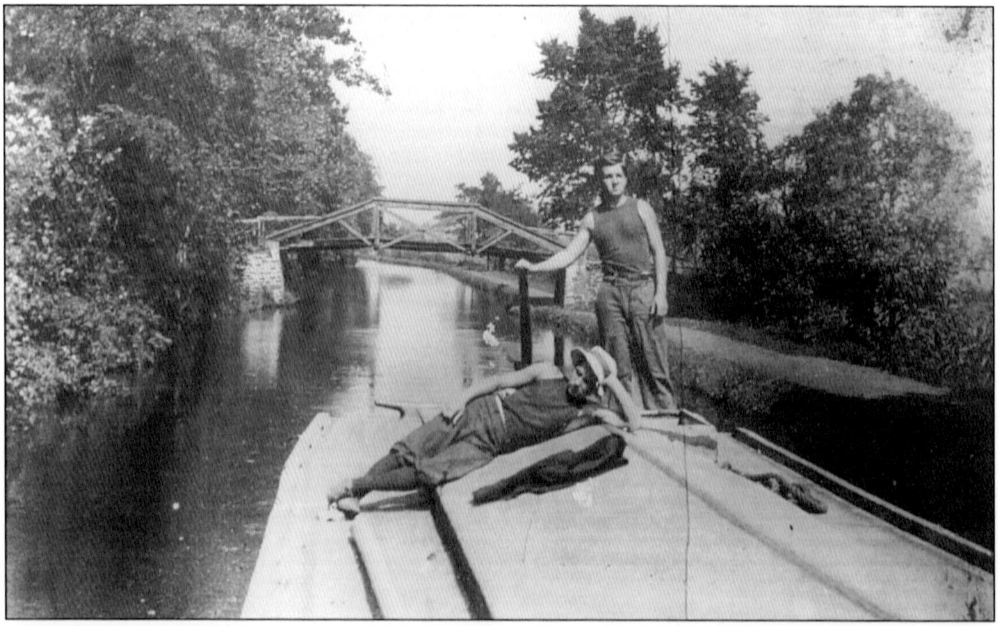

These canal boatmen photographed near Yardley seem to be enjoying the good life. In reality, a boatman's working day was long and hard—from 4 a.m. to 10 p.m. Crews were usually two men, or father and son. Sometimes an entire family lived on the boat during the season, which ran from April through December.

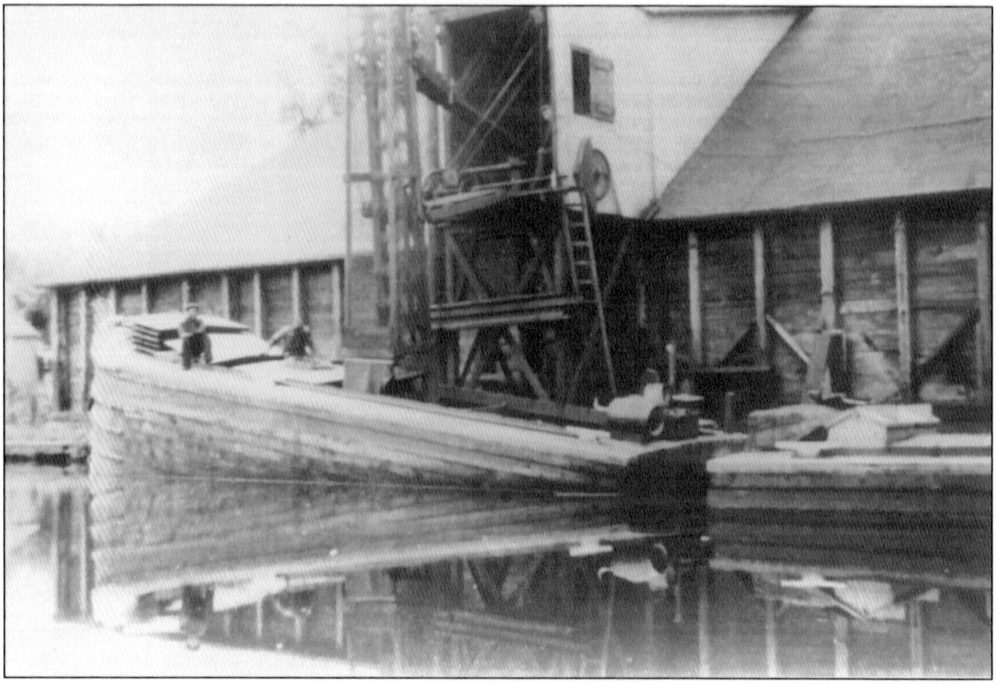

Lumber and coal yards were established in Yardley after the canal opened. Coal, lumber, and other products were unloaded at the Leedom yard on Canal Street until 1932. The standard boat was 87.5 feet long, 10.5 feet wide and drew 5 feet of water. Pictured is a "snapper," or hinge boat, built in two sections so that it could be turned around in the narrow canal.

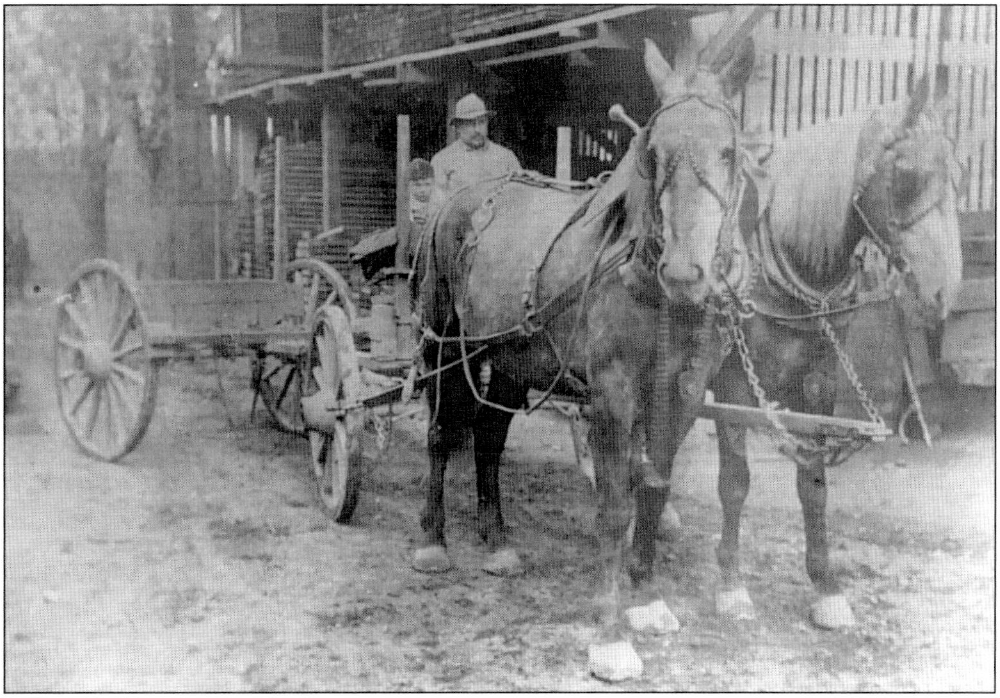

Horses pulled carriages, sleighs, and all types of wagons and carts through the streets of Yardley into the early part of the 20th century. A young boy gets a ride with Barry Hibbs, a teamster for the Leedom Lumber and Coal Company.

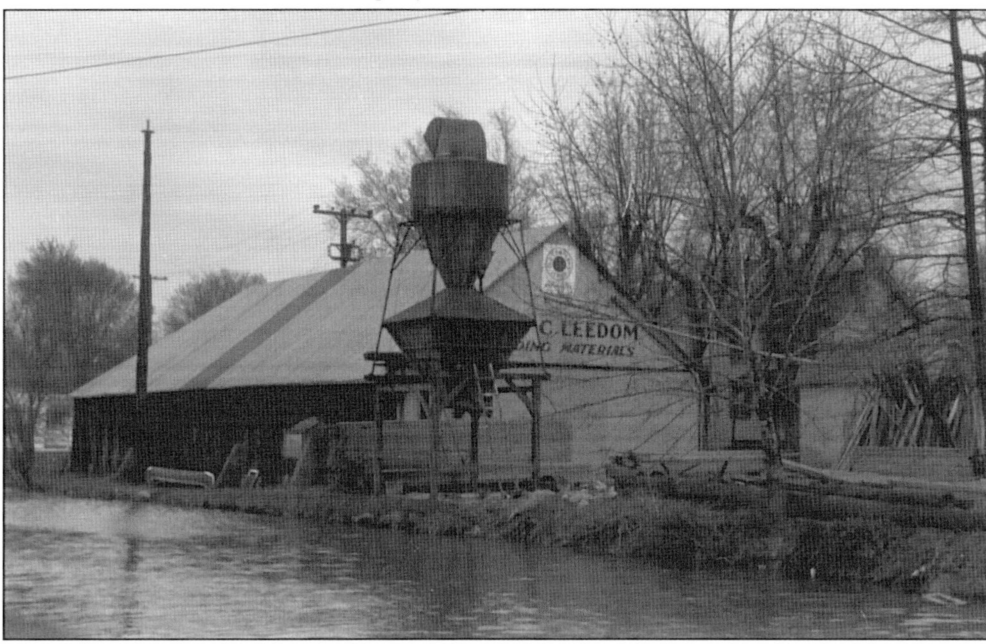

The "Old Company's Lehigh" bull's eye logo over the Louis C. Leedom sign is a reminder of the flourishing anthracite coal business that existed in Yardley for one hundred years. At one time, buckets attached to a ship's mast (on the left) were used to unload coal. By the 1950s, Leedom's was primarily a lumberyard. The last shed was torn down in 1998.

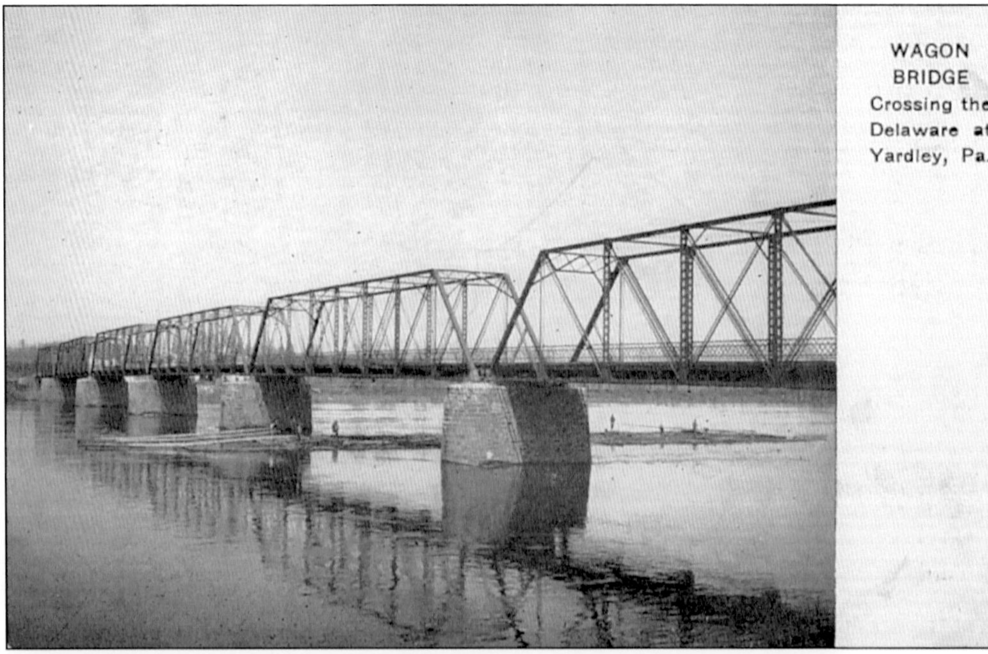

In 1903, the covered bridge at Yardley washed away in a flood. A new steel bridge was constructed. Gardner Girton, a local butcher, was given the honor of being the first to cross the new structure. In 1922, the Yardley Bridge became part of the Delaware River Joint Bridge Commission. It was destroyed in the 1955 flood.

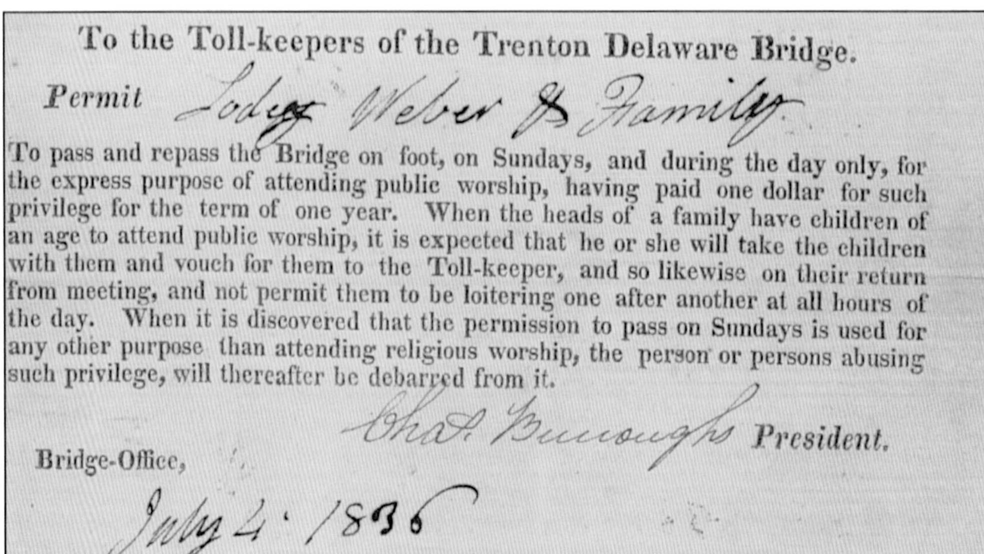

To the Toll-keepers of the Trenton Delaware Bridge.

Permit Lady Weber & Family

To pass and repass the Bridge on foot, on Sundays, and during the day only, for the express purpose of attending public worship, having paid one dollar for such privilege for the term of one year. When the heads of a family have children of an age to attend public worship, it is expected that he or she will take the children with them and vouch for them to the Toll-keeper, and so likewise on their return from meeting, and not permit them to be loitering one after another at all hours of the day. When it is discovered that the permission to pass on Sundays is used for any other purpose than attending religious worship, the person or persons abusing such privilege, will thereafter be debarred from it.

Chas. Burroughs *President.*

Bridge-Office,

July 4 · 1836

This free pass to cross the bridge was issued on July 4, 1836 to "Lady Weber & Family," African-American residents of Yardley. Passes like this were issued on Sundays to attend religious services.

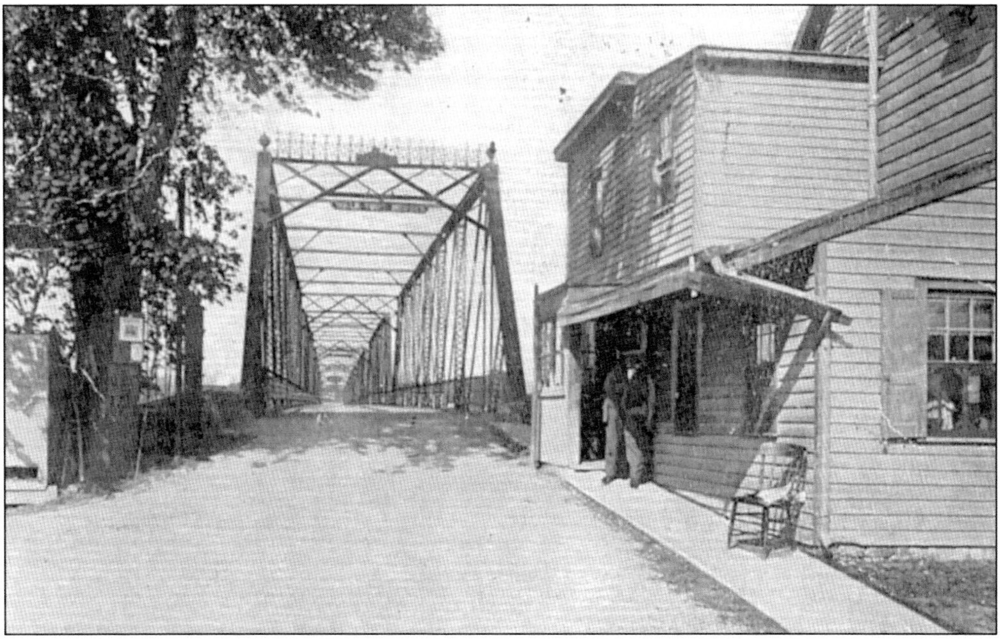

Elisha Scattergood, toll collector for 24 years, resigned in 1904 during construction of the new bridge that connected Yardley to Wilburtha, New Jersey. The new toll collector, John Wetzstein, and his family arrived in Yardley from Point Pleasant on a canal boat. The tollhouse is on the right in this *c*. 1920 postcard.

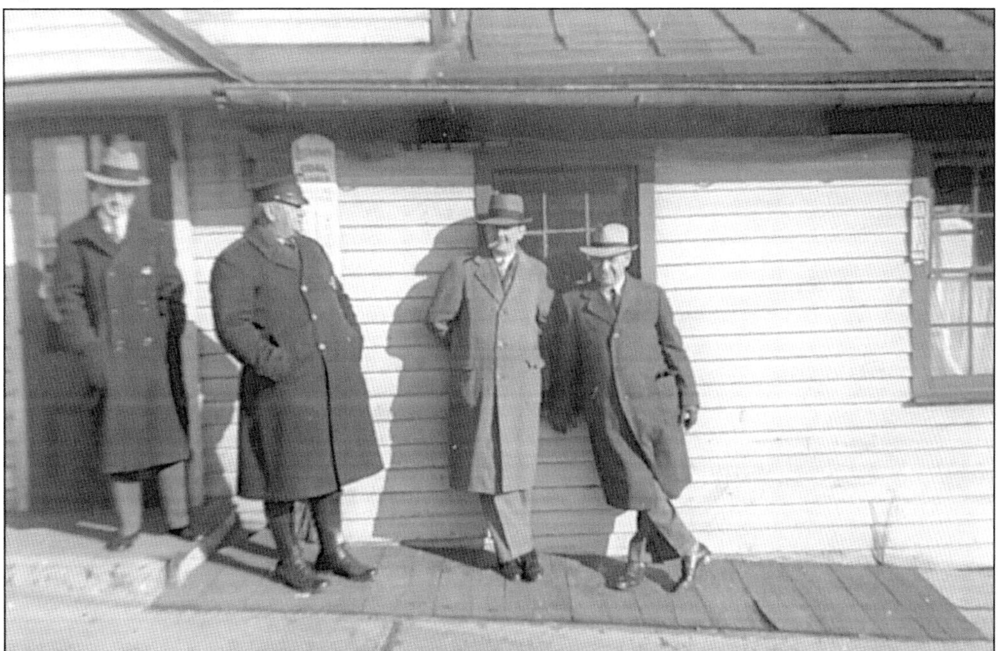

Chester Wetzstein was hired as collector on the Yardley Bridge when his father retired in 1921. The following year, the state purchased the bridge, and fares were eliminated. Chester's job was then to enforce speeds and weight limits. In this photograph from the 1930s are pictured the following gentlemen, from left to right: Ralph Bushong, Chester, Tom South, and Jack Smith.

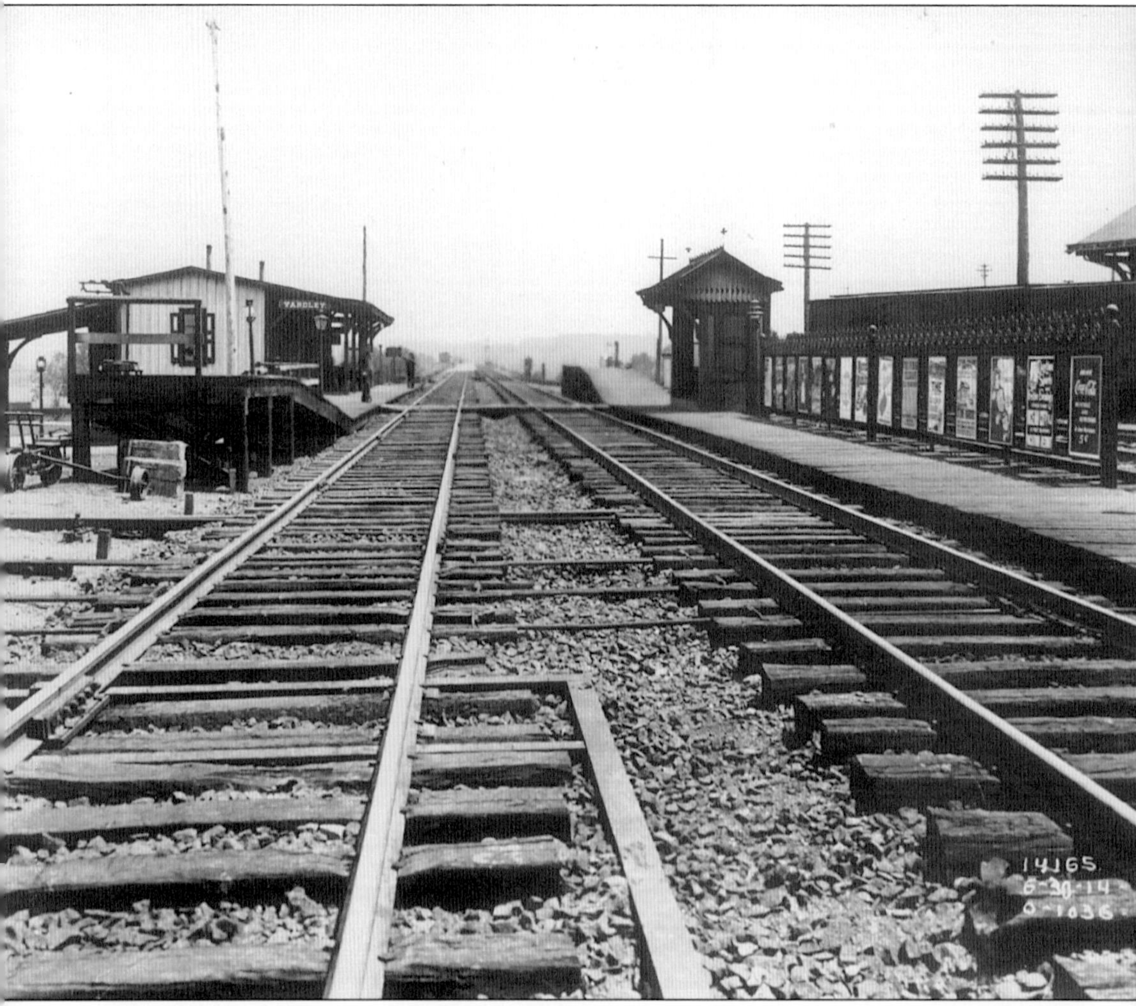

The railroad came to Yardleyville in 1876, just in time to take visitors to the Centennial Exhibition in Philadelphia. William Schively, the editor of the *Village Luminary* wrote, "We in Yardleyville want the railroad . . . no village can remain stationary or dull as long as it has a free and swift communication with a great city. The presence of the railroad within or in close proximity to a village will have the effect of changing entirely for the better its character." The name of the station and the town were soon changed to Yardley. The railroad sparked a boom in both housing and business, leading to incorporation as a borough in 1895. This photograph, taken in 1914, shows the Victorian station and waiting booth built in 1876. On the right is the freight house; a sign advertises Coca-Cola for 5¢.

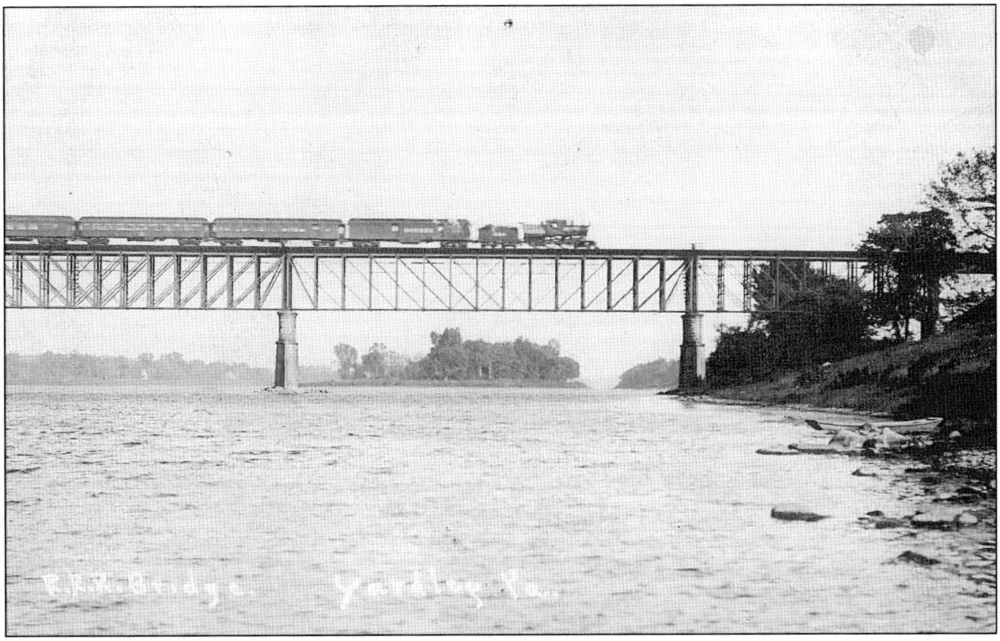

This turn of the century photo postcard by Linford R. Craven shows a train passing over the 1876 Yardley Railroad Bridge. During construction of the bridge, a local paper reported: "Last Sabbath's sunshine attracted many pedestrians to the railroad bridge. One elderly Friend in her drab garb was specially noticeable, walking the trestle work with confidence and disdaining all masculine assistance."

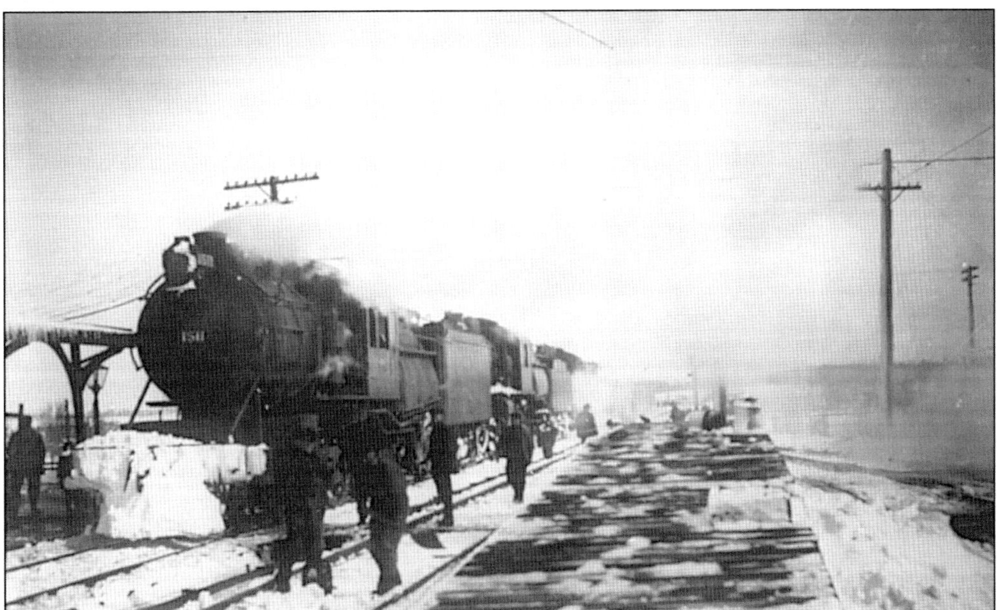

Steam locomotives with their clouds of dark smoke, shrieking whistles, and blasts of steam passed through Yardley until the 1930s when the Reading Railroad line was electrified. By then, the Yardley yard included the original station, a north-bound waiting booth, water pump, scale, freight house, switching tower, cattle chute, coal trestle, and electrical substation.

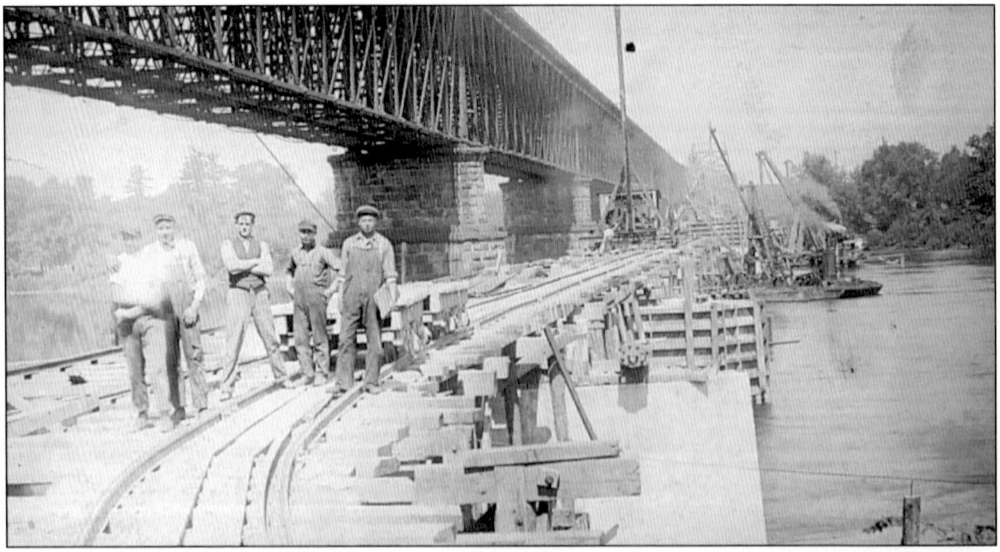

In 1911, the Reading Railroad began construction of a new stone and concrete bridge. About 50 men were employed to construct a small temporary railroad, place pilings, and complete other preliminary work. The workers in this photo postcard are, from left to right, William Hendrickson, Leonard DeSau, John, Charles and Eddie Morier. Newspapers reported that another worker, Harry Hendrickson, fell 20 feet into the river. He sustained a broken leg and sprained ankle.

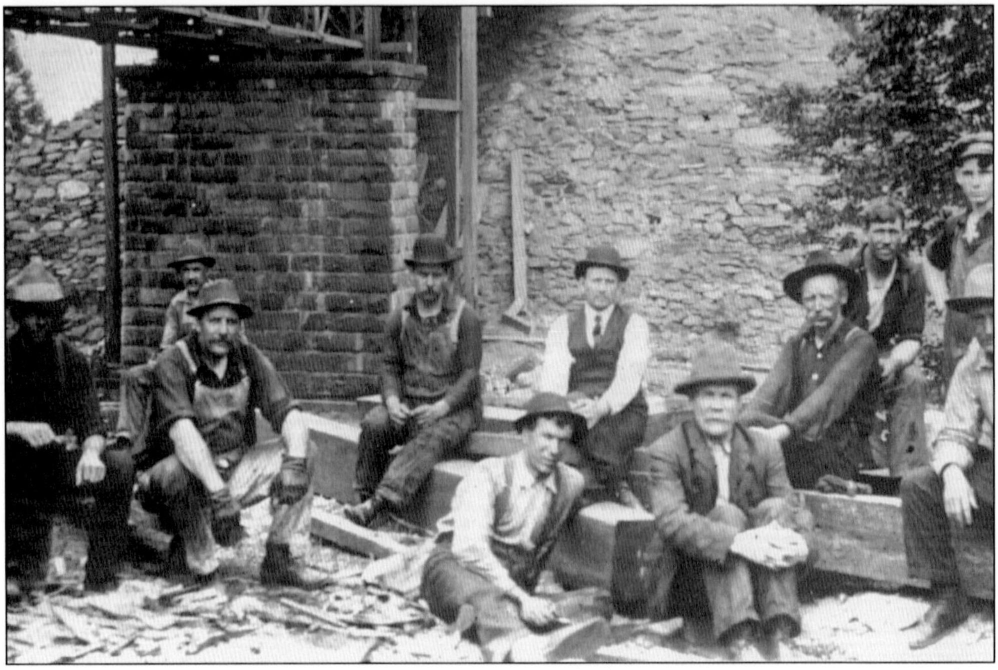

Construction of the new Reading Rail Road Bridge took three years, 1911-1913. Many workers made Yardley their temporary home. Older residents, who remembered the carousing and fighting of workers when the original bridge was constructed in 1876, requested the services of the state constabulary. Their fears, however, were unwarranted. Not a single case involving workers was brought before local justices.

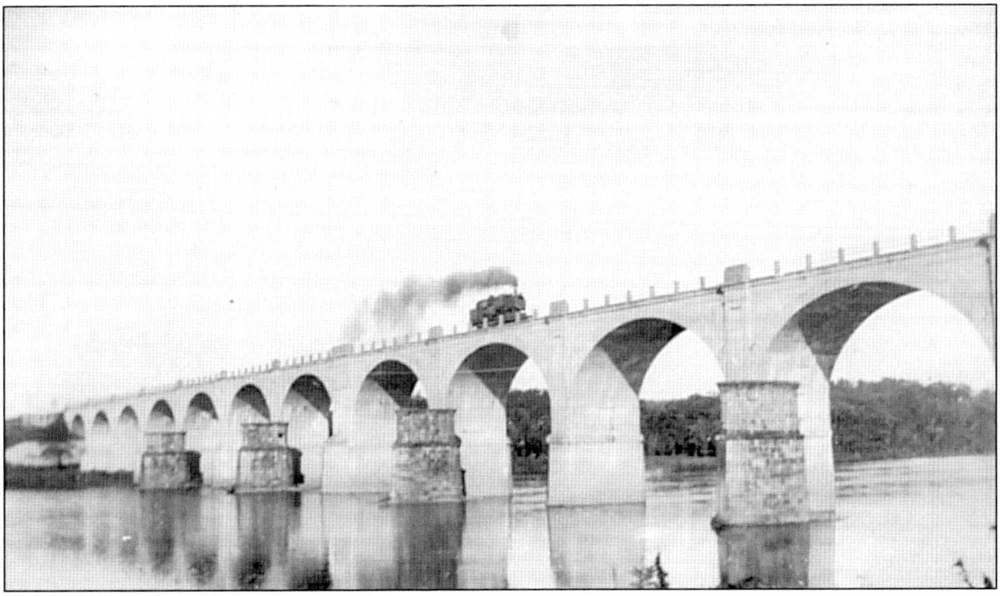

The Yardley Railroad Bridge was described architecturally "as a thing of beauty. Its long graceful arches (rose) far above the flowing river . . . Of modern reinforced concrete construction, the new bridge (was) a fine type of up-to-date-engineering and its durability (was) expected to make it last far into the coming generations." The stone piers from the old bridge were never removed, and are seen in this photograph.

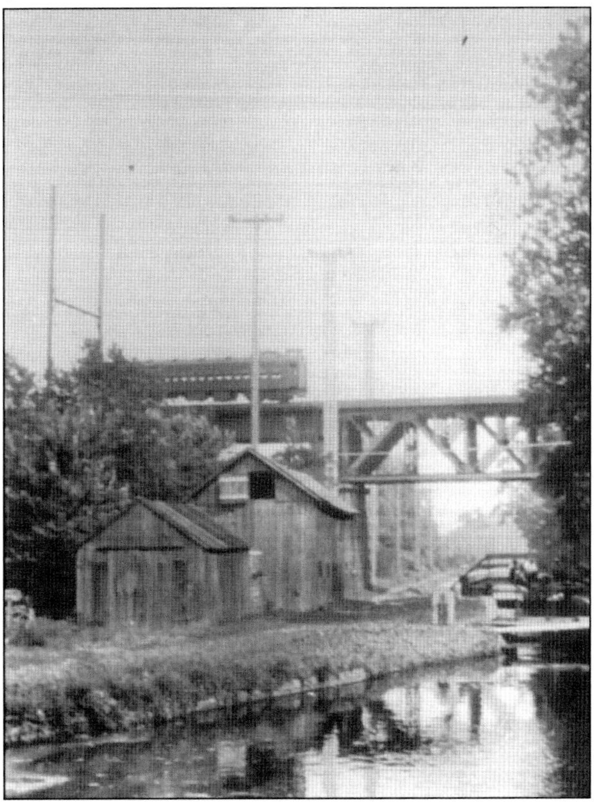

Transportation was in transition in the early 1930s when this photograph was taken. This scene is Lock Five on the Delaware Canal where the Reading Railroad passes over the canal. It was the end of an era. The canal ceased commercial operations in 1932, and the railroad passed from steam to electric about the same time.

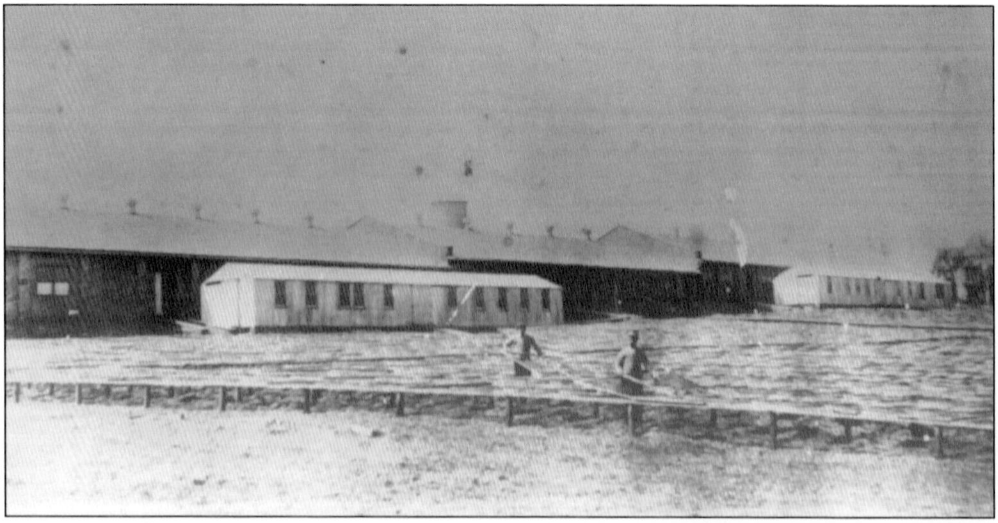

In 1902, Yardley Borough Council exempted manufacturing companies that employed fifteen workers from taxes for a period of ten years. One of the concerns that benefited was the Century Leather Enameling Company, established on the College Avenue in 1902 to process goat and sheepskins into patent leather. This *c.* 1902 photograph shows skins stretched out on racks to dry.

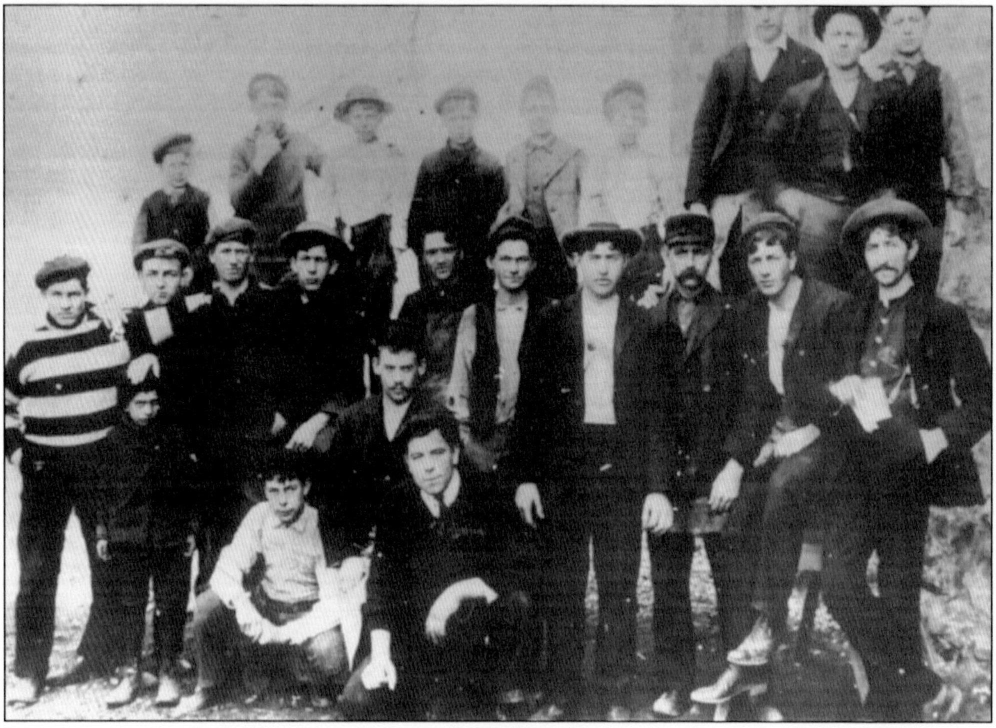

The Century Leather Enameling Company employed many local men and boys. Pictured in this *c.* 1902 photograph, from left to right, are as follows: (front row, kneeling) William Coffin, ? Miller, and Dan Hickey; (middle row) Joe White (second), Joe Shanahan (fourth), Bill Long (fifth), R. Cadwallader (seventh), Michael Heffern (eighth), Ed DeSau (ninth), and Frank Cadwallader (tenth); (back row) Jack Shanahan and Ray Lear (first and second).

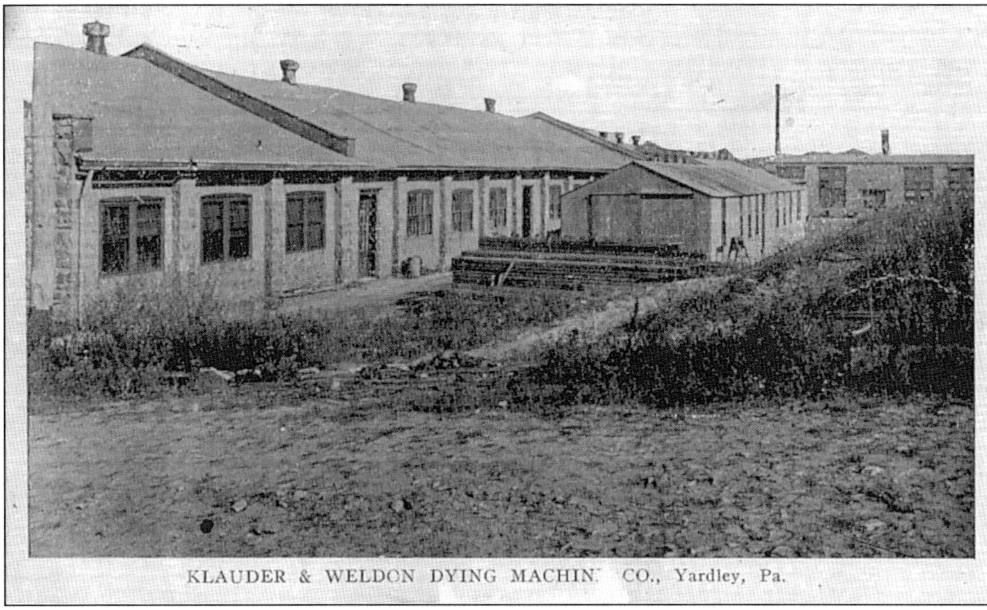

In 1916, the Klauder & Weldon Dying Machine Company, which manufactured machines for dying and finishing material, occupied the Century Leather Enameling Company building. They constructed a railroad spur from the Reading Railroad to the plant. In 1919, the Keystone Bolt and Screw Company took over the property.

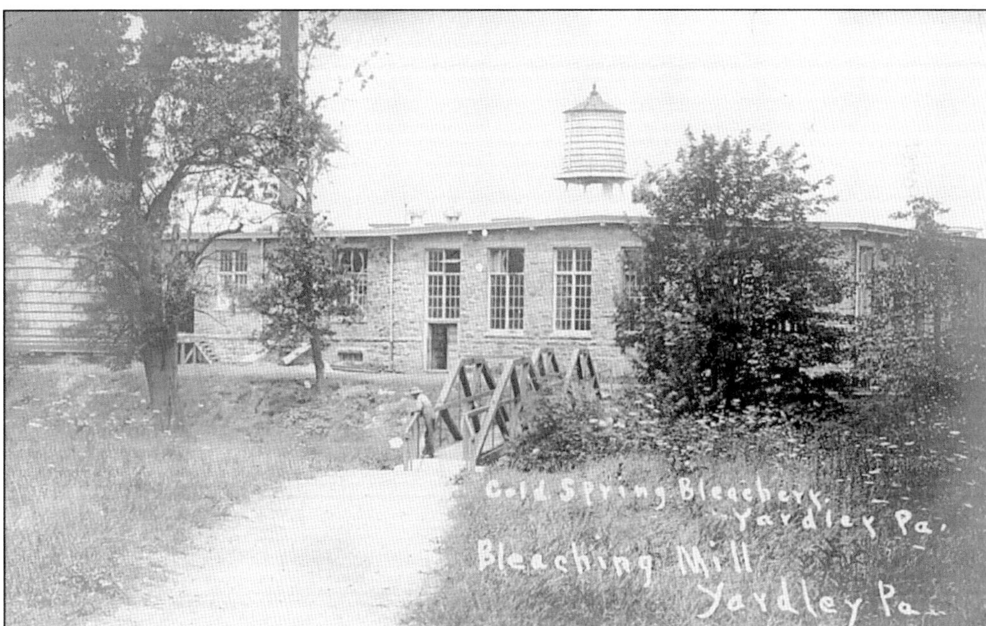

The biggest manufacturer in Yardley was the Cold Spring Bleachery, located off of North Main Street near Lake Afton. The founders, Theodore Search and O. W. White, chose the site based on the available clean water from the lake. The Bleachery finished white cotton goods and dyed materials. This photograph (*c.* 1920) shows the main building and water tower.

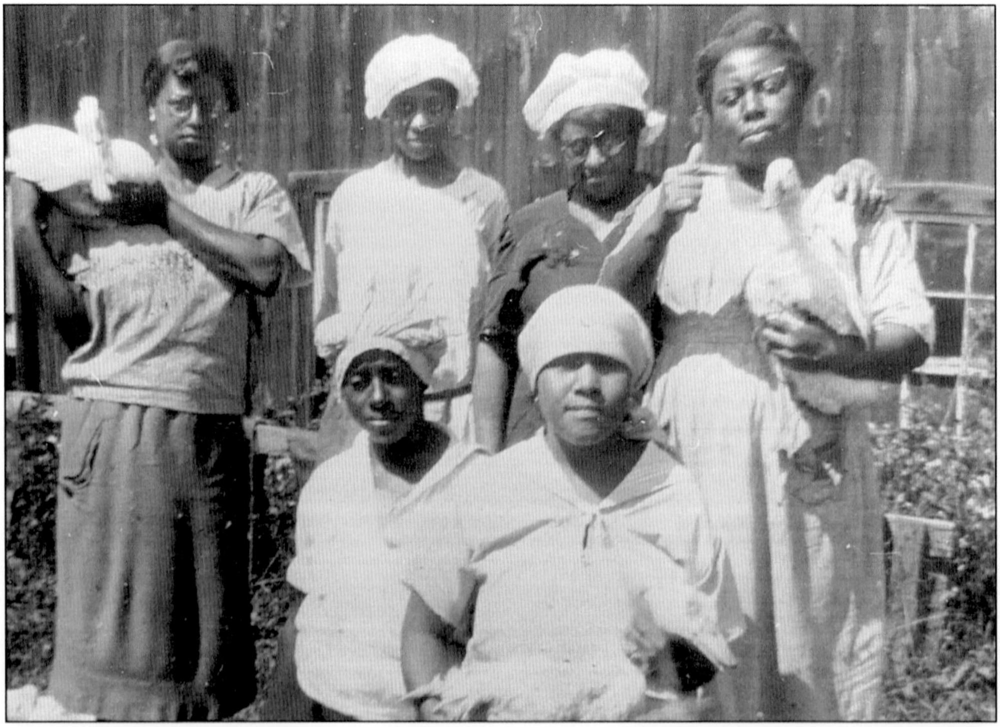

Many African American women were employed plucking and preparing ducks at McCormick's Yardley Duck Farm, one of the largest duck farms in the country. This photograph probably dates from the 1920 to 1930s. George Worrell was a manager. Residents were sometimes invited to the farm to shoot pigeons that ate duck food. During the 1930s, pigeon, not duck might grace a Yardley dinner table.

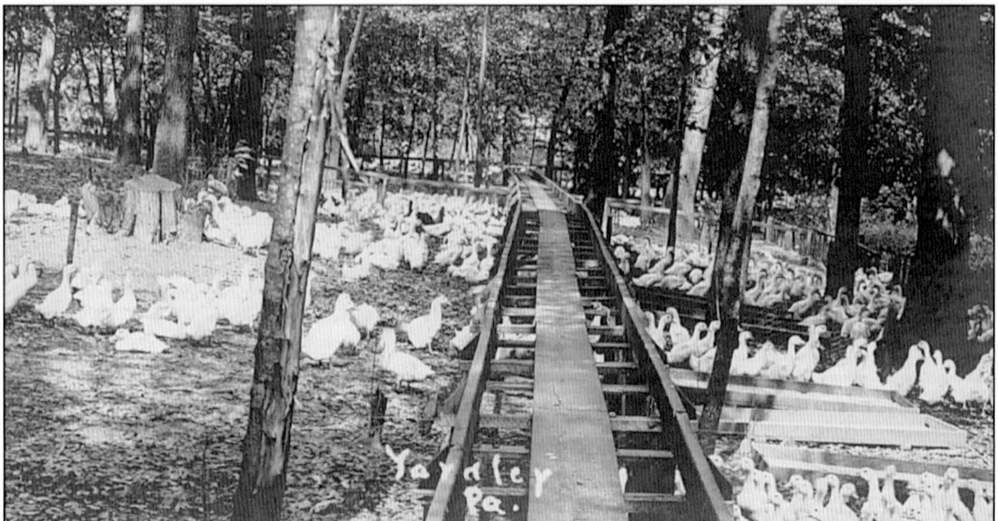

This Linford R. Craven photo postcard mailed from Yardley in 1908 shows the mini-railroad of McCormick's Duck Farm. McCormick's ducks were shipped throughout the East Coast. From the Poconos to New York City, patrons of fine restaurants could order a "Yardley duck." In more recent years the duck has become a symbol of Yardley.

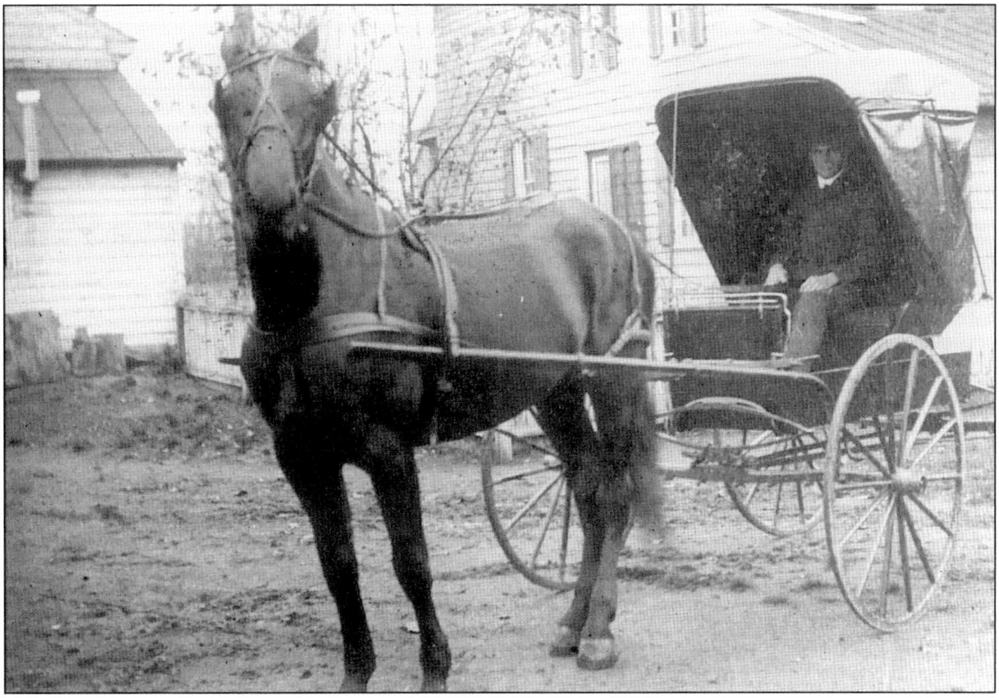

At the turn of the century, J.C. McCormick was the owner of the Yardley Duck Farm. The farm was located on Dolington Road on land that was part of William Yardley's Prospect Farm. McCormick drove his carriage from the farm to his home at 55 West Afton Avenue.

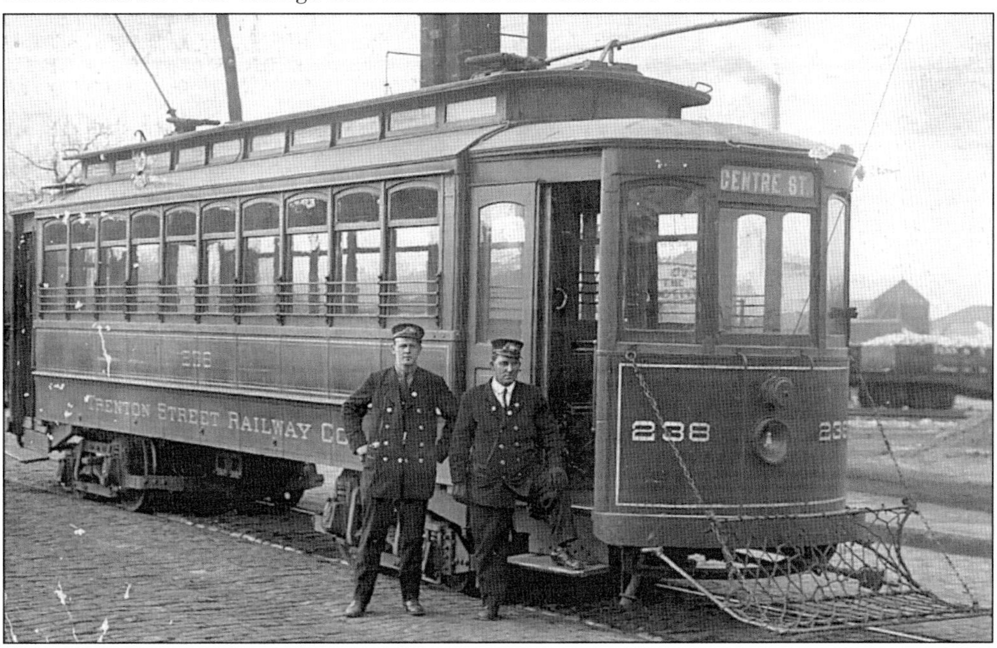

Horse-drawn carriages and wagons were still common on the streets of Yardley during the first two decades of the 20th century. But there was competition. Streetcars and automobiles had arrived. Motorman Chester Wetzstein (left) and the conductor posed for this photo postcard, c. 1913.

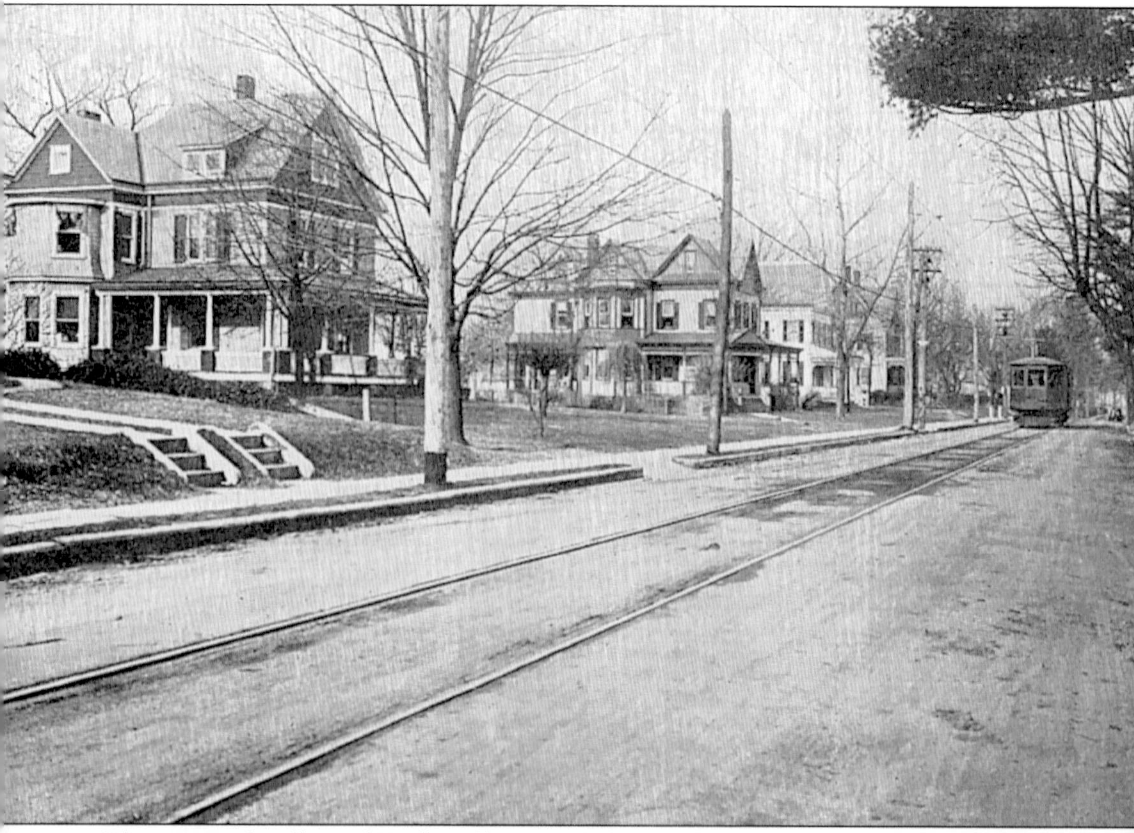

The crossroads village of Yardleyville expanded, even flourished, in the 19th century as the canal and later the railroad passed through town. In 1895 Yardley was incorporated as a borough. Growth would continue in the early 20th century fueled by new industries and a streetcar line. Despite failed contracts, changing franchises, and a torn-up and sometimes dusty Main Street, the streetcars linked Yardley with the rest of Bucks County as well as Trenton and Lambertville, NJ. In the early 1900s, trolley cars traveled down South Main Street past a line of new Victorian homes.

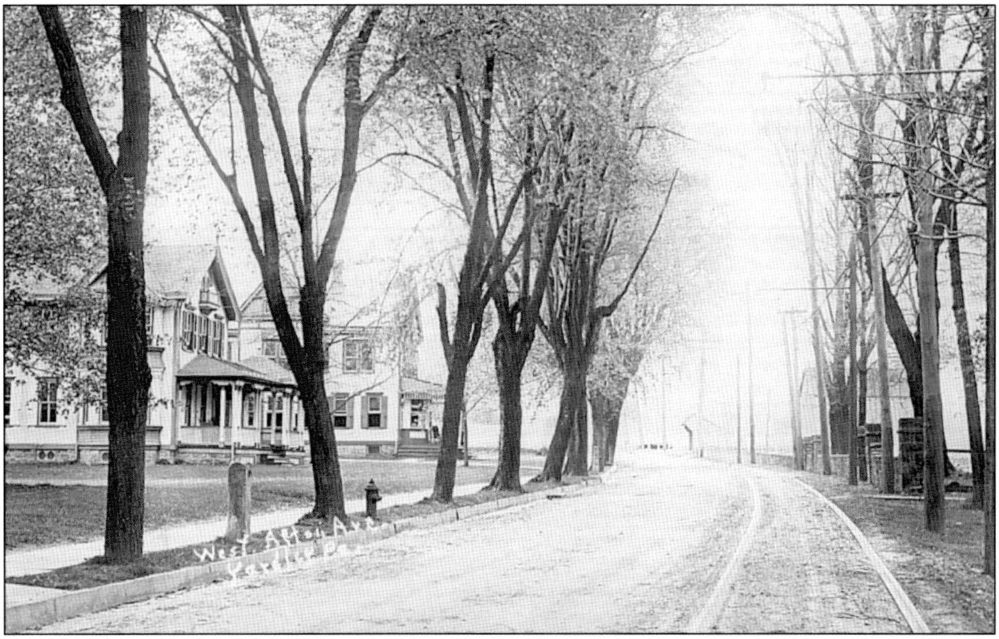

The line between Morrisville and Yardley was completed in 1900. The line was extended up West Afton to Newtown. Tracks are visible in this postcard view of West Afton Avenue, c. 1910. When the system was completed, a Yardley resident could take a streetcar to Trenton, Newtown, or New Hope.

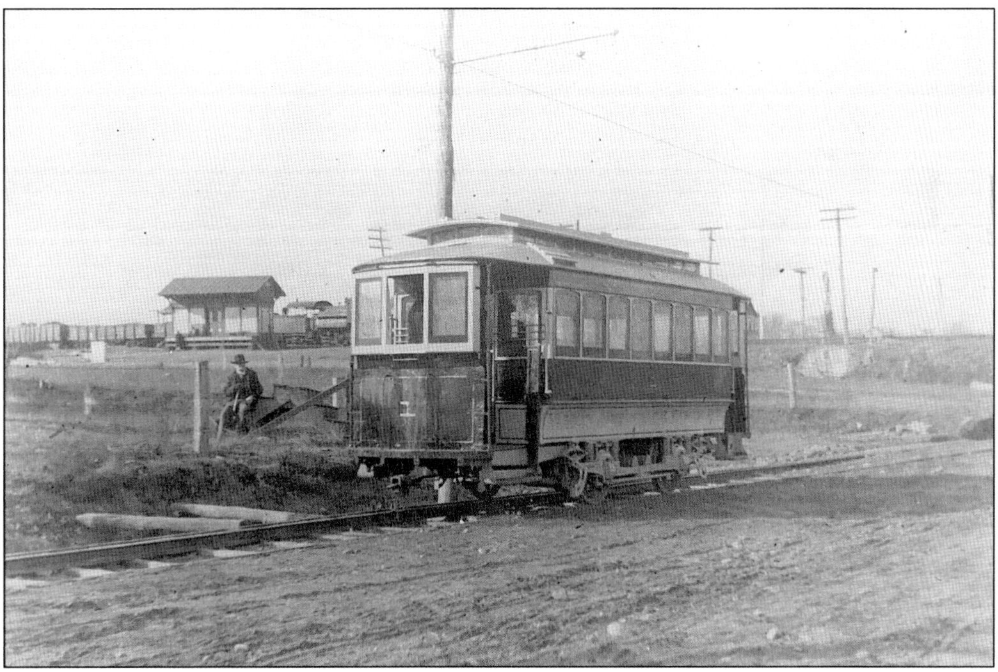

Old Number 1, an 18-foot, single truck "dinky" painted red was the first trolley car used on the Morrisville-Yardley line. It was put into service on December 28, 1900. The motorman was Owen Moon, one of the company owners; manager Wilbur Sadler acted as conductor. The Reading Railroad freight house and station can be seen in the background.

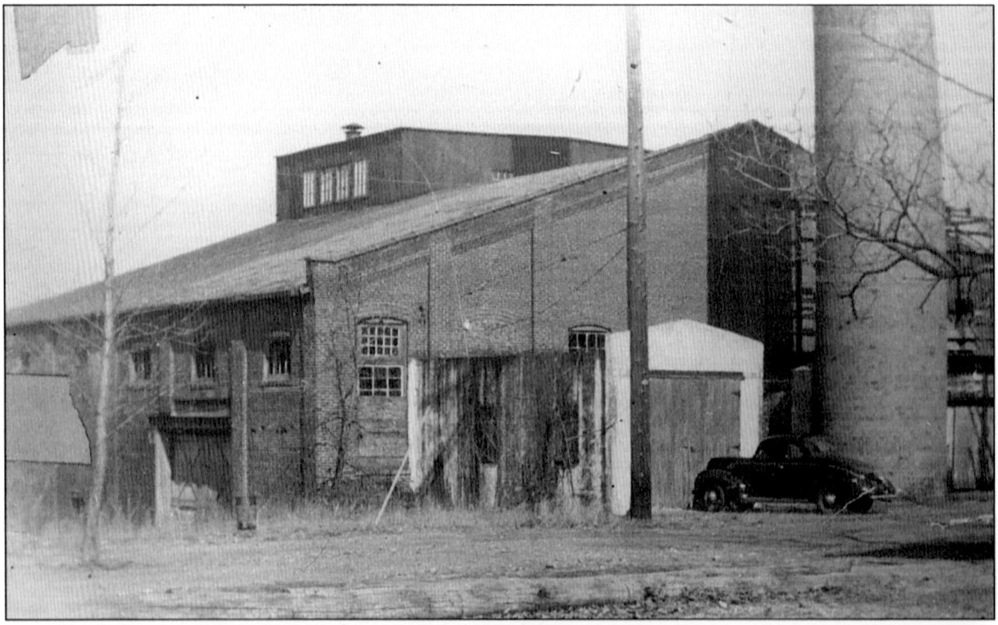

A.L. Smith erected the Yardley Power Generating Plant in the 1890s on the site of the Yardley sawmill on East Afton Avenue. In 1900, the Yardley, Morrisville, and Trenton Street Railroad was granted a franchise to lay track on Main Street. The company purchased the generating plant from the Yardley Power and Light Company. This photograph, c. 1940, shows the abandoned plant before its conversion for retail business.

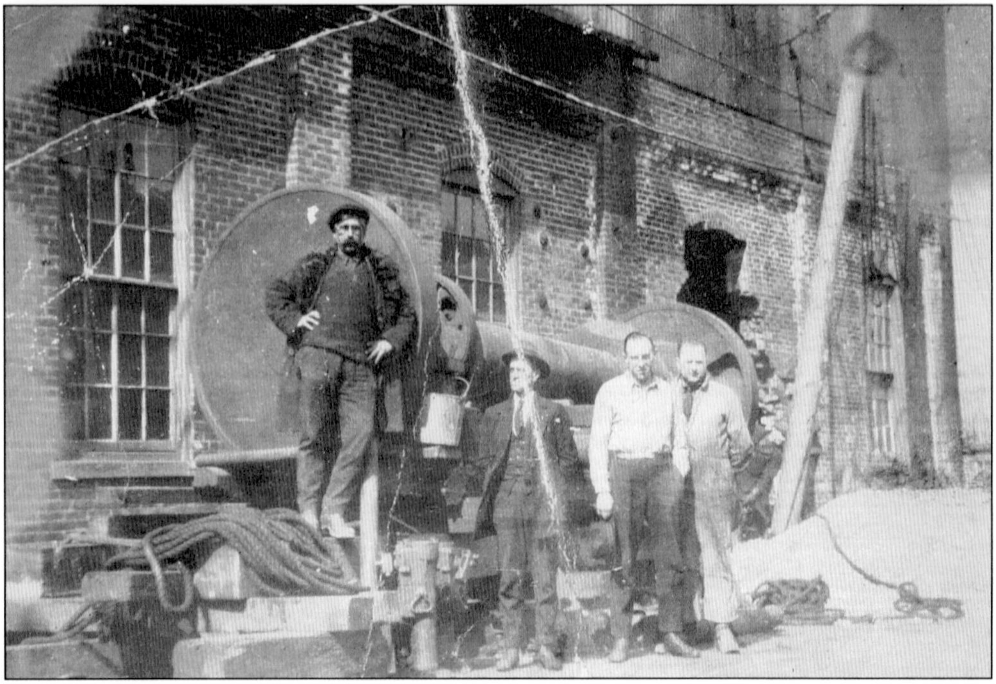

Electric power station employees stopped their repair work on East Afton Avenue in this undated photograph. By 1924, trolley service between Yardley and Newtown had stopped. The power station continued to operate until about 1934, when all service was suspended.

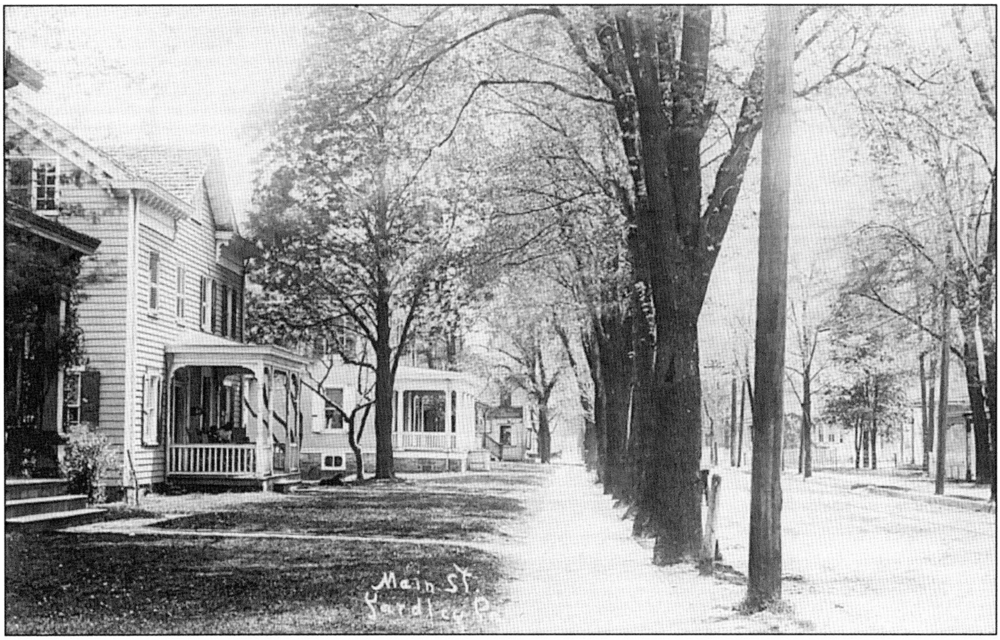

Yardley didn't change much from 1900 to the 1940s. The trolley tracks, which were laid in about 1900, were torn up in the late 1930s, but Main Street in the 1940s didn't look all that different from this photograph taken *c.* 1910. There would be some major changes in the 1950s.

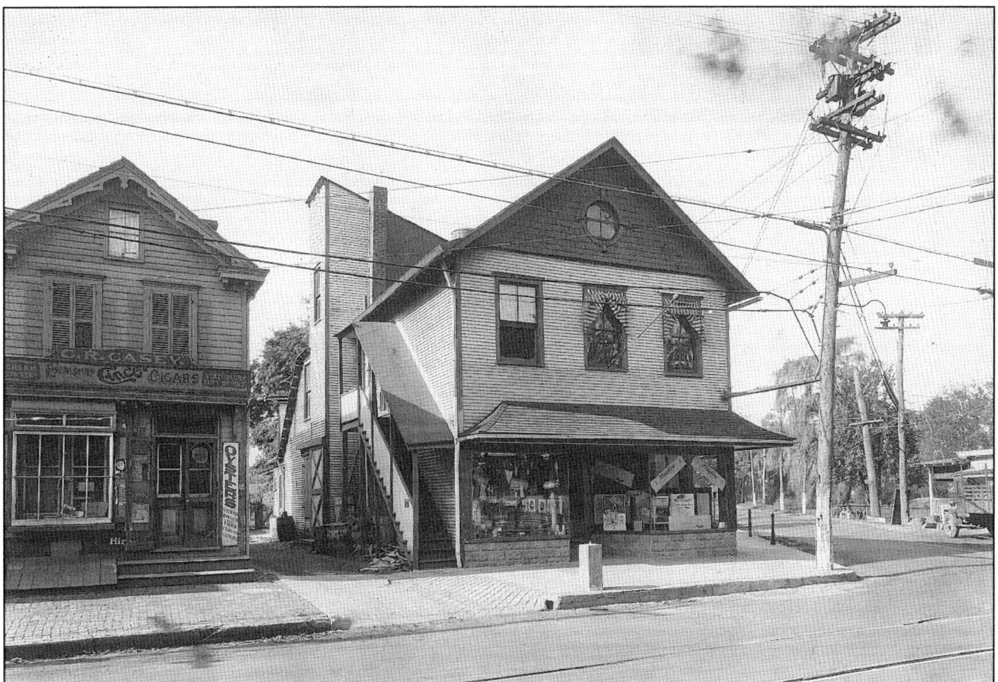

The Beener building, right, was built in 1900 after a fire destroyed Cadwallader's general store. Casey's Ice Cream Parlor is on the left-signs advertise ice cream, soda drinks and oysters. Main Street is lined with a tangle of electric and telephone lines. Streetcar tracks are still present in this *c.* 1930 photograph.

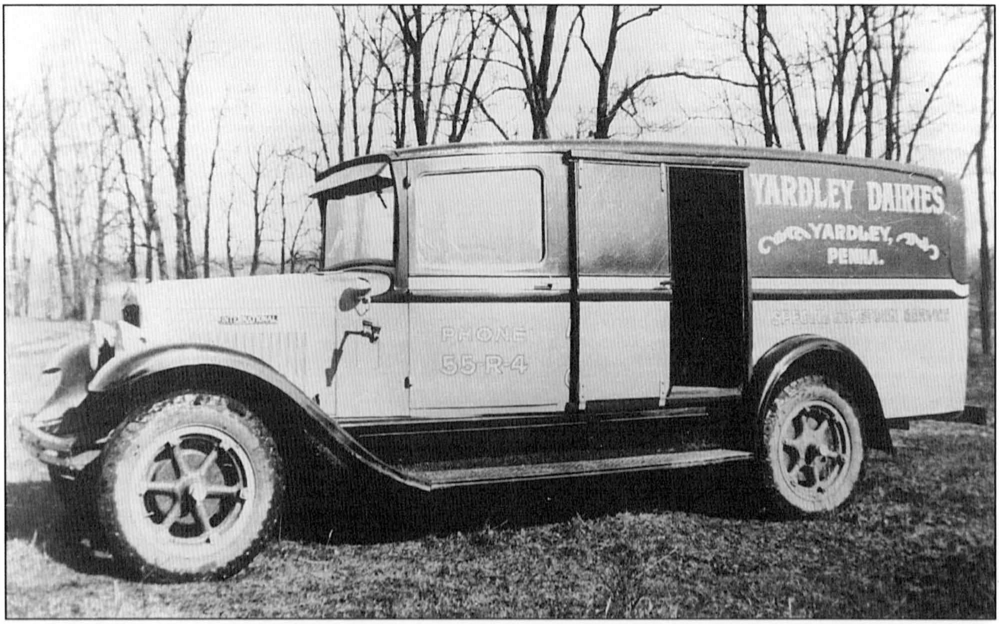

In the 1930s, buses replaced trolley cars, and trucks began to replace the many horse-drawn wagons and carts that made deliveries in Yardley. The Eggleston family operated Yardley Dairies, located in the Maplevale section of Lower Makefield. The number for service was 55-R-4.

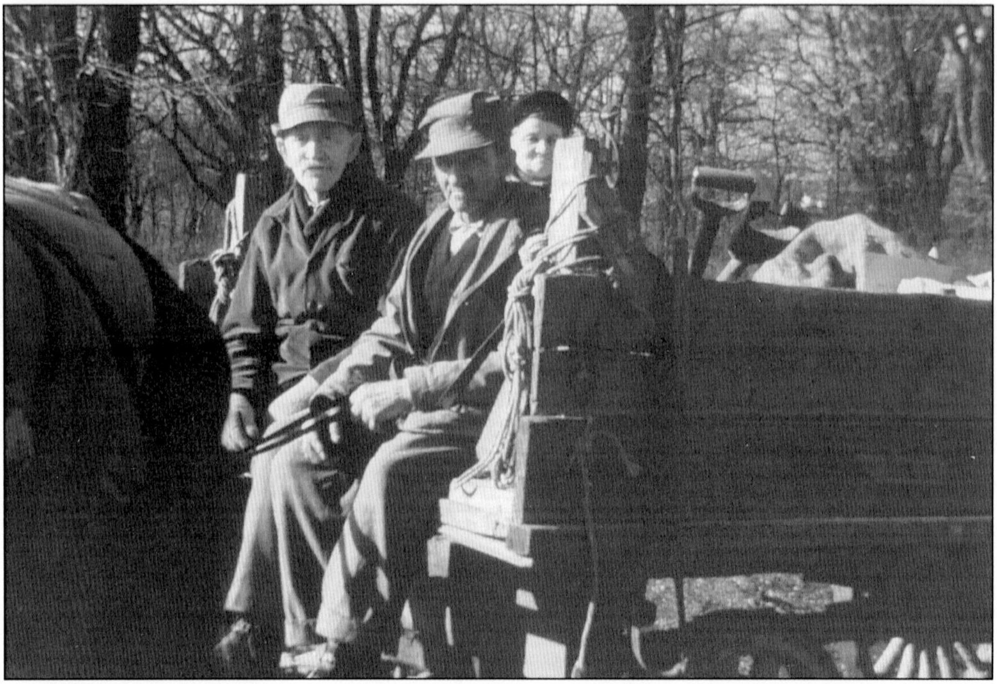

It wouldn't be until 1955 that a gasoline fueled truck would replace Tommy Todd's horse-drawn trash wagon on the streets of Yardley. It is said that Todd's horses could find their way home from the Continental Tavern. This photograph of Tommy (the driver) John White, and Alice Burhley is from a color slide shot in 1948

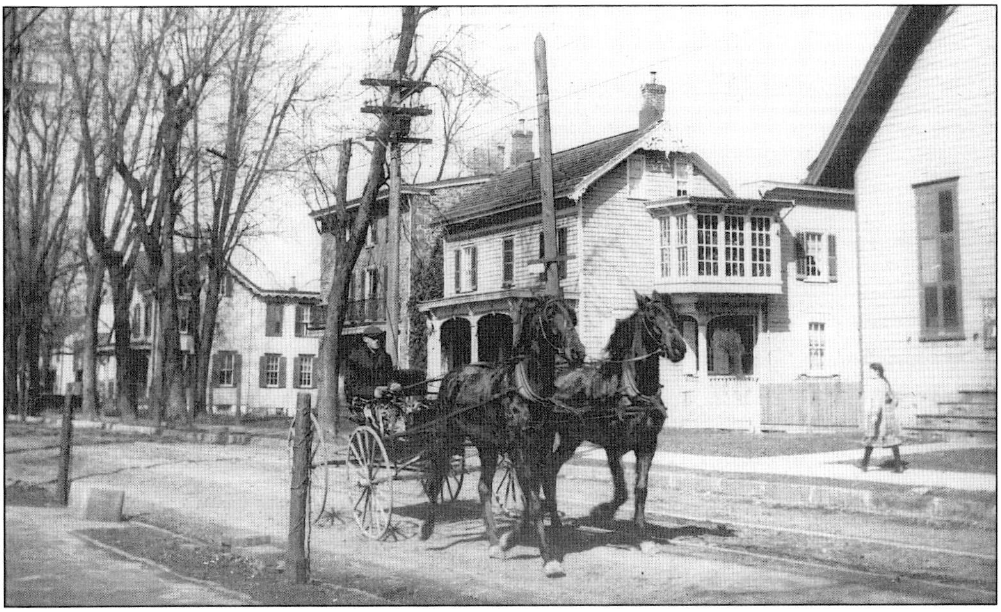

"Skylark" and "Star" clip along Main Street. Harry South is pictured in the buggy owned by Dr. Henry Linn Bassett who lived and practiced medicine at 70 South Main Street. In 1909 Dr. Bassett purchased a new Buick and joined the small number of automobile owners in the Yardley area. In the background on the right is the Yardley Community Center, the Ella Moon House, and Yardley Borough Hall.

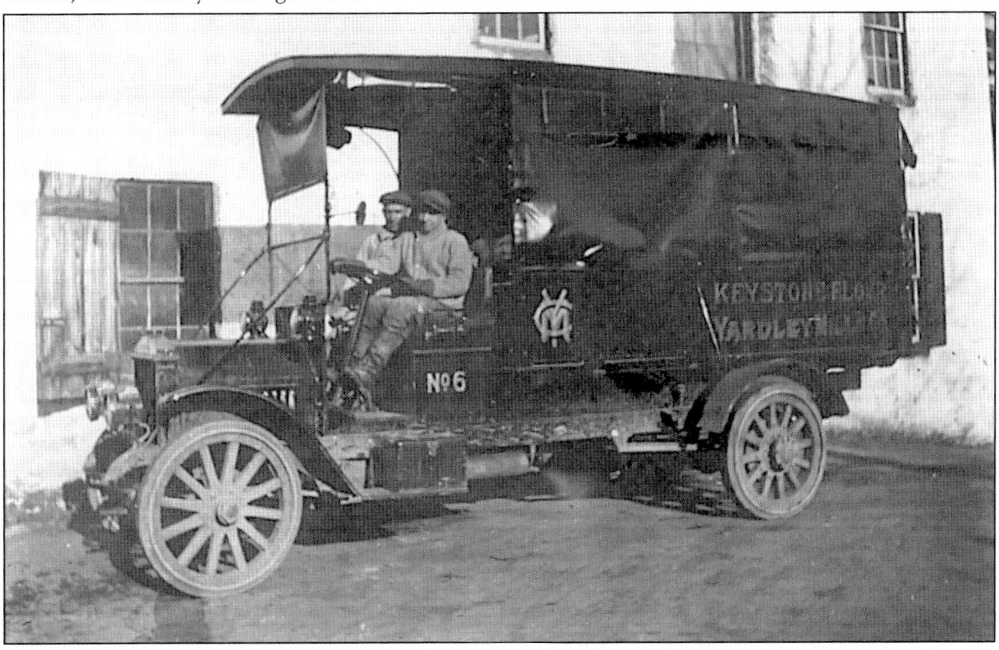

An undated photo postcard documents the change from horse-drawn wagon to motorized truck for the Yardley Mills Company. The driver is a Gallagher; the helper is Joseph B. Johnson. During the early decades of the 20th century, the Yardley Mill Company, owned by T. Sidney Cadwallader, was a prosperous business—buying, storing, and selling grain, flour, and feed in Lower Bucks County.

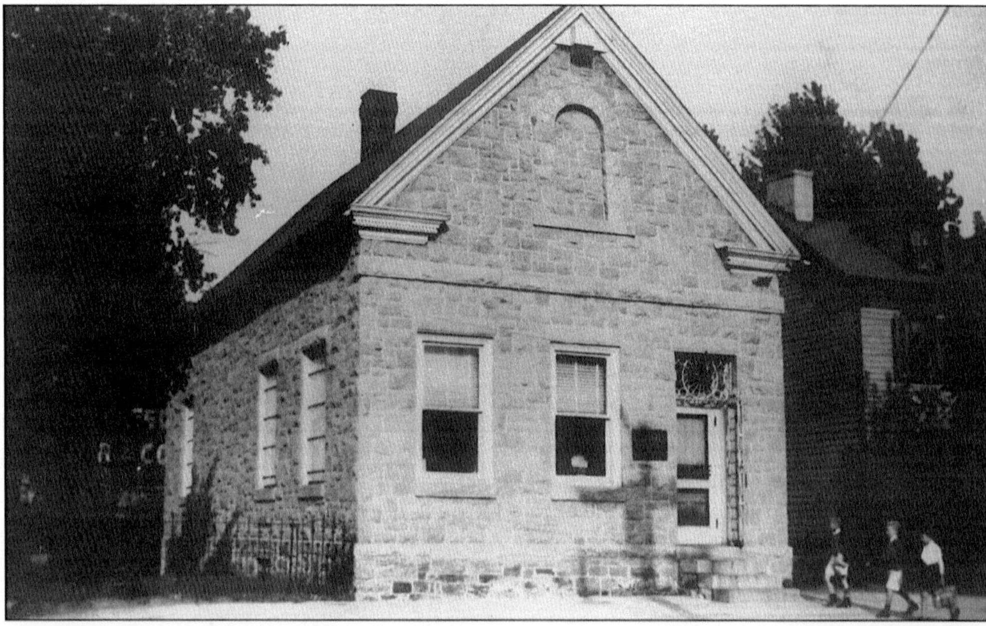

The Yardley National Bank was established in the 1890s. An addition was later added to the stone building constructed on South Main Street.

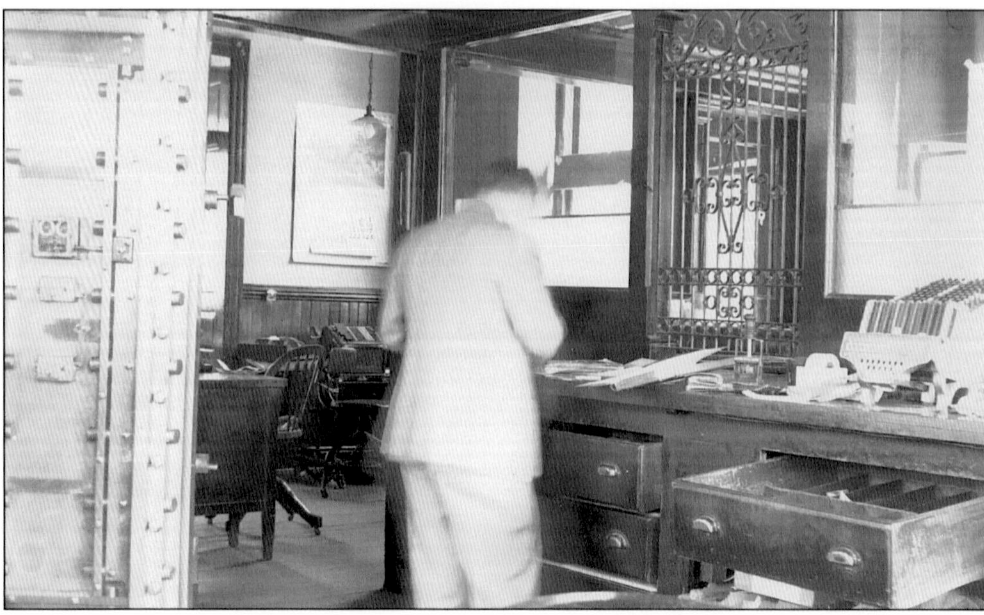

During the 1930s, the Yardley National Bank joined a long list of banks that failed. A new bank under a different name was immediately chartered. For several months, depositors were able to withdraw depreciated assets from the old bank, and deposit them in the new bank without ever leaving the building.

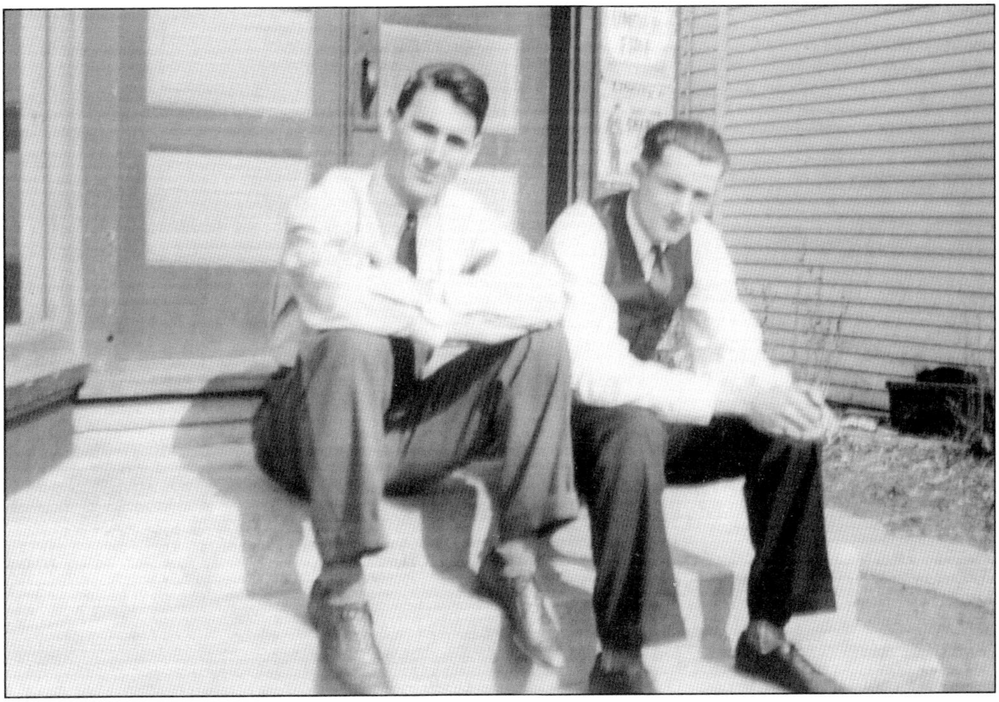

Jack Rembe and Raymond Yantz were employees of the Yardley National Bank, 1936.

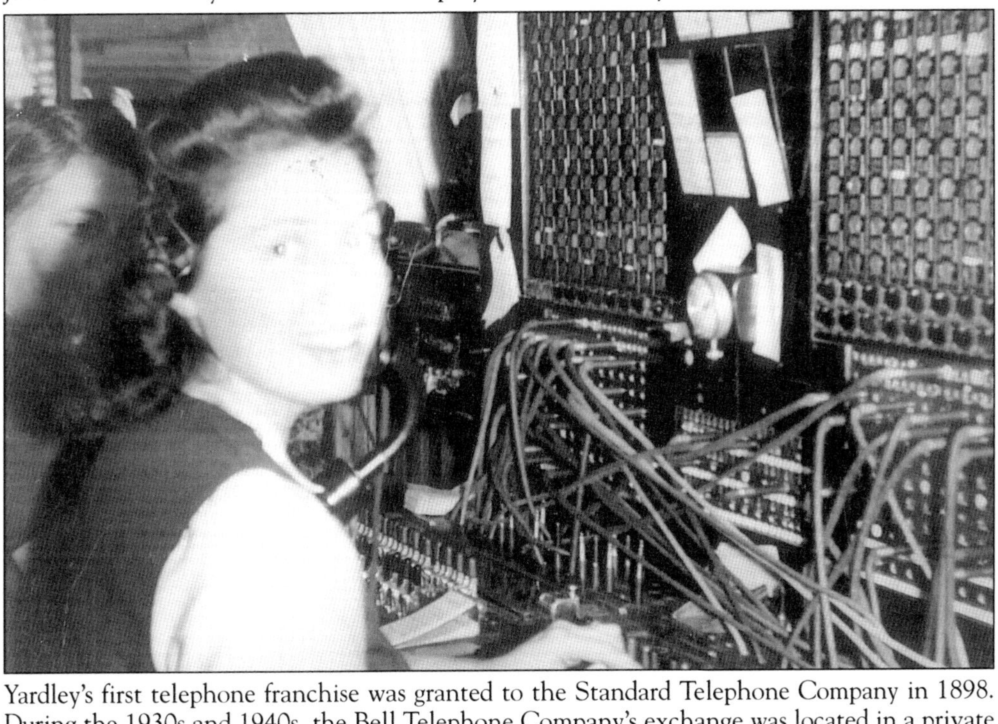

Yardley's first telephone franchise was granted to the Standard Telephone Company in 1898. During the 1930s and 1940s, the Bell Telephone Company's exchange was located in a private house at 57 West Afton. Anne Hackett was the chief operator. Rachel Smith DeSau was one of several high school students who worked at the switchboard. Another high school operator, Connie Schmidt, took this photograph of Rachel in 1939–40.

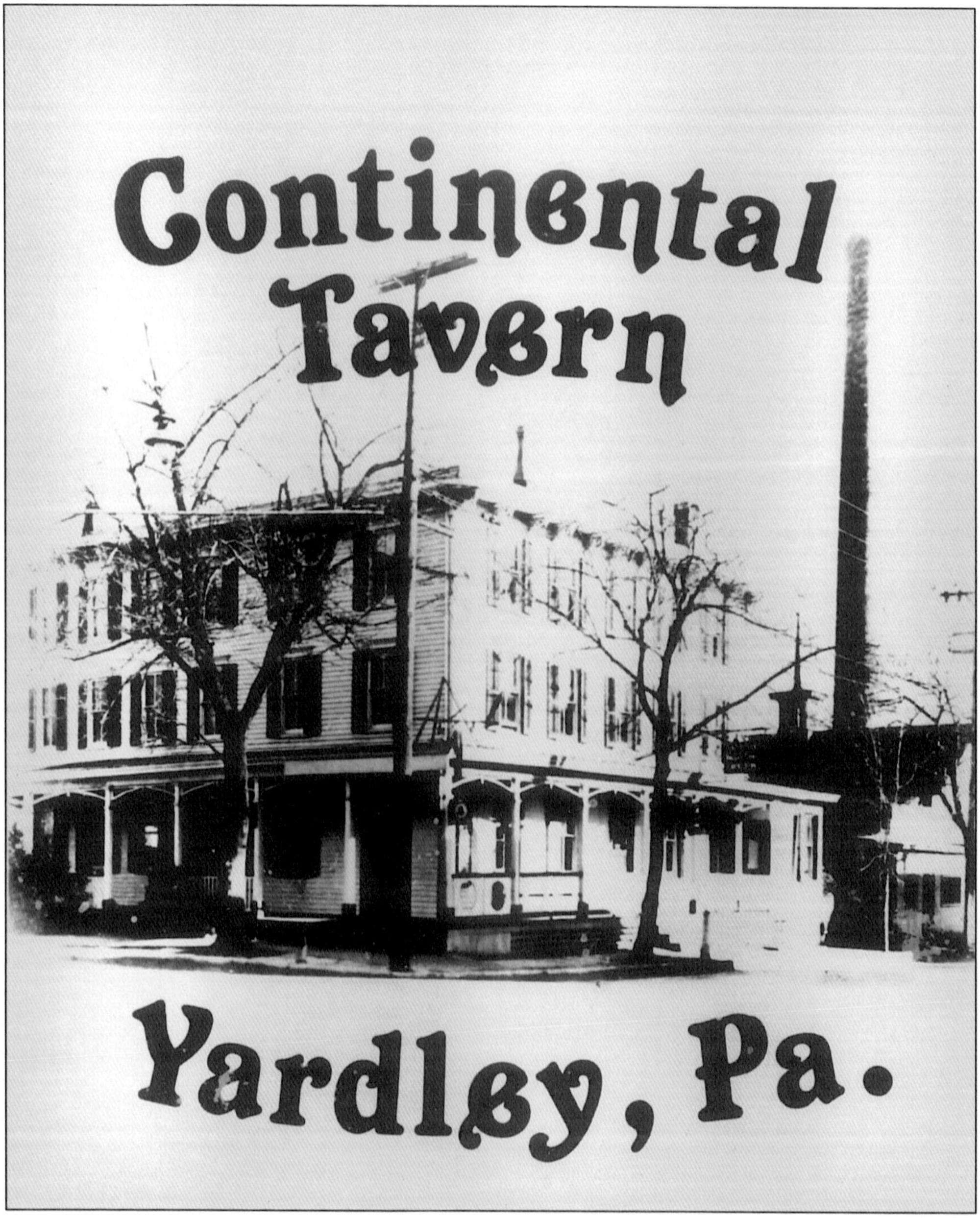

In 1845, Samuel Slack operated a Temperance House and store on the northwest corner of Main and Afton. In 1866, Aaron Slack obtained a license to operate a hotel there. To fulfill the requirements for a license, Slack built four bedrooms over the barn. By this time, another store and barbershop had been added to the main building. A fire caused by the barber, Henry Brown, drying hair in his stove, destroyed the entire corner, and this hotel was built in 1876. Notice the Yardley Power Company smoke stack behind the hotel.

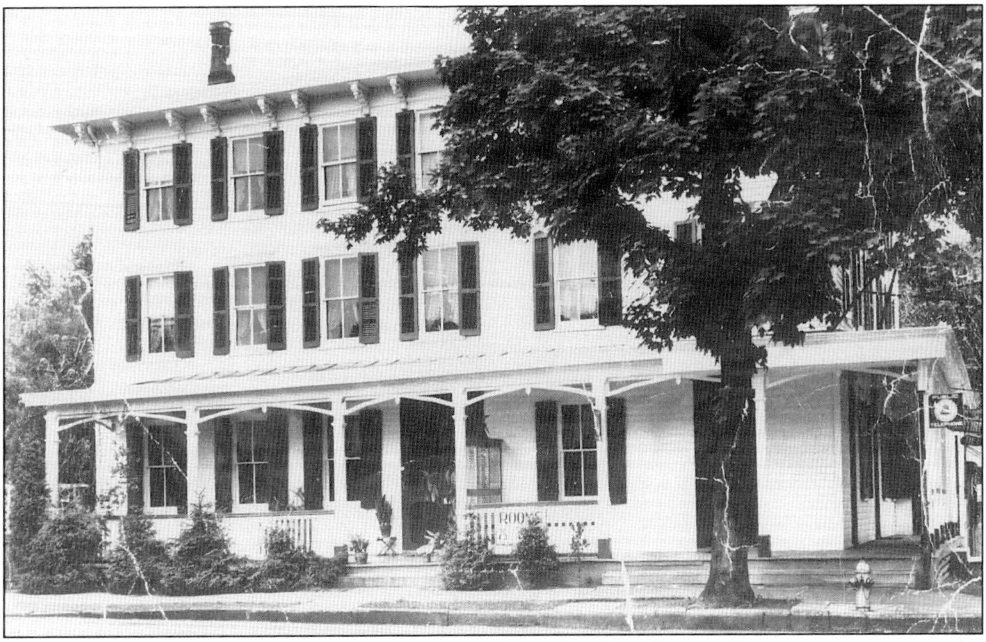

In the late 19th and early 20th centuries, Yardley developed a small summer tourist trade. One destination was the Continental Hotel. Visitors could enjoy a stroll down Main Street and spend quiet hours on the Continental's porch. Beginning in 1899, they had access to telephone service.

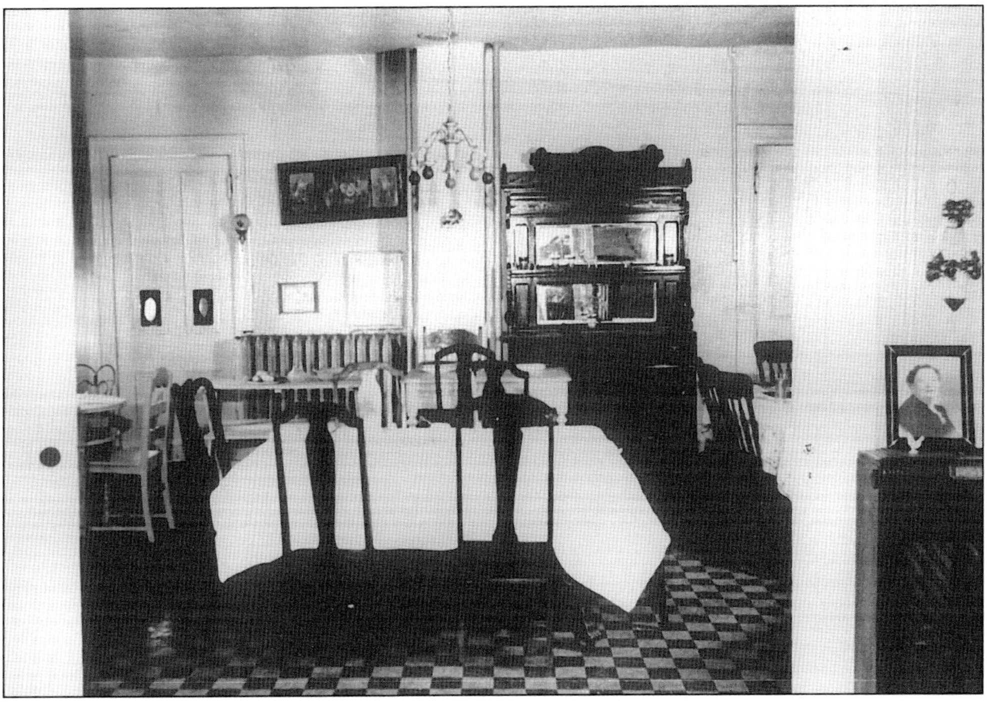

A local newspaper described the Continental as "a first class stopping place." Its proprietor Aaron Slack was described as particularly attentive to the wants of everyone. Oysters and snapper soup were favorites on the menu.

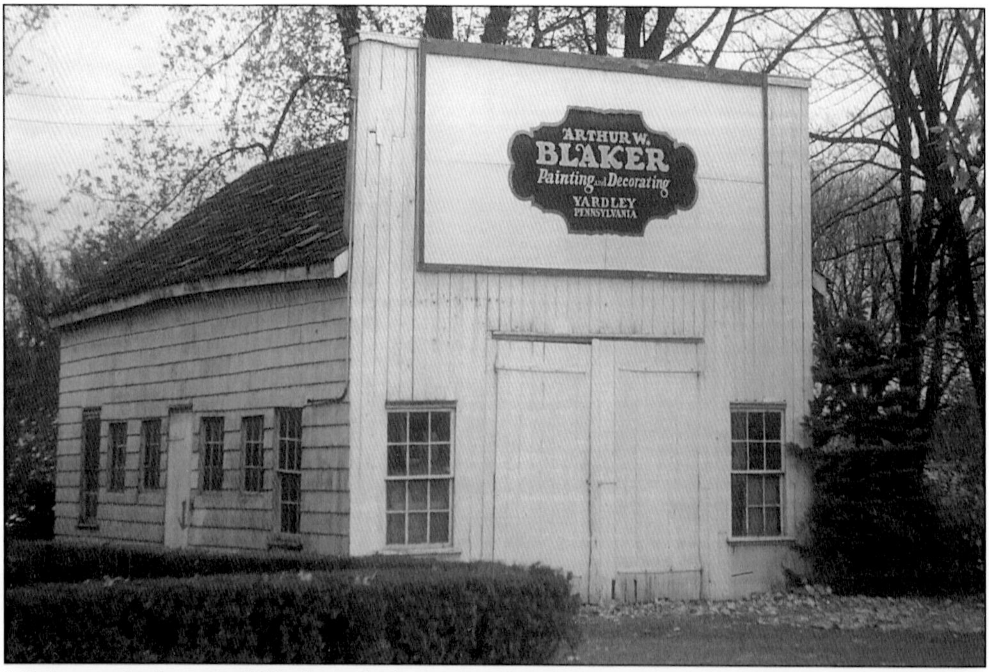

J.S. Lovett built a small blacksmith shop at 42 South Main Street in 1855. In the early years of the 20th century Walter Gallagher operated the shop. During the 1940s, Arthur Blaker's Painting and Decorating Shop was located in the building. In the 1980s, the renovated building was Harriet's, an interior design shop; late in the 90s, it was a cigar and coffee shop.

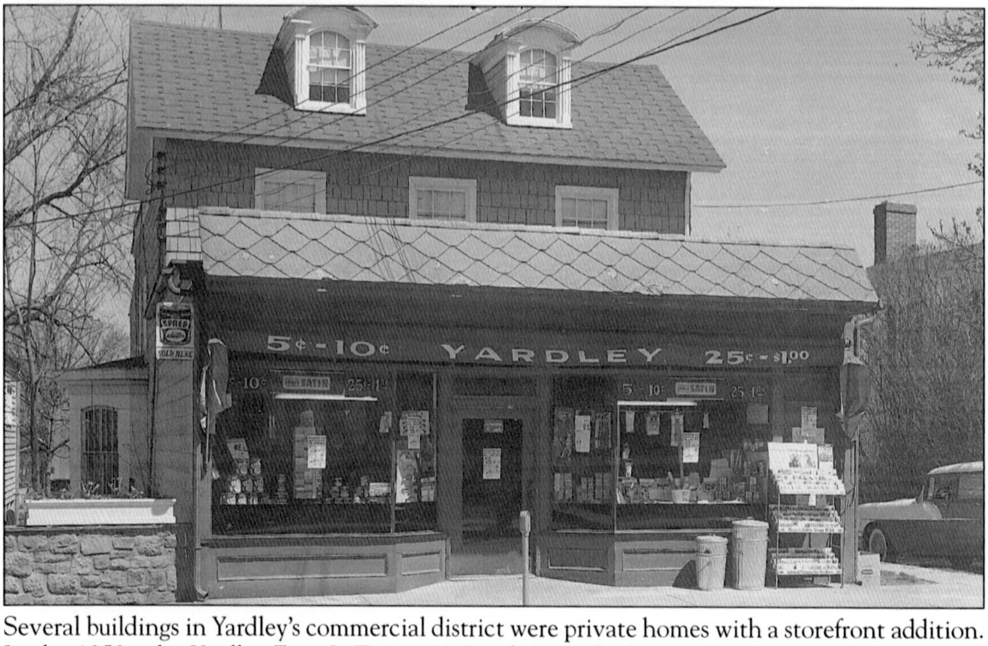

Several buildings in Yardley's commercial district were private homes with a storefront addition. In the 1950s, the Yardley Five & Ten at 20 South Main had a wooden facade. In 1958, it was replaced with a stone facade, striped awning, and "colonial windows." The owners, Mr. and Mrs. Len Murray, advertised "Variety is Our Specialty, A Dozen Stores in One—Open During Alterations—We're Helping to Beautify Yardley."

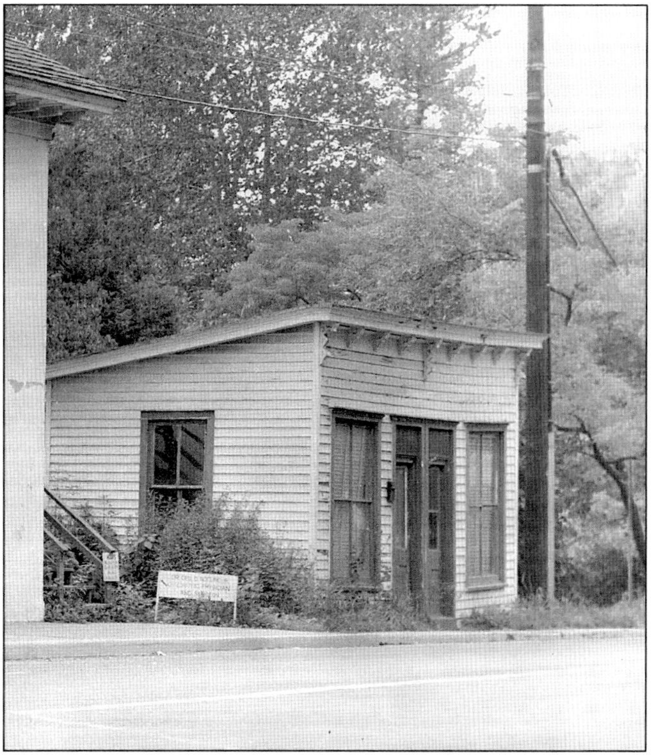

Archie Gallagher's barbershop, once located on North Main Street behind Wist's Corner, was one of several quaint, small buildings in downtown Yardley. In 1958, as part of a town improvement campaign, the building was demolished.

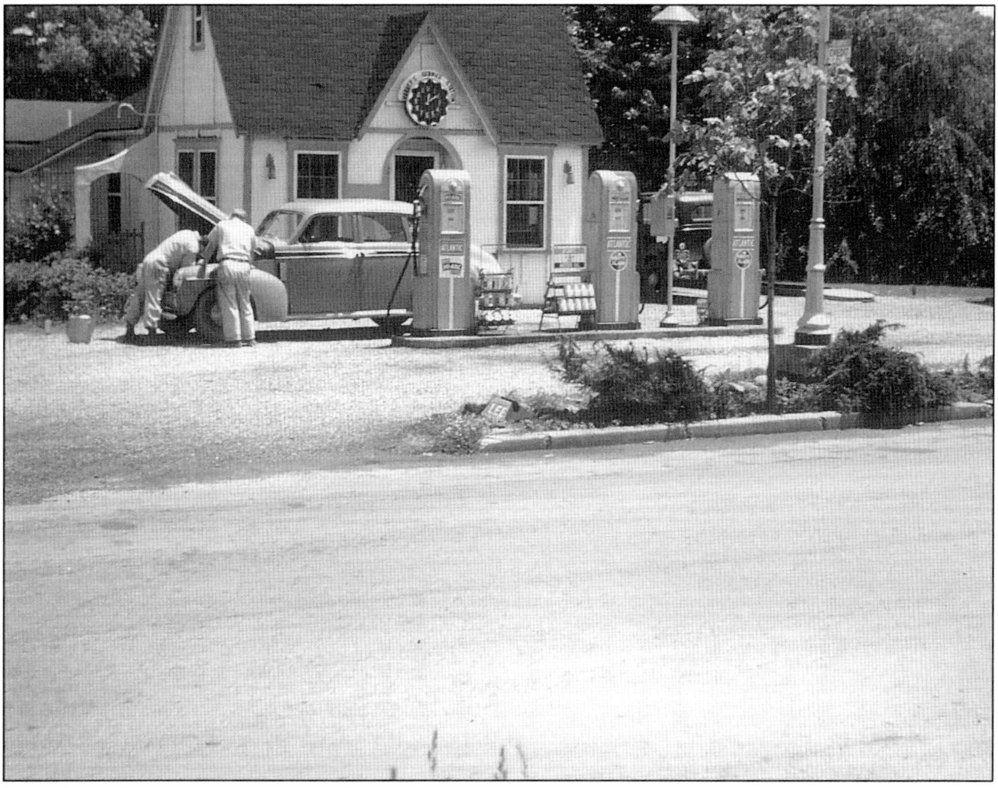

This photograph was taken in 1948 when the Yardley Service Station located on South Main Street near the Railroad pumped Atlantic gasoline.

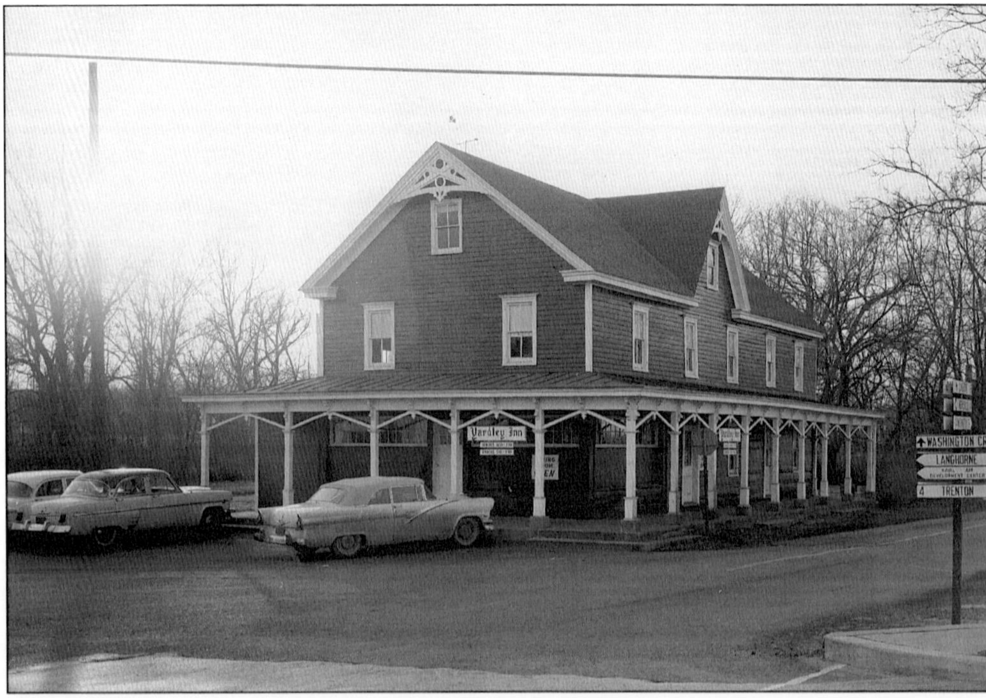

The Yardley Inn was on River Road near the ferry crossing. It was originally known as the "White Swan." Yardley, however, was a strong temperance community. Activists frequently attempted to close public drinking establishments. In the 1890s, the Swan was refused a liquor license and became a summer boarding house and way stop for cyclists.

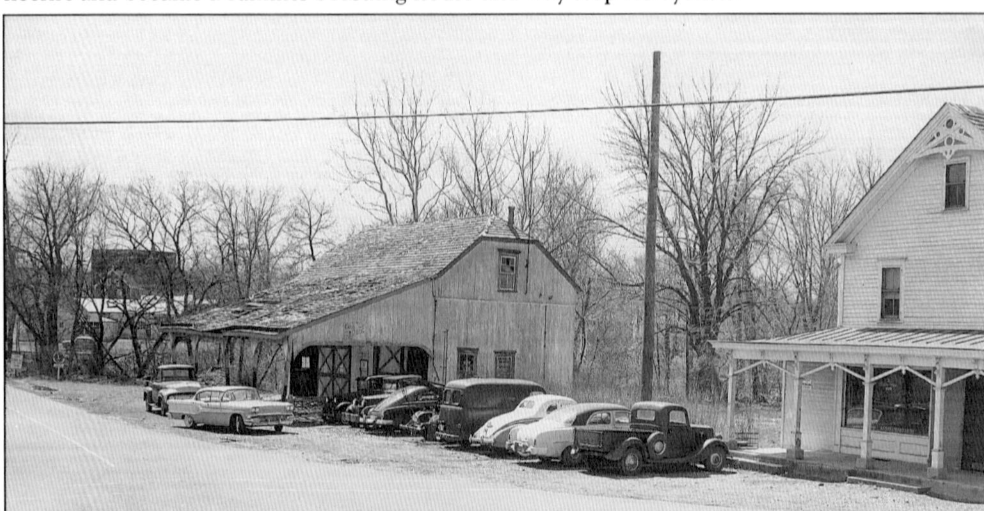

The White Swan had several names. In the 1890s, the proprietor was Jonathan Shoemaker. The first borough elections were held in Shoemaker's Inn in 1895. At one time it was Dugan's Swan Hotel, and in the early 20th century it was Cryne's Hotel. In 1958 the old barn was removed and the historic riverside inn and tavern was renamed the Yardley Inn.

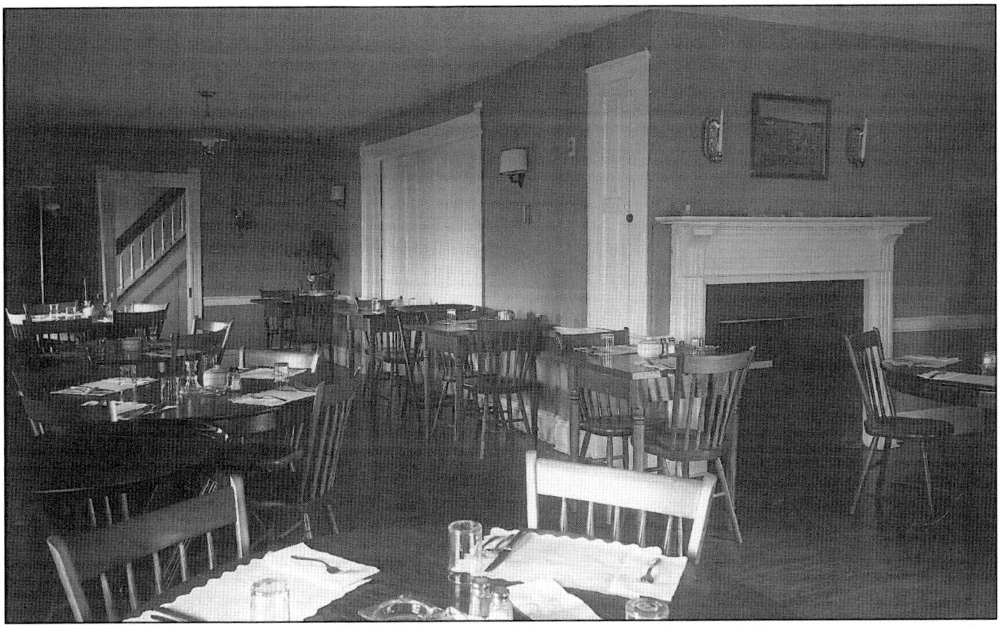

The main dining room in the Yardley Inn was ready for customers after renovations in the 1950s. During the renovations, workers found Prohibition-era corks and labels under a false floor.

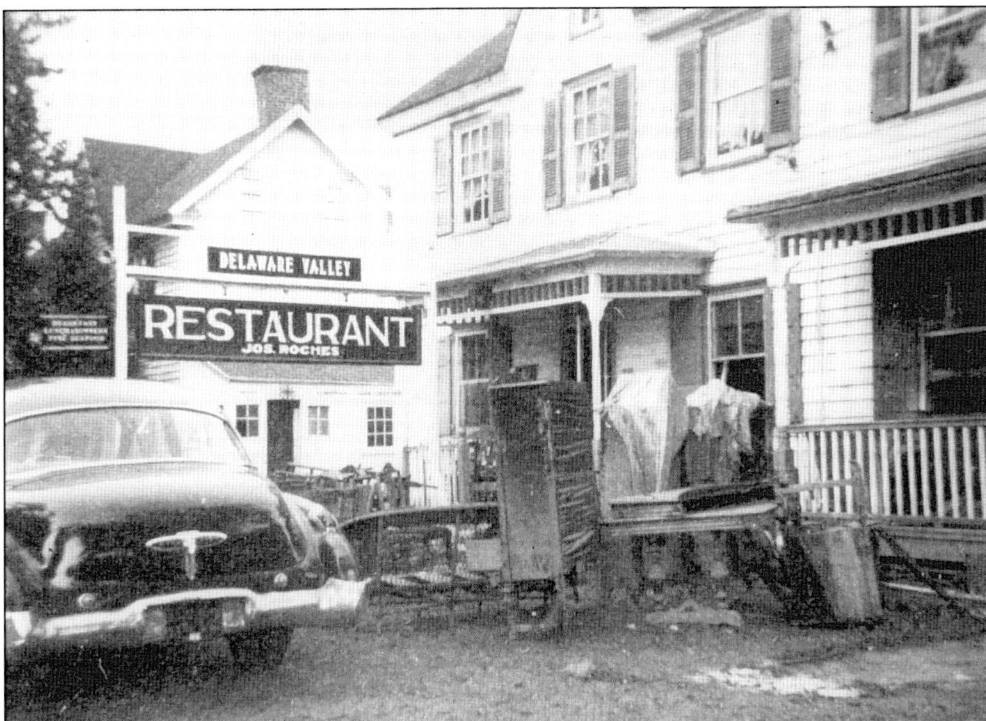

Joseph Roches operated the Delaware Valley Restaurant on East Afton Avenue. This photograph was taken after the 1955 flood, as the Roches cleaned up and attempted to salvage furnishings. Mrs. Roches also operated a small dress making business in the building.

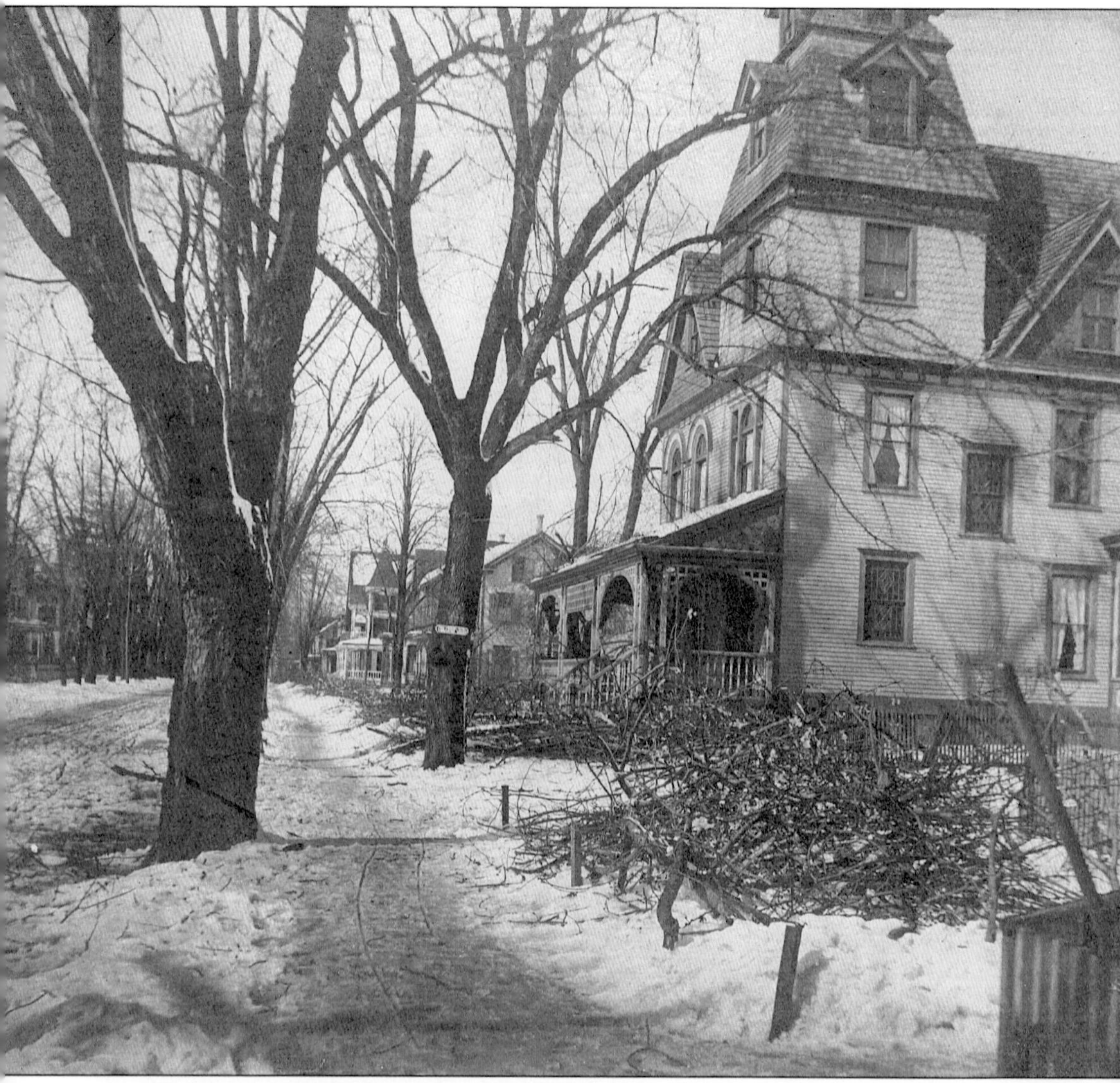

During the late 19th century, the railroad ushered in a new period of prosperity in Yardley. On South Main Street, older homes were renovated and new homes were constructed in a variety of Victorian styles. In 1890, Joseph H. Martin erected a Queen Anne Victorian on the corner of College and Main. The large elaborate turret seen in this turn-of-the-20th-century photograph was later removed to save maintenance costs. Martin's home replaced a frame house and log kitchen built on the site in the 1830s by Ralph Lee. Ralph and his son David were local carpenters.

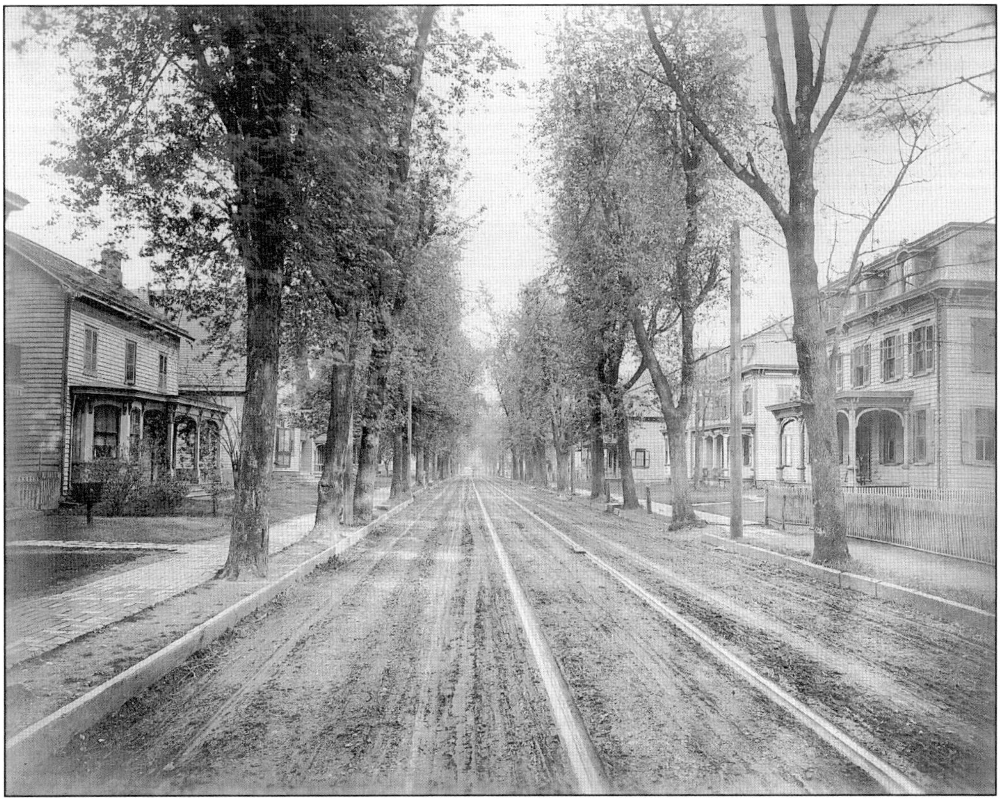

Trolley tracks were laid on South Main Street in 1900. Trees lined the newly graded street and shaded the new brick sidewalks. Two large French Second Empire-style homes are on the right. The style, popular during the 1860s, featured a distinctive roof designed by Francoise Mansart in the 17th century. The Ella Moon house is on the left, followed by the Yardley Community Center.

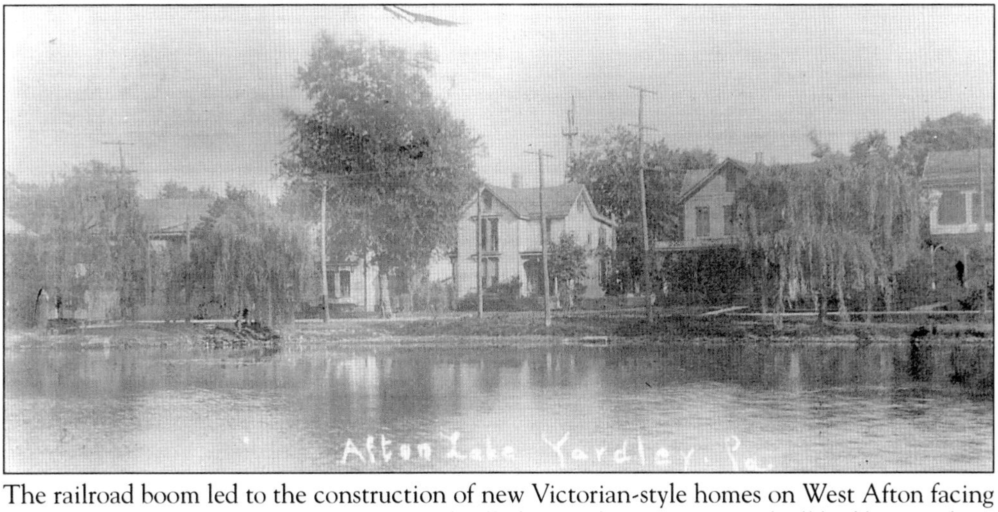

The railroad boom led to the construction of new Victorian-style homes on West Afton facing the lake. The Twinings, Swartzlanders, Cadwalladers, and J.C. McCormick all had homes along the avenue. For several decades in was "the place" to live in Yardley.

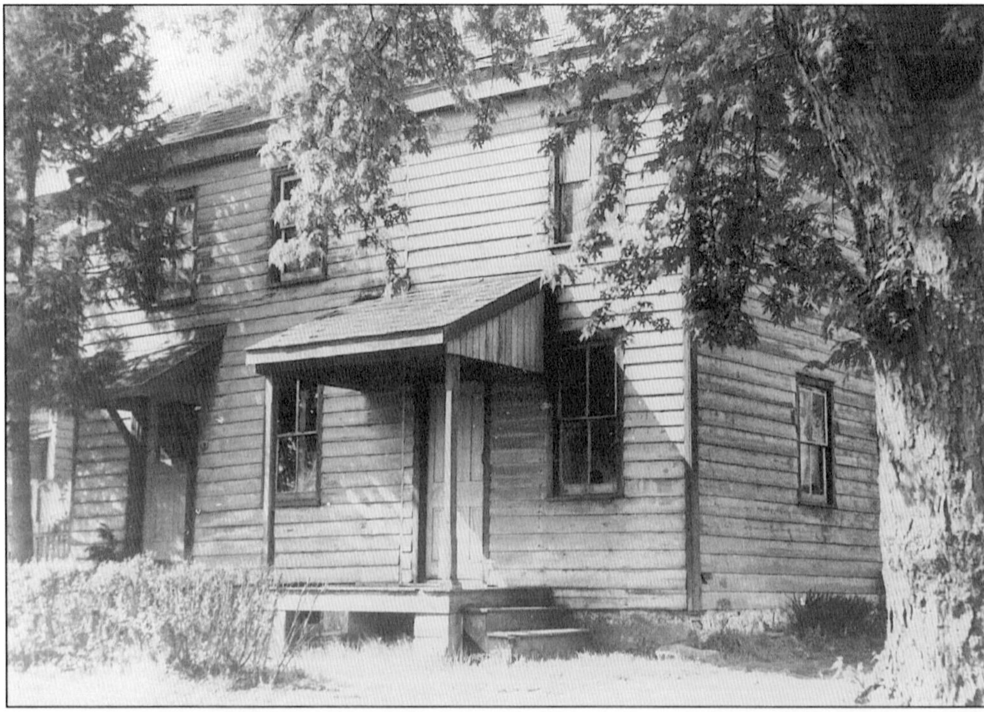

Homes were built on Back (later Canal) Street in the 1830s and 1840s after the construction of the Delaware Canal. This photograph of 21 Canal Street was taken during the Canal Street Renaissance in the 1960s, during which many homes were renovated.

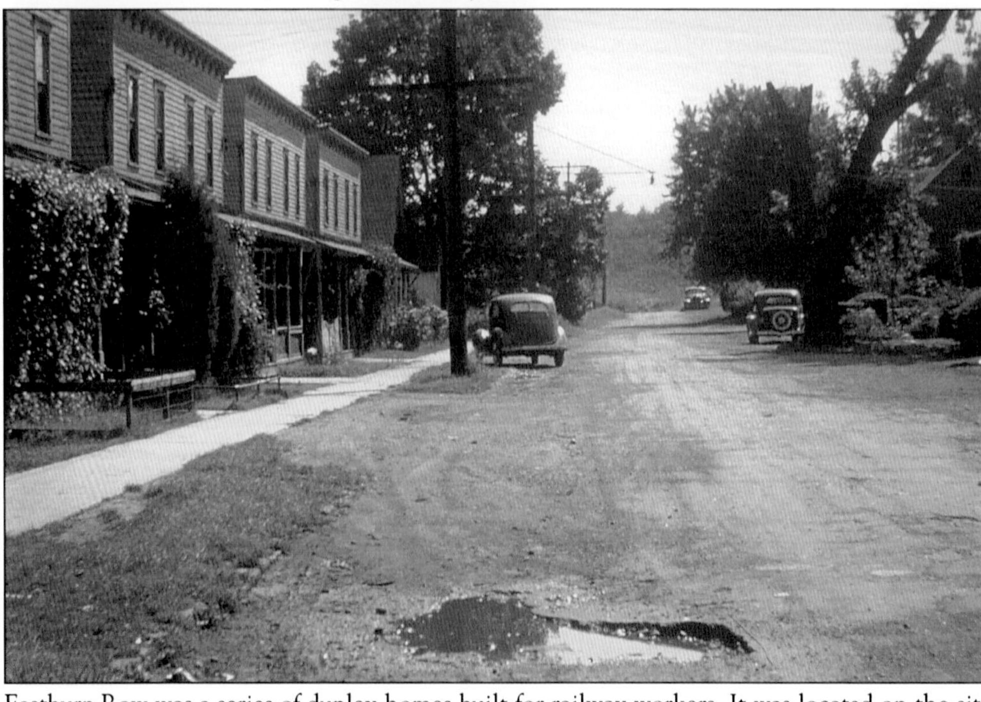

Eastburn Row was a series of duplex homes built for railway workers. It was located on the site of a canal boat yard. This photograph was taken in 1948.

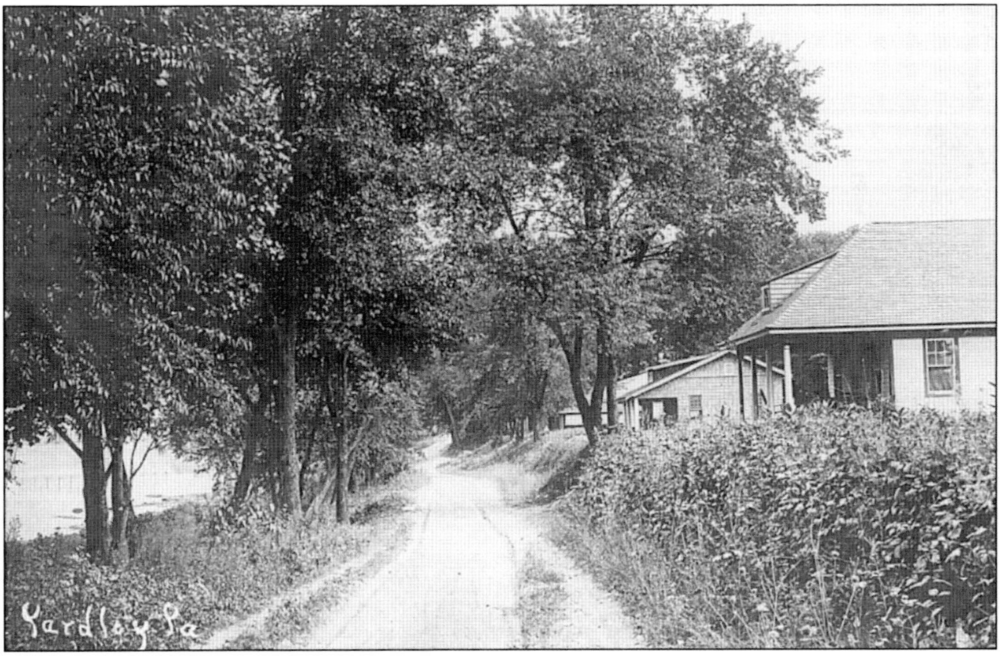

In 1908, Mary Yardley sold developers Morgan and Fuld land between Brown Street, the canal, and the Delaware River. They created a subdivision of summer bungalows. An unpaved River Road dominates this photo postcard by Doylestown photographer Linford R. Craven, c. 1910.

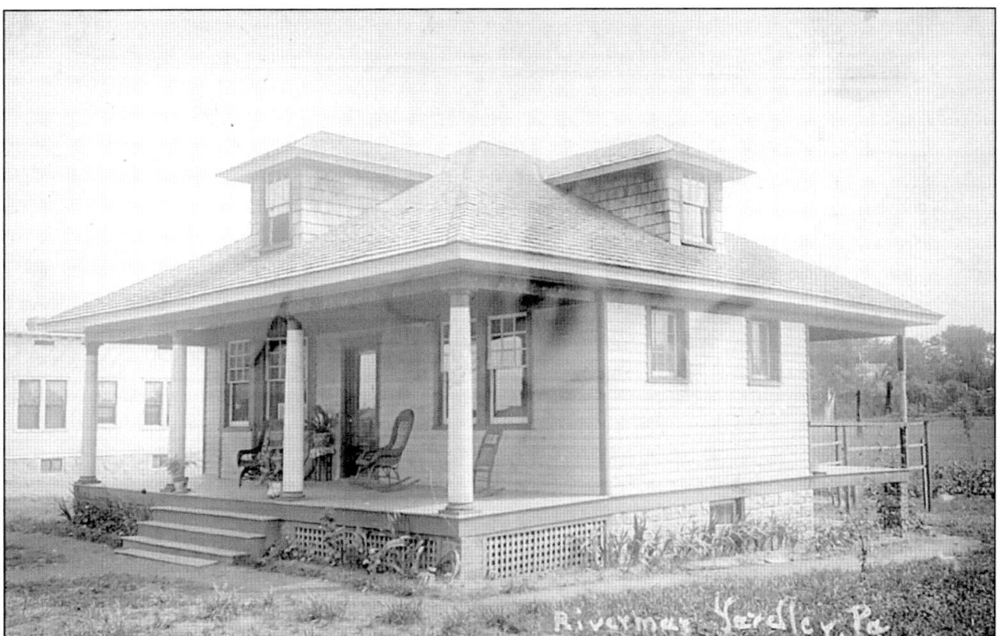

Morgan and Fuld named their development Rivermawr, and in an agreement of sale required that houses on River Road cost at least $1,500. On back streets, less expensive bungalows were allowed. Fences and the manufacturing of spirituous liquors were forbidden in the neighborhood.

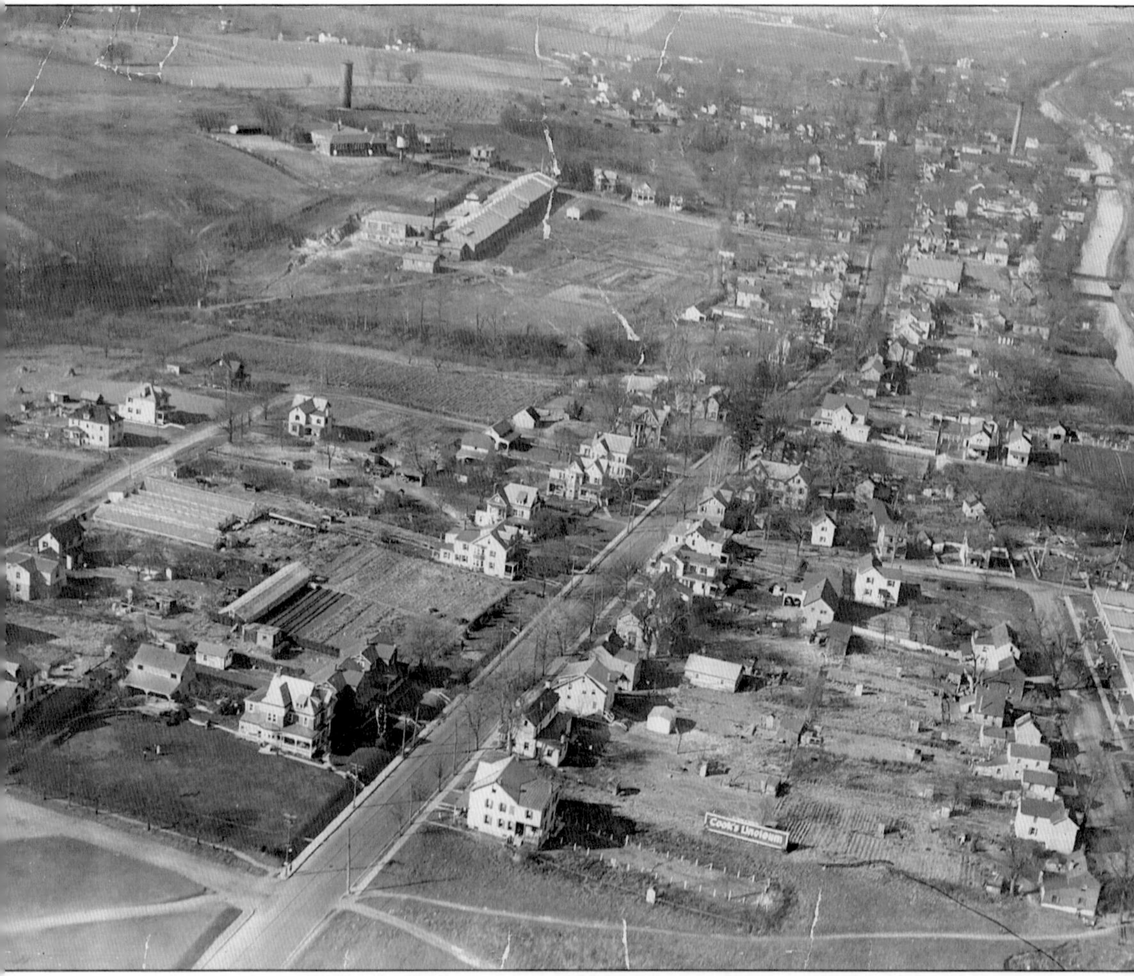

In 1682, William Yardley settled in Lower Makefield Township. A little more than 200 years later, in 1895, the village of Yardleyville was incorporated as an independent borough. The ferry crossing, canal, railroad, and trolley had led to the town's growth as a commercial hub for area farmland. Beginning in the 1950s, Yardley faced new challenges. Interstate 95 was constructed, opening up former farmland for development. Yardley's commercial district would face increased competition from suburban stores. Despite these changes, Yardley remained a small town with a rich historic past, traditions, and unique spirit. Main Street cuts diagonally across this aerial photograph taken by Virgil Kauffman before the 1955 flood washed away the Yardley Bridge.

Three

Institutions and Organizations

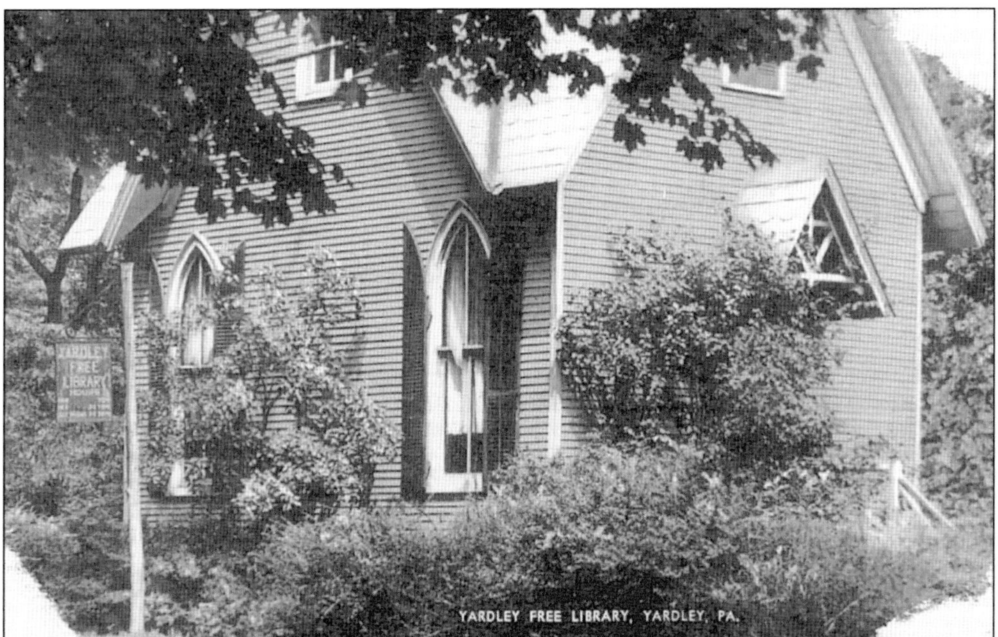

The "Old Library" by Lake Afton has become Yardley's most treasured landmark. The building dates to 1878 when the citizens of Yardleyville donated money, labor, and materials to construct a library. The heirs of founder William Yardley donated land along the lake. The Carpenter Gothic-style library with its pointed, arched windows and steep, decorative slate gable roof has been a subject for countless photographers and painters.

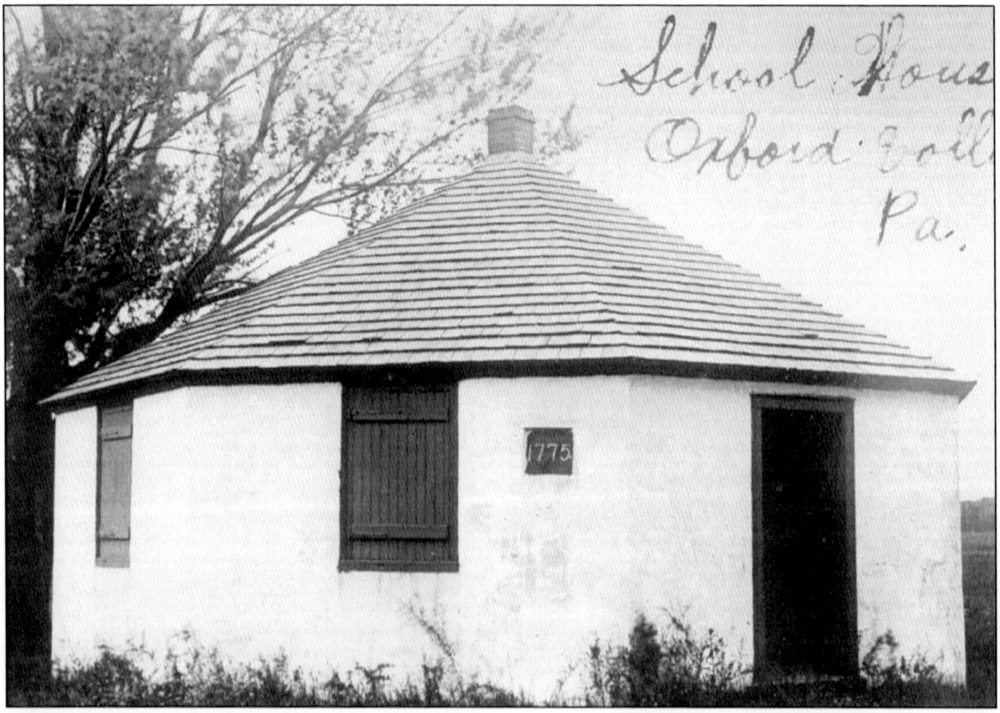

An octagonal school was built at "Oxford Valley" in Lower Makefield Township in the 1770s. Children in Yardleyville went to the school until a similar school building was built at "Oak Grove," now the American Legion property. Justin Stradling took this undated photograph of the "Oxford Valley School."

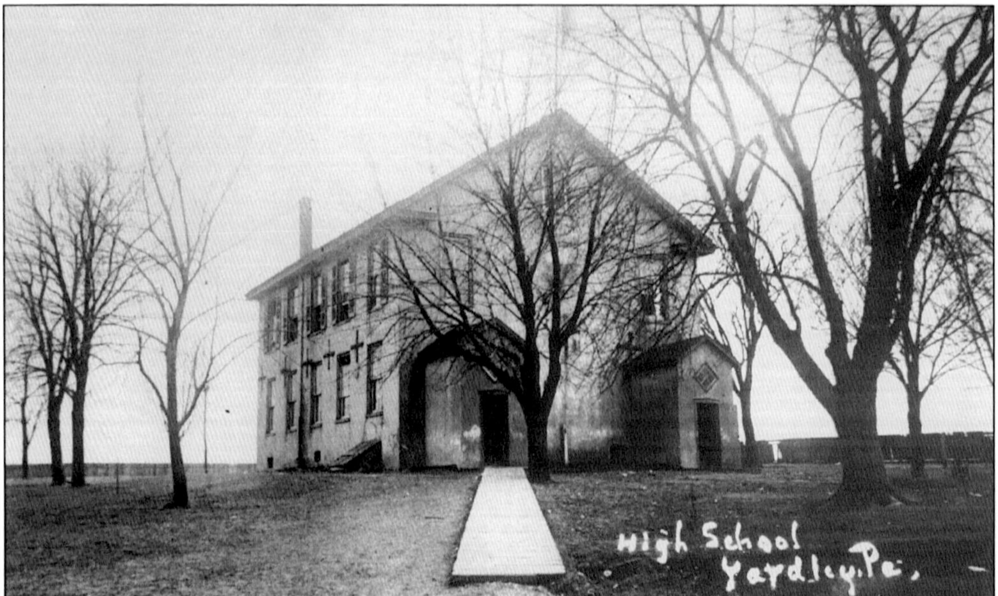

In 1874, a two-story elementary and secondary school was built on College Avenue. Notice the board sidewalk and two entrances, one for boys and one for girls. The school burned to the ground in 1916. Lost in the fire were the minutes of the Yardley School Board.

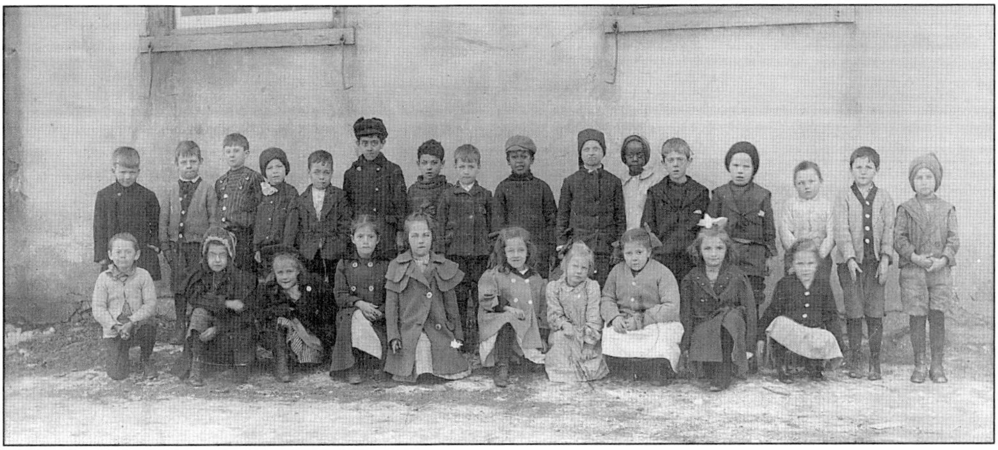

Yardley's second and third grade classes were photographed outside of the old school, *c.* 1905–10.

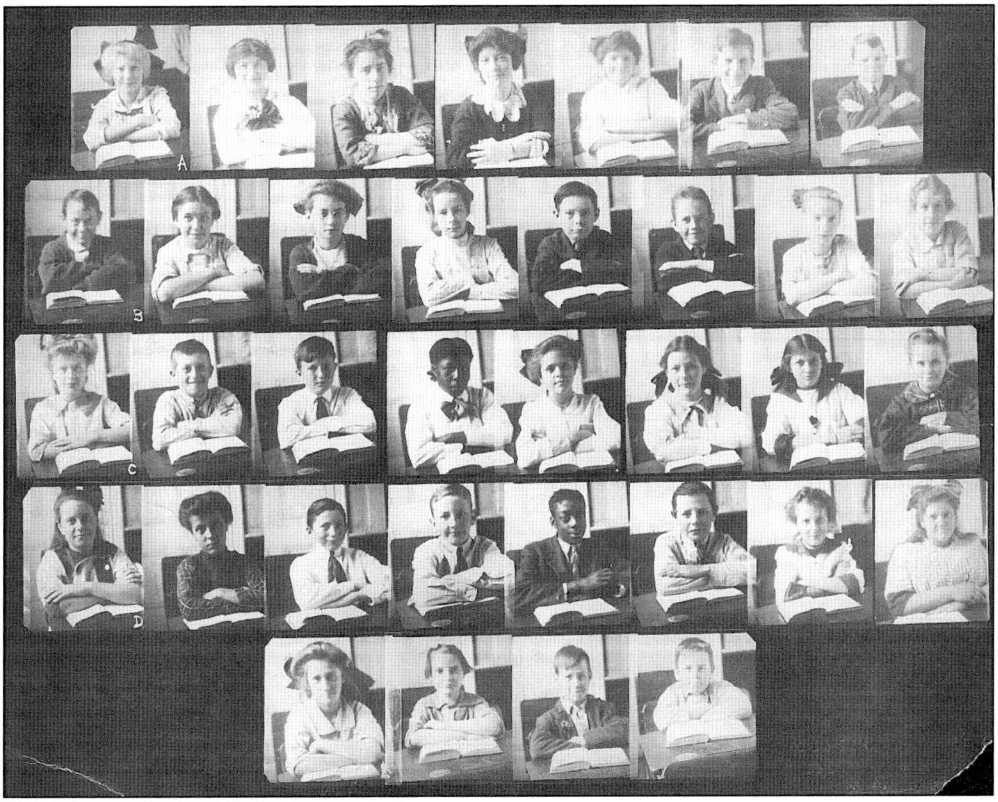

Yardley School students had individual photographs taken, *c.* 1911. Some of the students are, from left to right, as follows: (top row) Catherine Arnold, Dorothy Lynn, Margaret Cryne, Catherine Shannahan, two unidentified students, and Harry Baird; (second row) Theodore Smith, unidentified, Albert Van Hart, Anna Smith, and four unidentified students; (third row) unidentified, Edward Gallagher, two unidentified students, Anna Clark, unidentified, Anna Berry, and unidentified; (fourth row) unidentified, Martha Brady, Vince Casey, Thomas South, two unidentified students, Emma Borden, and unidentified; (fifth row) Gladys Bergen, and three unidentified students.

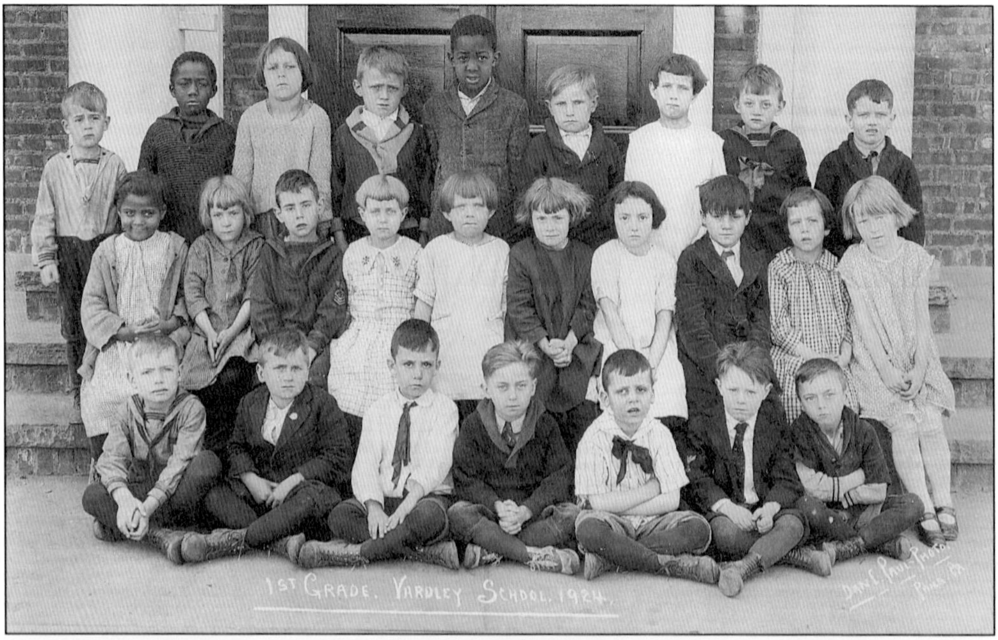

The 1924 First Grade class at the Yardley School lined up for a picture in 1924.

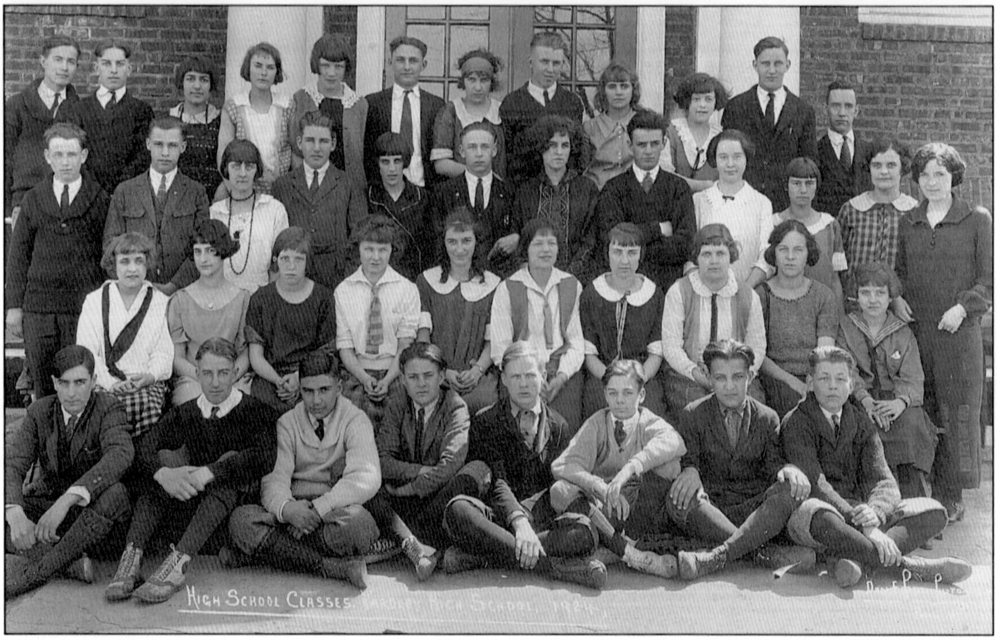

Yardley High School students pictured in 1924, from left to right, are as follows: (bottom) Bill Mulhern, Bill Gibbs, five unidentified students, and Henry Stover; (second row) Marian Harvey, Marie Jamison, unidentified, Helen Kauffman, Louise Cadwallader, Caroline Bassett, Alma Miller, Elsie Sands, Laura Weber, and unidentified; (third row) Nelson Dilliplane, Raymond Hampton, Margery Williamson, Elliot Eggleston, Gertrude Slack, Jessie Davis, Madaline Hartman, unidentified, Anna Wright, and three unidentified students; (top row) John Bilbee, Morris Eisenberg, unidentified, Helen Wilson, Kathleen Kauffman, Harry Dilliplane, Iva Kane, Newton Balderston, Ruth Allen, Katherine Gallagher, and unidentified.

Miss A. Baker, perhaps a teacher, was photographed on the grounds of the Yardley School in 1915. The Century Leather Enameling Company is in the background.

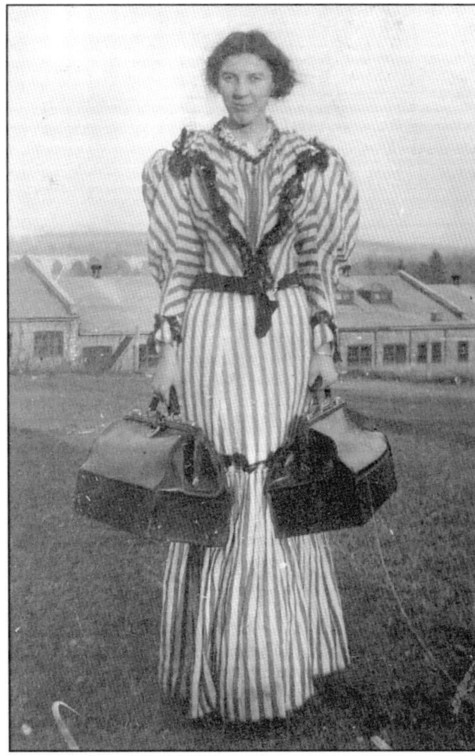

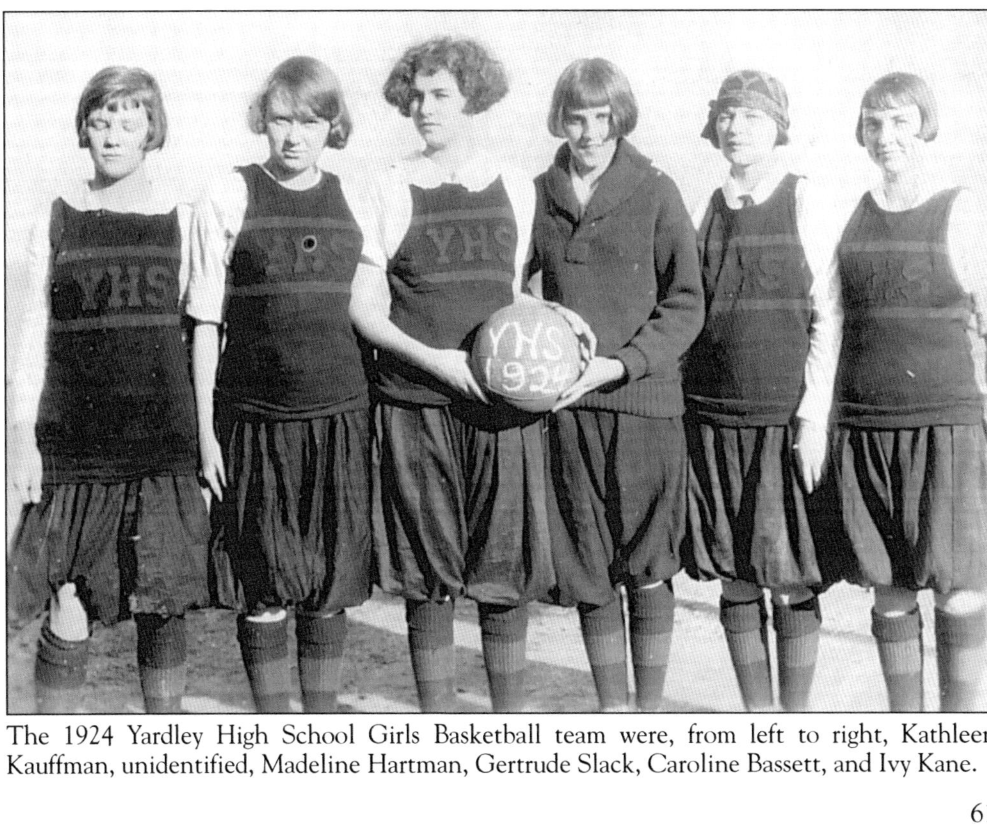

The 1924 Yardley High School Girls Basketball team were, from left to right, Kathleen Kauffman, unidentified, Madeline Hartman, Gertrude Slack, Caroline Bassett, and Ivy Kane.

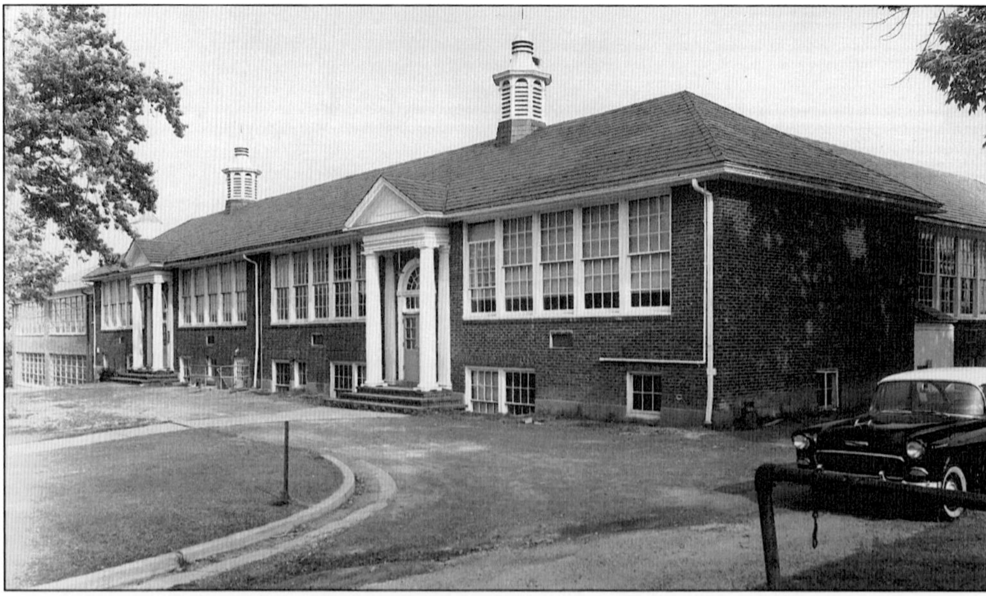

The Yardley School, built in 1917, served students from first grade through high school until 1948 when the Pennsbury School District was formed. In 1980, Pennsbury sold the College Avenue building to Abrams Hebrew Academy.

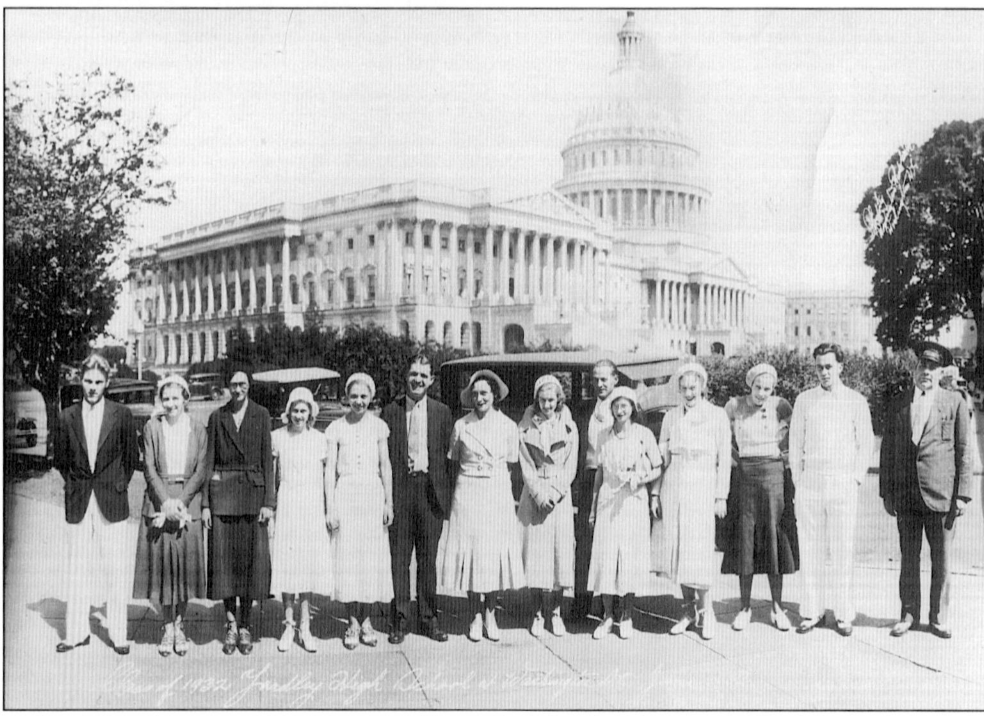

Each year, graduating students from Yardley High School took a trip to Washington, D.C. The class of 1932 had this traditional photograph taken in front of the Capitol Building. Pictured here, from left to right, are Alton Dilliplane, Marian Smith, Gladys Scott, Evelyn Lear, Helen Clark, unidentified, Cora Holsclaw (class advisor,) Anna Woolman, unidentified, Marjorie Dinges, Alice Ross, Harry Gilmore, and the driver.

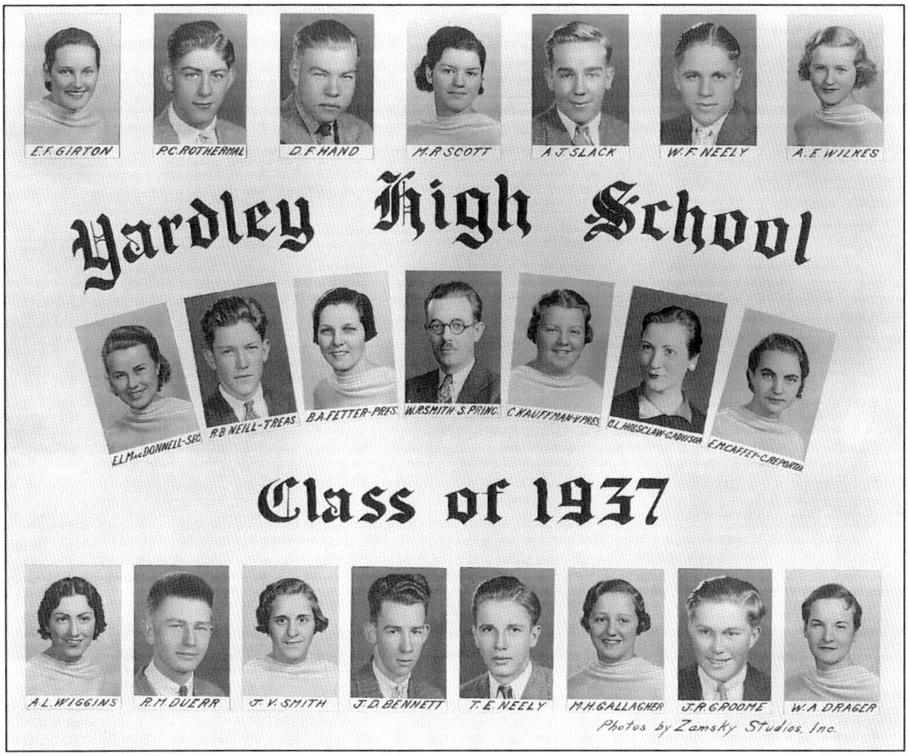

The Yardley High School, Class of 1937, is shown here. The photograph includes the following, from left to right: (bottom row) A.L. Wiggins, R.M. Duerr, J.V. Smith, J.D. Bennett, T.E. Neely, M.H. Gallagher, J. R. Groome, and W.A. Drager; (middle row) E.L. MacDonnell, R.B. Neill, B.A. Fetter, Warren R. Smith (Principal), C. Kauffman, Clora L. Holsclaw (Class Advisor,) and E.M. Caffety; (top row) E.F. Girton, P.C. Rothermal, D.F. Hand, A.J. Slack, W.F. Neely, and A.E. Wilkes.

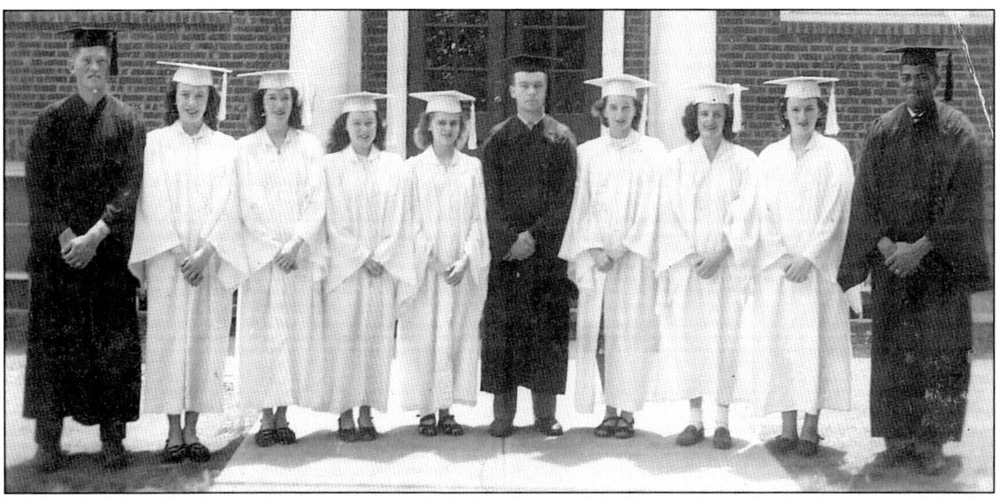

The class of 1948 was the last to graduate from the Yardley High School. The members of the class were, from left to right, Raymond Dansbury, Odetta Dougherty, Ruby Smith, Joy Mae Dilliplane, Grace Neaman, Keith Caffey, Lois Felger, Patricia Kinney, Martha Bennett, and Robert Galloway.

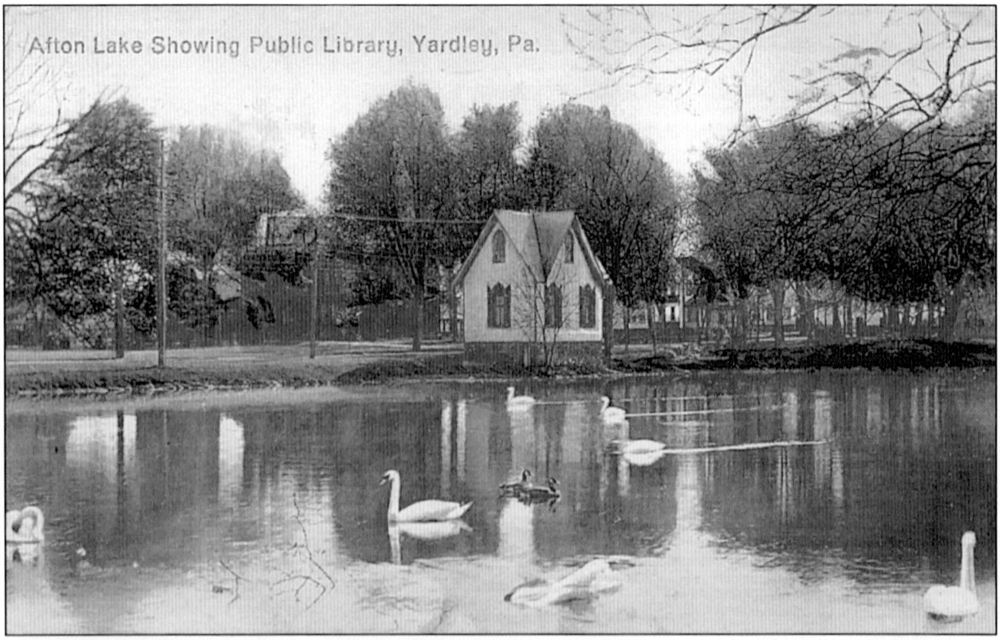

"The Old Library by Lake Afton," with swans and ducks in the foreground, made the perfect Yardley postcard, *c.* 1910. The Carpenter Gothic-style library was built in 1878 as a subscription library.

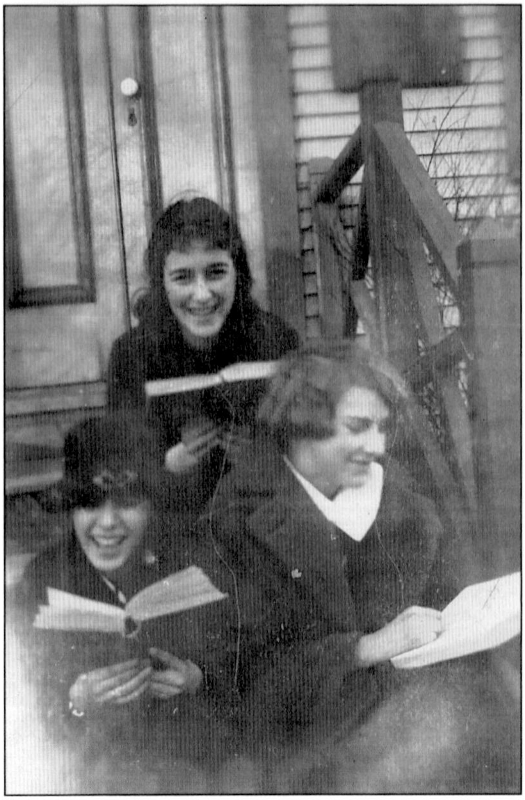

Louise Cadwallader (top,) Alice Cook (left,) and Helen Wilson were reading or maybe acting outside of the old library, *c.* 1923. Louise became an assistant to Mrs. Cook, the librarian.

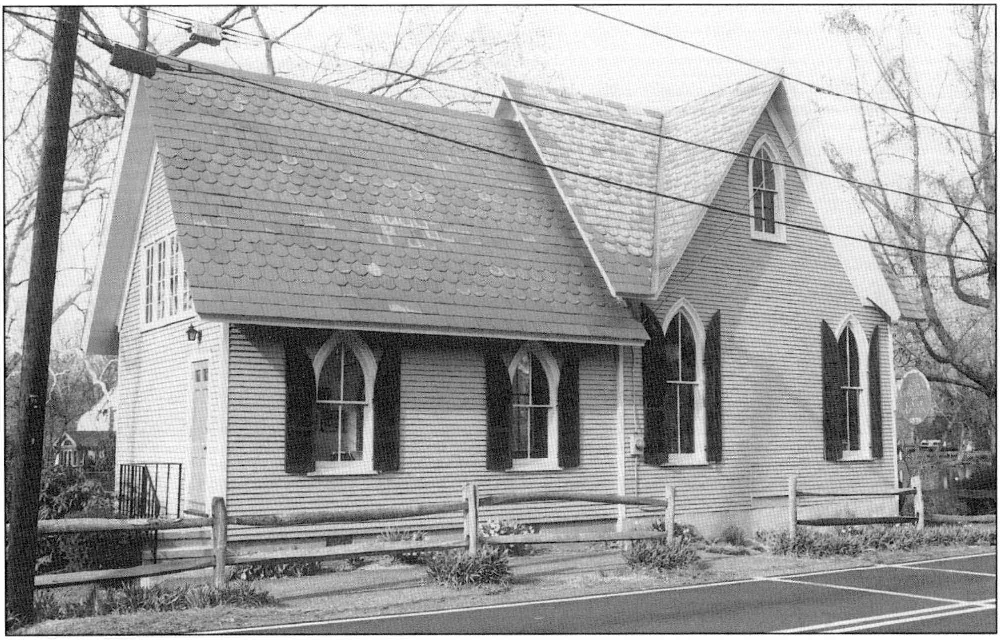

In 1955, an approach to the proposed new Delaware River Bridge would have led to the demolition of the Yardley Library. To discourage this, John L. M. Yardley donated funds for a major addition, provided the building remain a library. The rear section of the building was added, and the bridge site was moved to Scudders Falls.

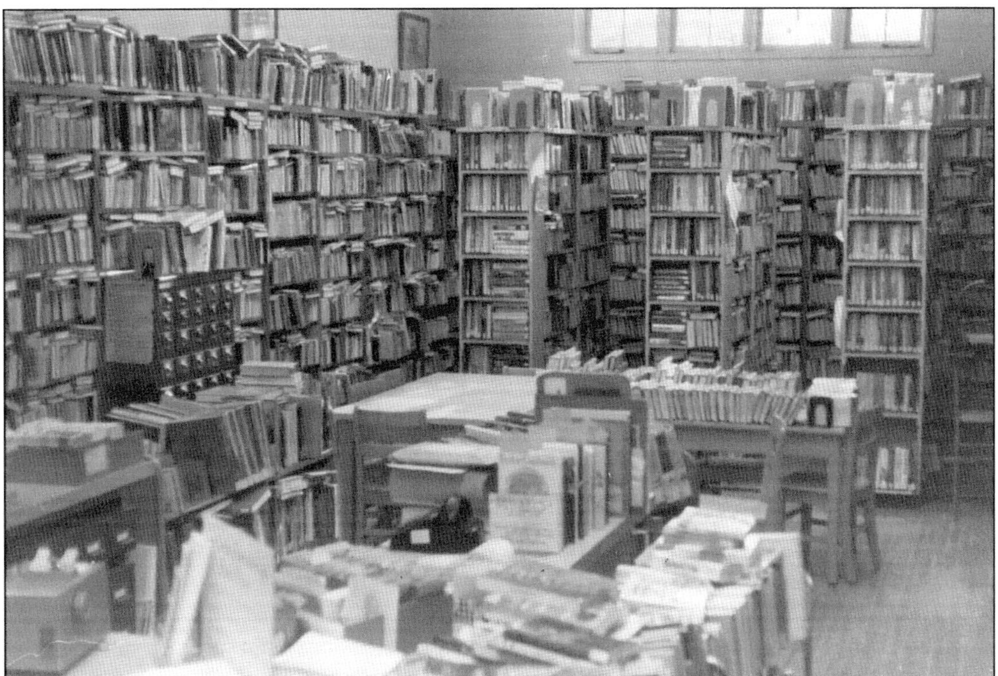

By the 1970s, the shelves in the Yardley Library overflowed with a collection of 22,000 volumes. In 1977, a new county library was constructed on Edgewood Road in Lower Makefield Township. The Old Library became the headquarters of the Yardley Historical Association.

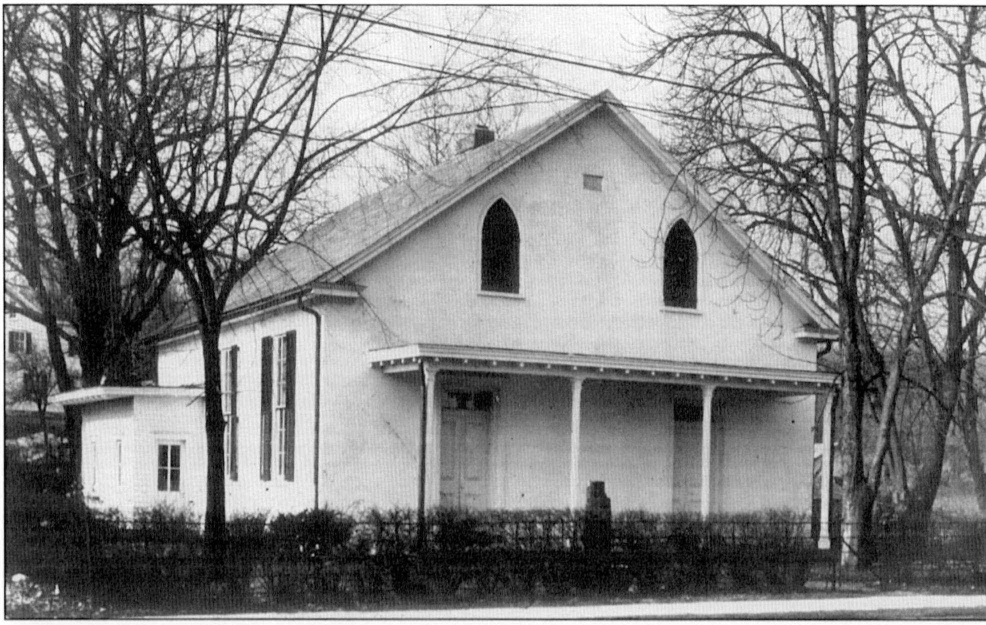

Quakers living in Yardley originally traveled to Fallsington for meeting for worship. Complaints about winter travel, however, led to the construction in 1752 of the Makefield Meeting House on Dolington Road. In 1869, Yardley Friends was established as a separate meeting. A meeting house was built on the corner of Main Street and College Avenue.

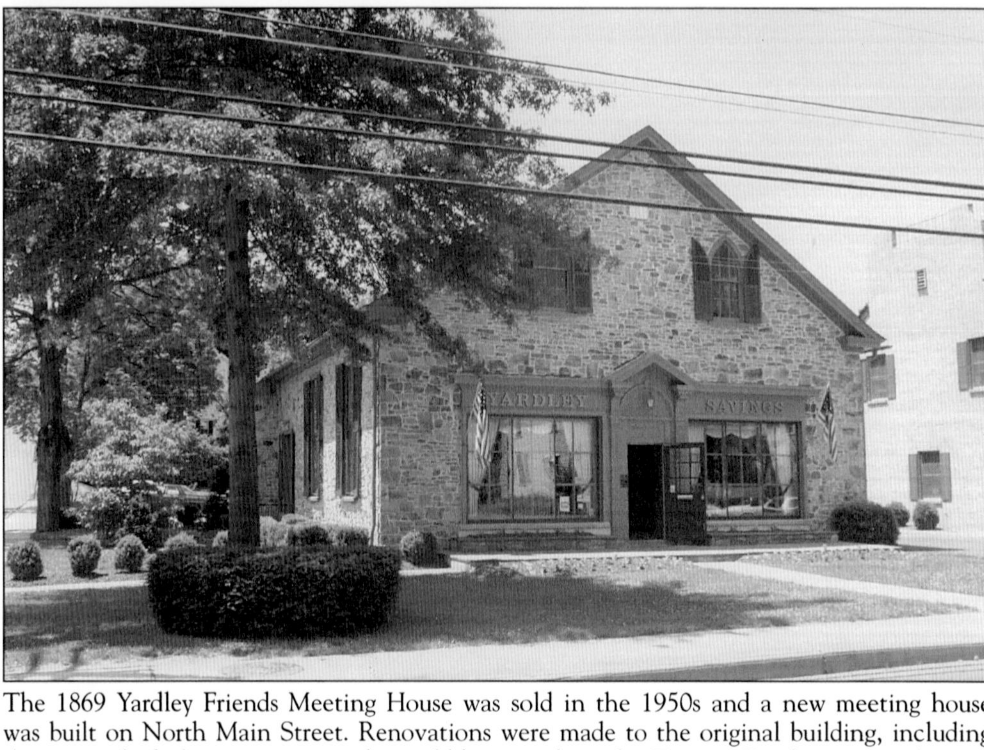

The 1869 Yardley Friends Meeting House was sold in the 1950s and a new meeting house was built on North Main Street. Renovations were made to the original building, including the removal of white stucco, revealing rubble stone from the Twining Brothers quarry located behind the meeting house property.

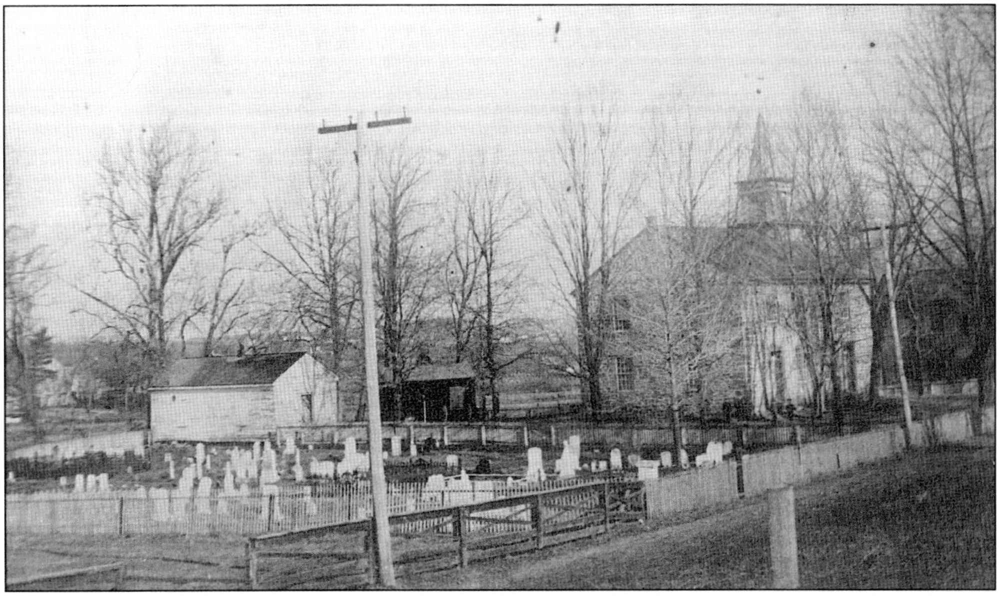

A Union Meeting House was built on West Afton Avenue in 1827. Missionaries from several denominations used the Meeting House until 1835 when it was taken over by St. Andrew's Episcopal Church.

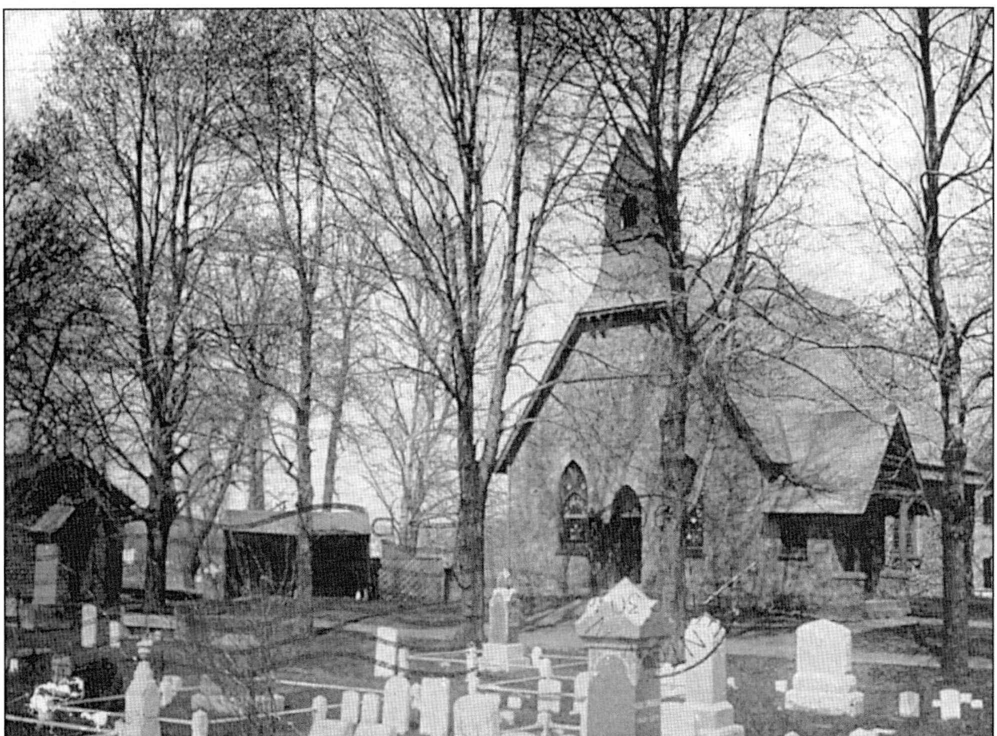

St. Andrew's consecrated a new church in 1890 on the site of the Union Meeting House. B. Frank Livezy, a local contractor, built the new Gothic Revival church shown in this *c.* 1907 postcard. Generations of Yardley men and women were buried in the adjacent cemetery.

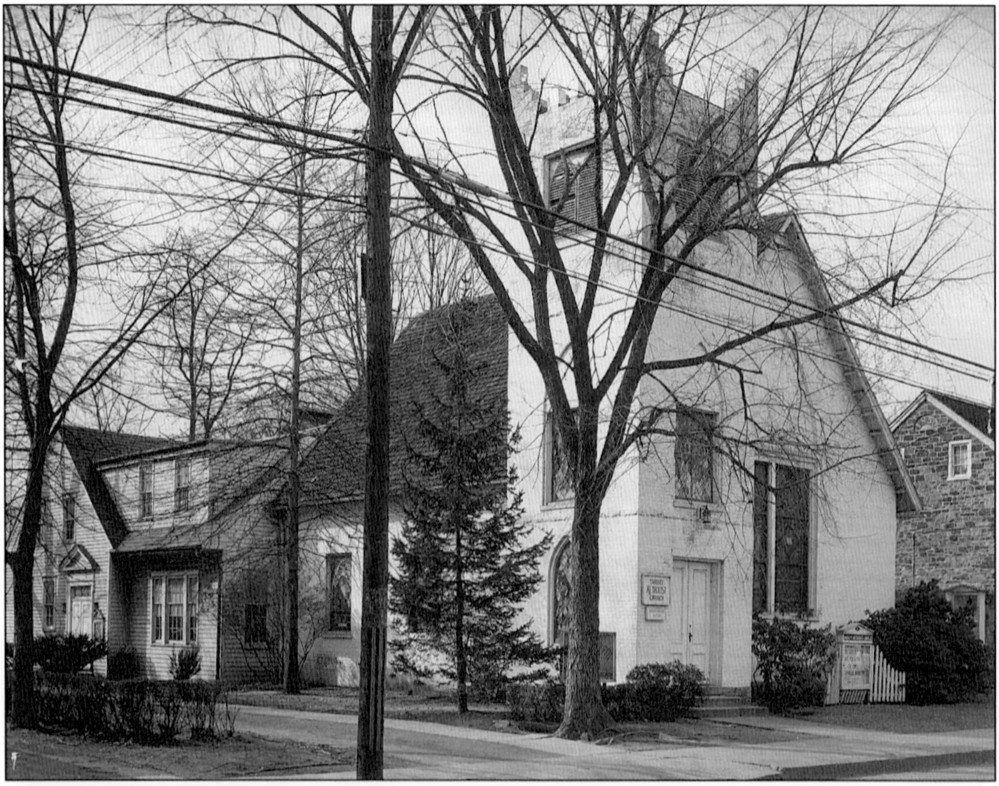

Methodist meetings were first conducted in the Canal Store on East Afton Avenue. In 1838, a brick church building was built on Main Street. This photograph of the church with its distinctive bell tower was taken in the 1950s.

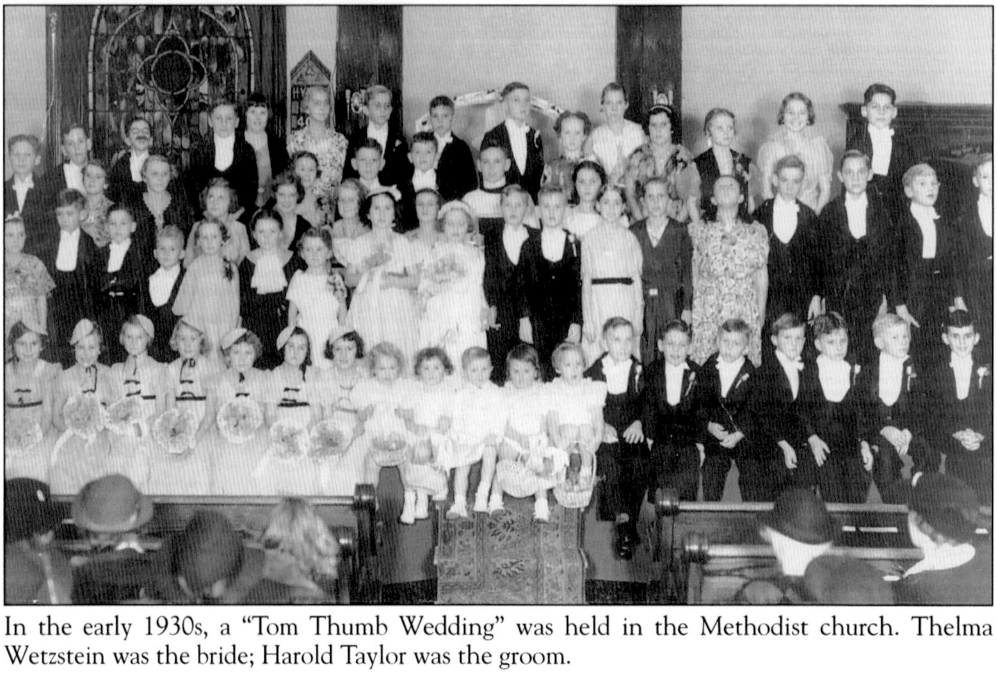

In the early 1930s, a "Tom Thumb Wedding" was held in the Methodist church. Thelma Wetzstein was the bride; Harold Taylor was the groom.

The St. Ignatius Roman Catholic Church was built at 110 South Main Street in 1904. There were about 25 families in the congregation. The white frame church replaced an old school house that had served the congregation since the 1870s.

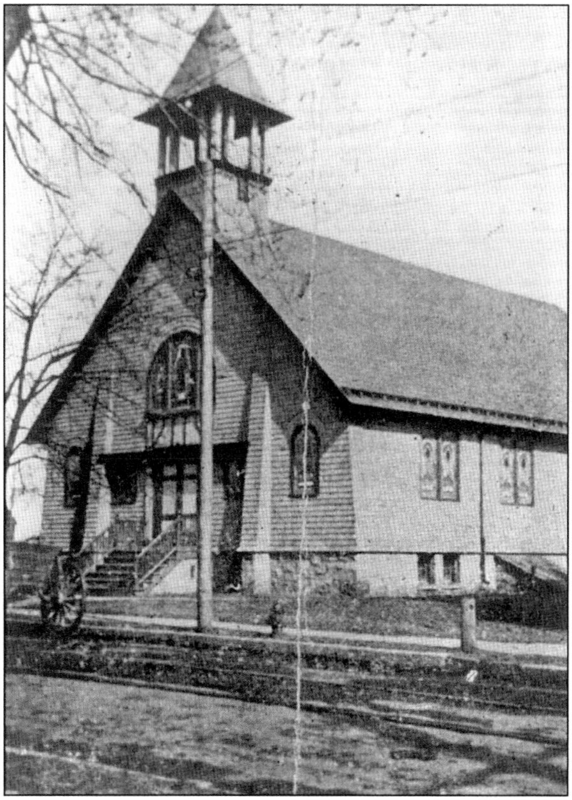

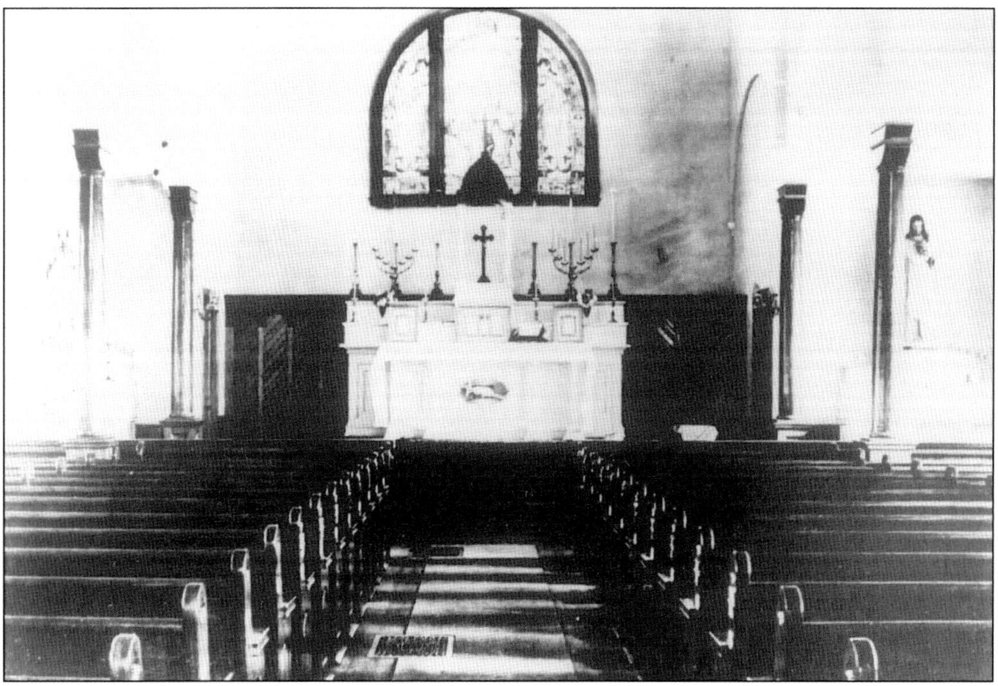

A newspaper article in 1904 described the "Tiffany style" windows, murals, brass gas fixtures, and dark, raised carved paneling around the white altar in the new church.

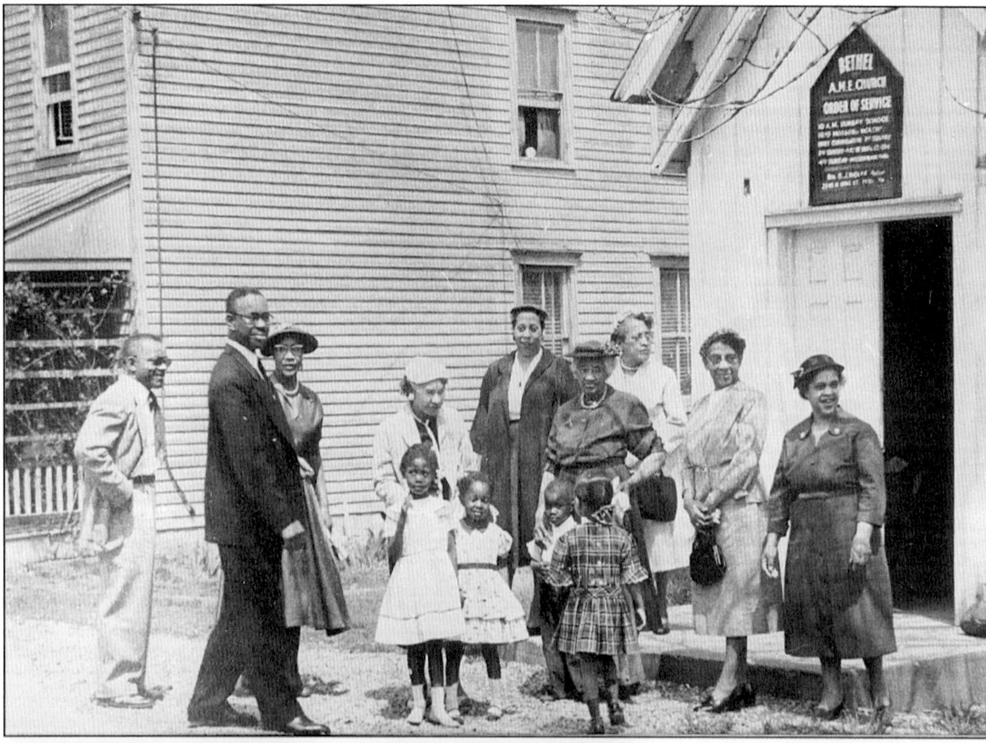

As early as 1817, a black congregation was meeting in an old hay barn in the "Flats." In 1877, a church was built on South Canal Street, and became part of the Bethel AME conference in 1893. Pictured in this photograph are the Reverend and Mrs. Gale, Florence Washington, Flossie Chapman, Mrs. Hodge, Helene Derry Giles, Julia Jacobs, and Edith McIntyre.

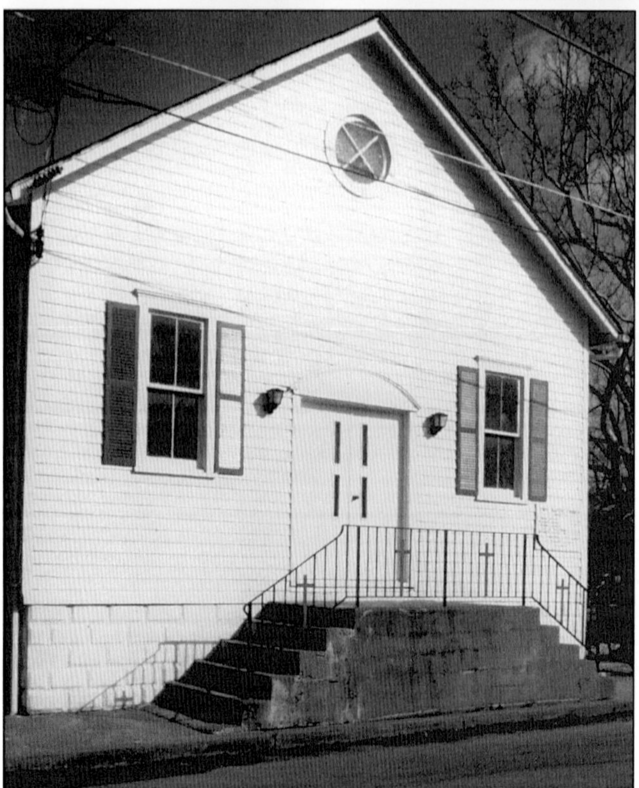

Members of Yardley's African-American community built the First Baptist Church on Canal Street in 1915. For many years, the congregation held baptisms in the Delaware River.

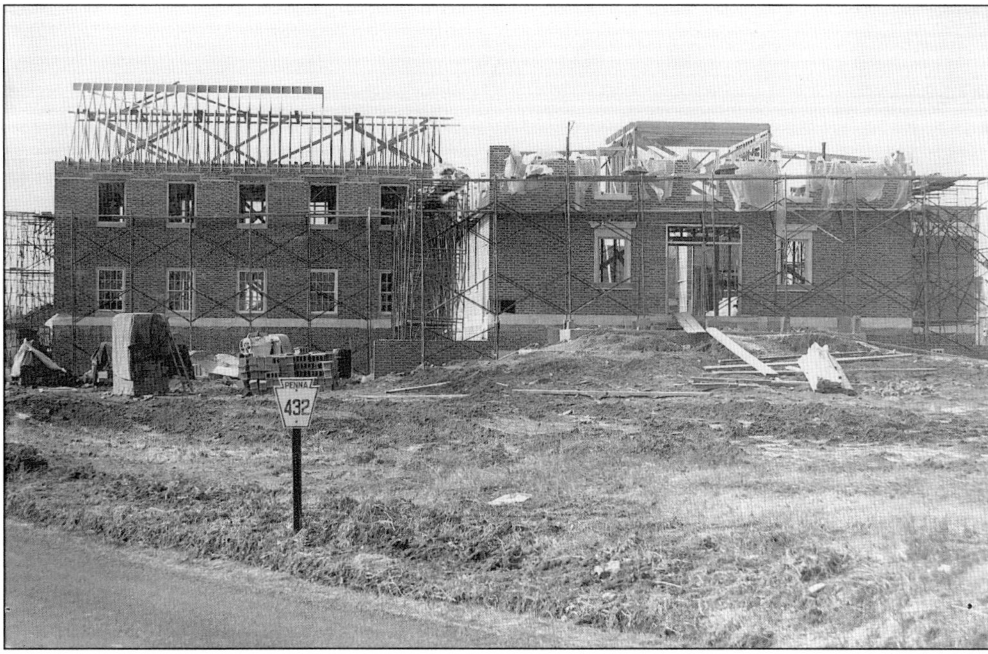

Suburban growth after WWII led several area congregations to build new facilities. In the late 1950s, Yardley Methodists sold their Main Street property (now part of the Yardley Town Center) and built a new church on the Langhorne-Yardley Road.

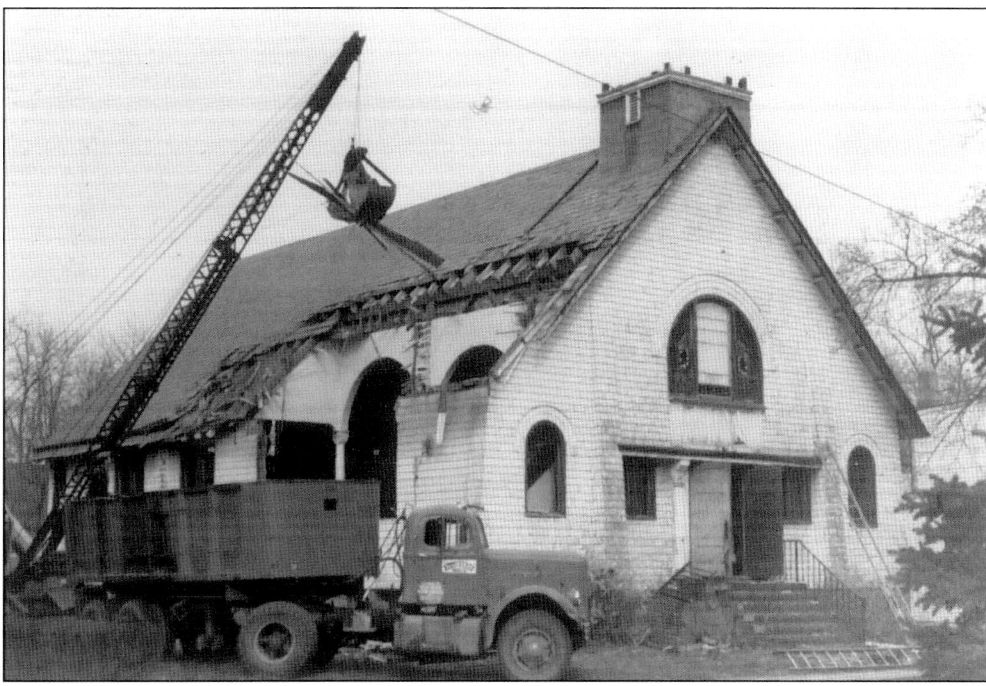

In April 1966, the deserted 62-year-old St. Ignatius church was torn down. Many residents mourned the loss of the picturesque landmark. The church bell, which had been cast in Belgium, was removed from the steeple and installed in the new church constructed on Reading Avenue.

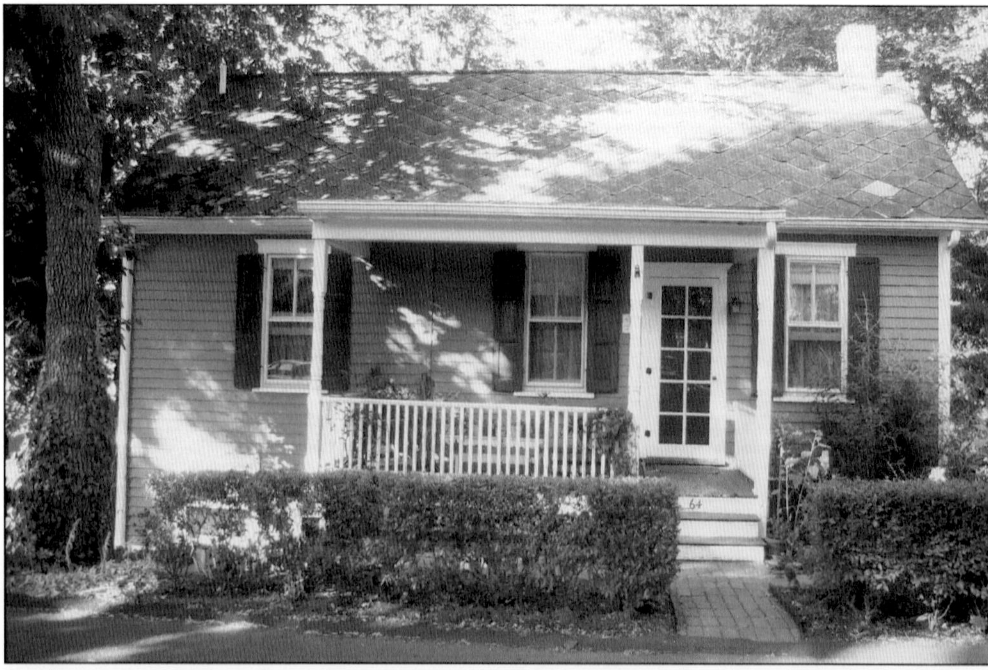

Yardley was incorporated as a borough in 1895. E.W. Twining was elected the first president; A.S. Cadwallader was the first burgess. The council purchased a small lot on Canal Street for $60 and paid Phineas South $443 for the construction of a lock-up and council rooms. Since 1916, the building has been a private home.

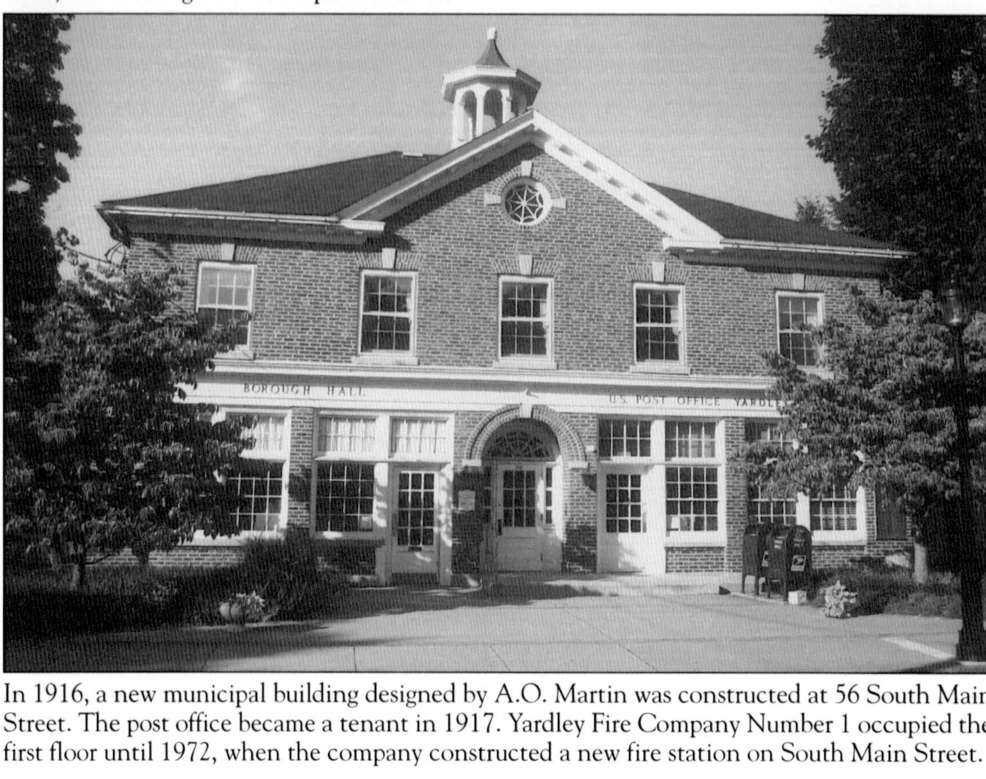

In 1916, a new municipal building designed by A.O. Martin was constructed at 56 South Main Street. The post office became a tenant in 1917. Yardley Fire Company Number 1 occupied the first floor until 1972, when the company constructed a new fire station on South Main Street.

Tom South (1902–1966) held up traffic at the intersection of Main and Afton, c. 1945. South served as constable, overseer of the poor, worked for the Delaware River Bridge Commission, and was a member of the Borough Police Department.

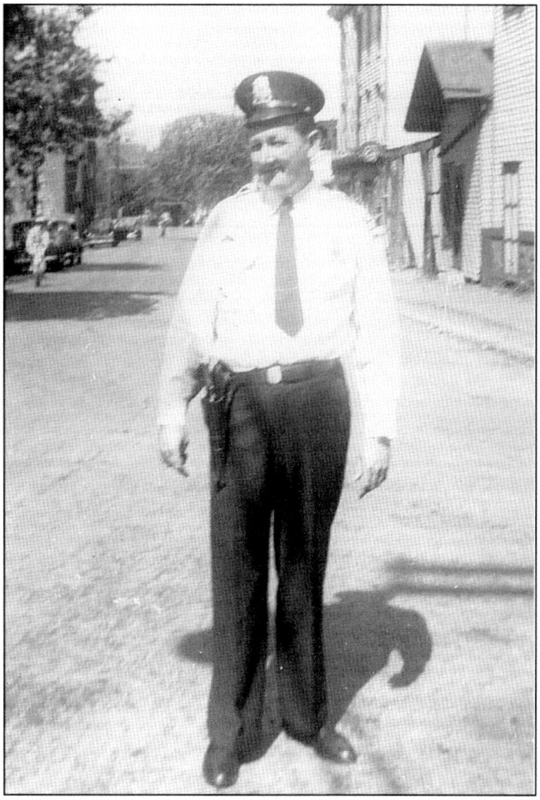

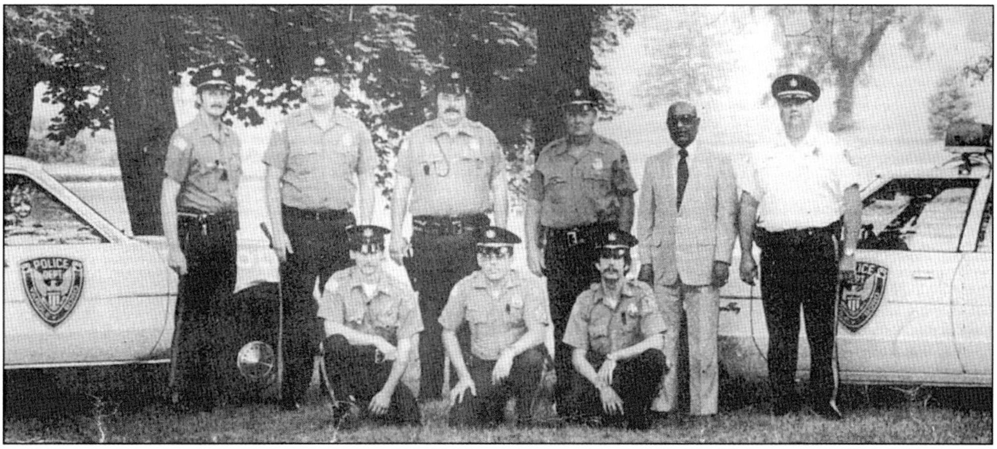

The Yardley Borough Police Department was established in the 1950s. Chief Lee Carroll (far right) stands next to Mayor Edward Robinson and members of the department, c. 1978. Mayor Robinson was the first African-American mayor in Pennsylvania.

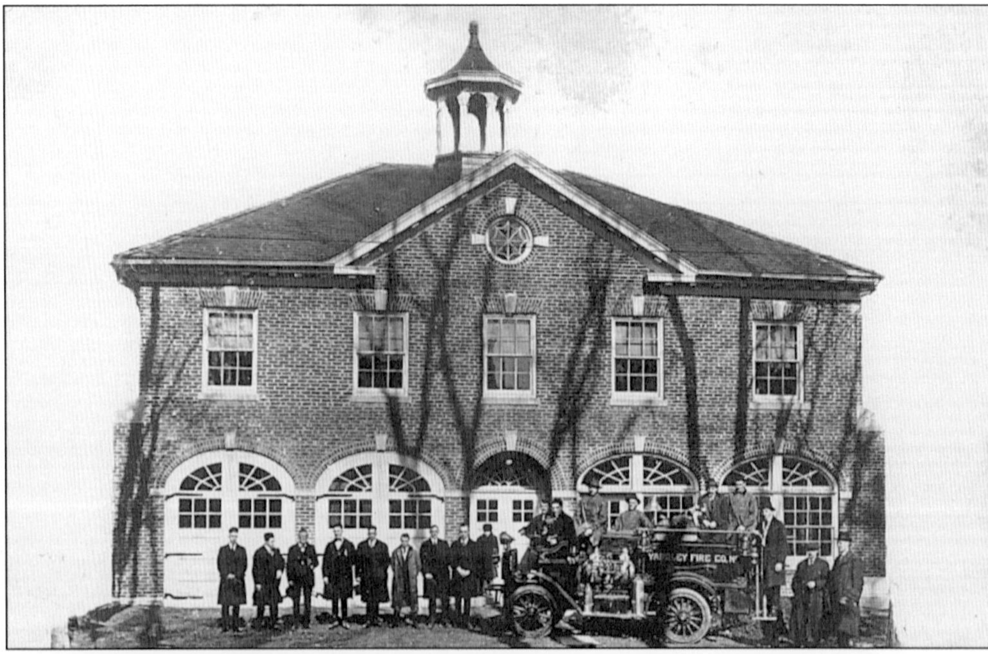

Members of Yardley Fire Company No. 1 were proud of their new Autocar Combination chemical truck. This 1917 photo postcard was taken outside of the new municipal building and firehouse. Notice the large swinging fire station doors.

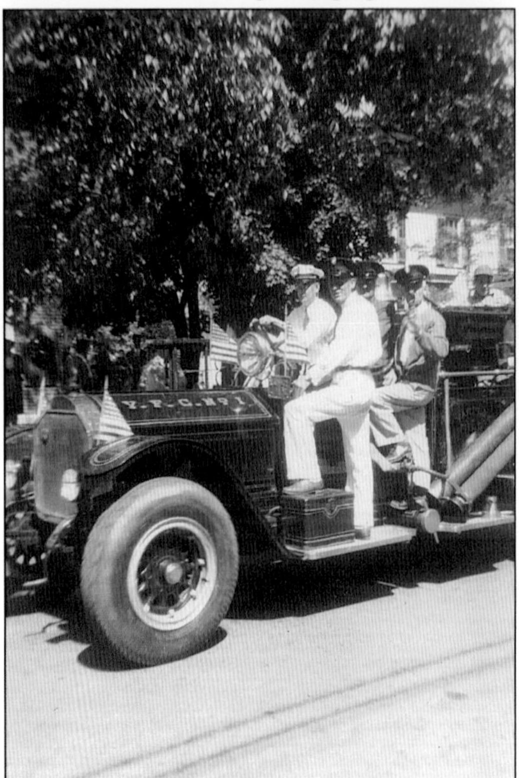

J. Satterwaite, Lewis C. Leedom, and Dick Kinny were photographed in an old fire truck in a Memorial Day Parade, *c.* 1947.

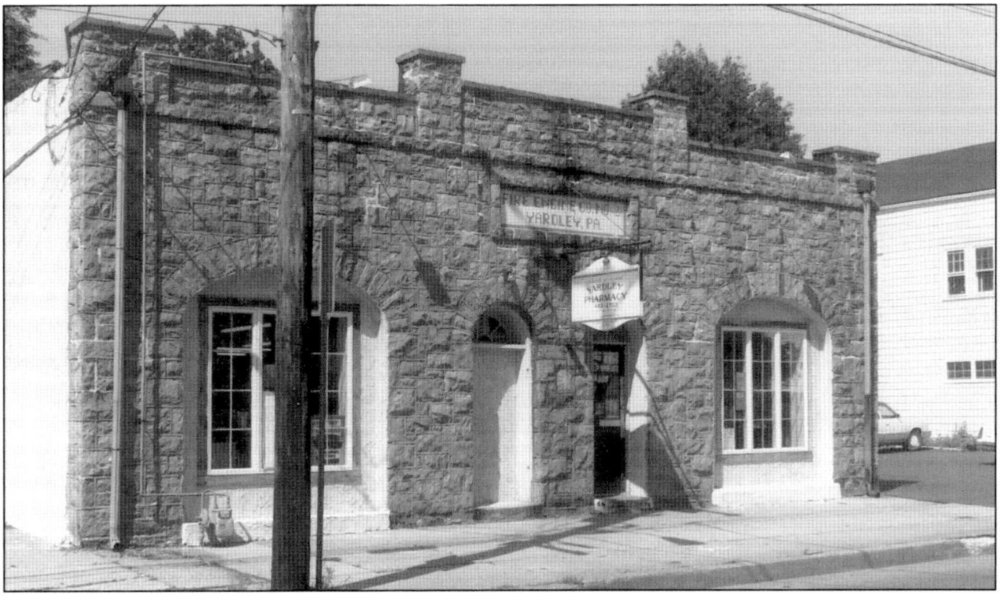

The bay windows and sign over the door are the remaining architectural traces of Yardley Fire Company No. 2, established in the 1920s. The company existed for several decades in friendly competition with Fire Company No. 1. When No. 2 was disbanded, the station building housed a drug store with a popular lunch counter.

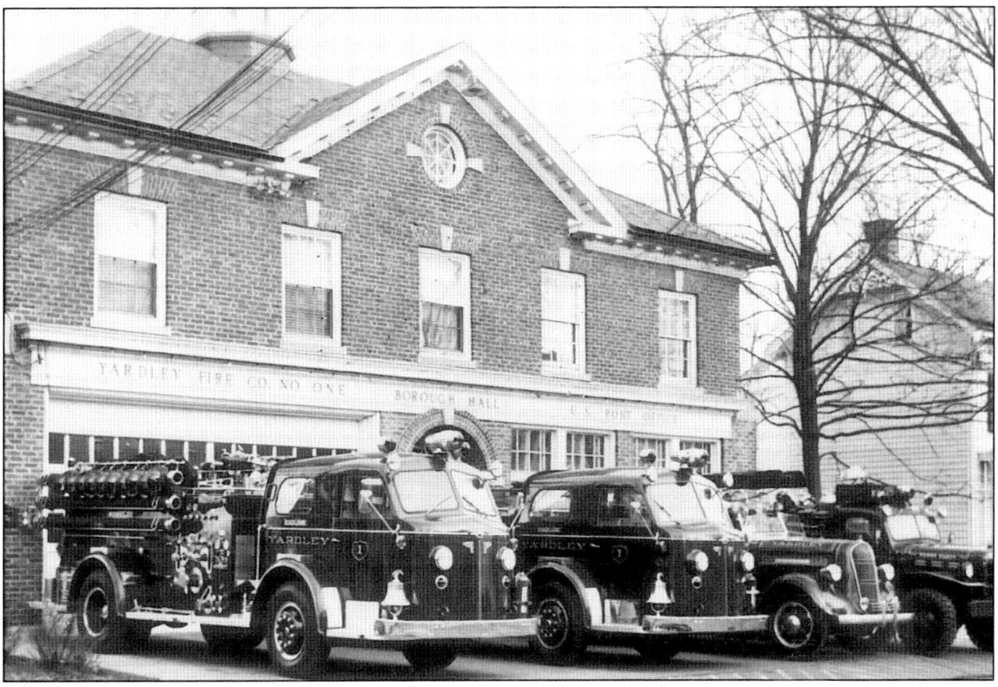

Yardley Fire Company No.1 was established in 1897. The first apparatus purchased was a $100 hook-and-ladder wagon, complete with fire buckets. In 1915, the company purchased an Autocar Combination chemical truck, followed by an American La France pumper in 1922, and a 75-foot ladder truck in 1957. More modern equipment is displayed in front of the municipal building and fire station, c. 1970.

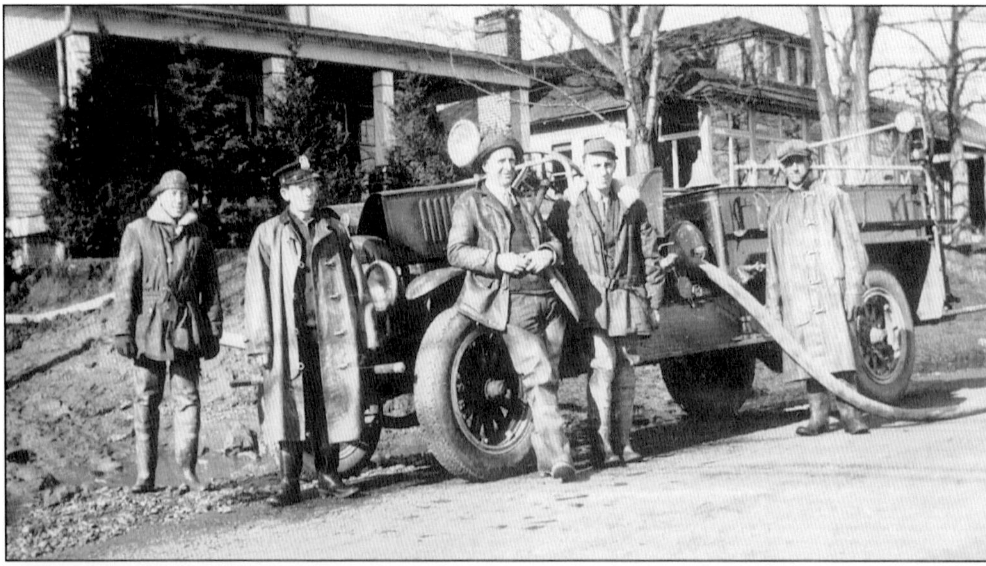

In the aftermath of the 1955 flood, crews of firemen and volunteers pumped basements and cesspools, removed mud and debris from roads, and chlorinated and limed the flooded areas. Fire Chief John Ziaylek directed local efforts. In this photograph, a group of rescue workers take a rest on North Delaware Avenue during the cleanup.

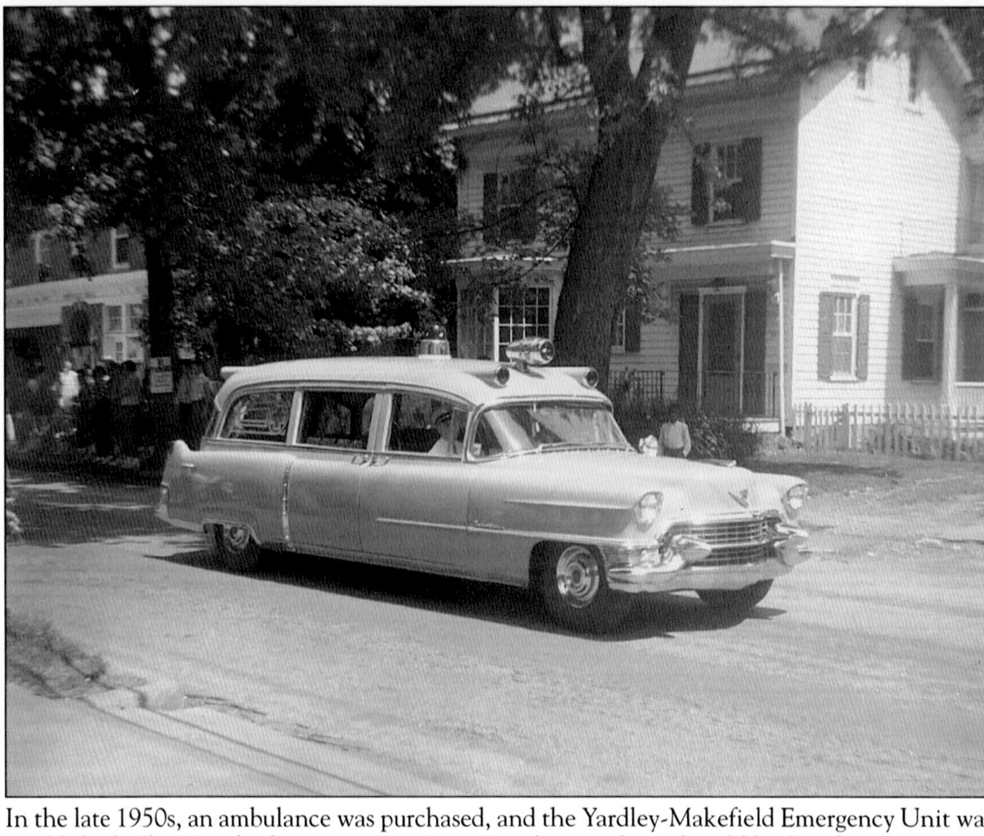

In the late 1950s, an ambulance was purchased, and the Yardley-Makefield Emergency Unit was established. The Unit built a station on River Road across from the old bridge abutment.

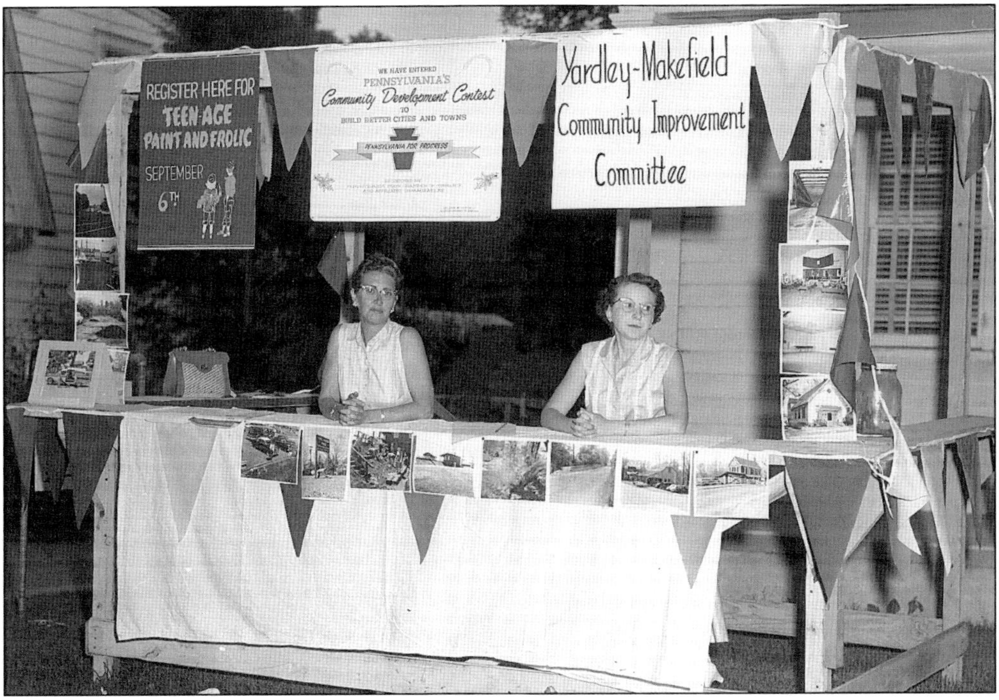

In 1958, the Yardley Lower-Makefield Improvement Committee was organized. The committee compiled a written and photographic record of their accomplishments, and then entered a statewide competition. Storefronts were painted and renovated, parking areas were paved, and Brock Creek was cleaned up.

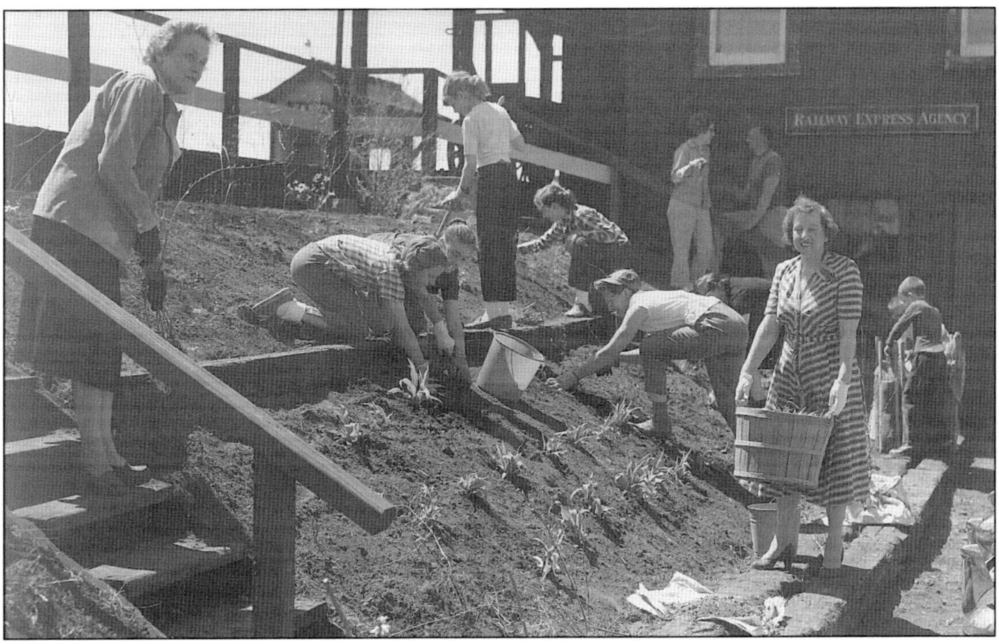

One community project in the 1958 campaign was the "beautification" of the Yardley Train Station. The Martha Washington Garden Club and local Girl Scouts landscaped the grounds; the Yardley Fire Company provided water.

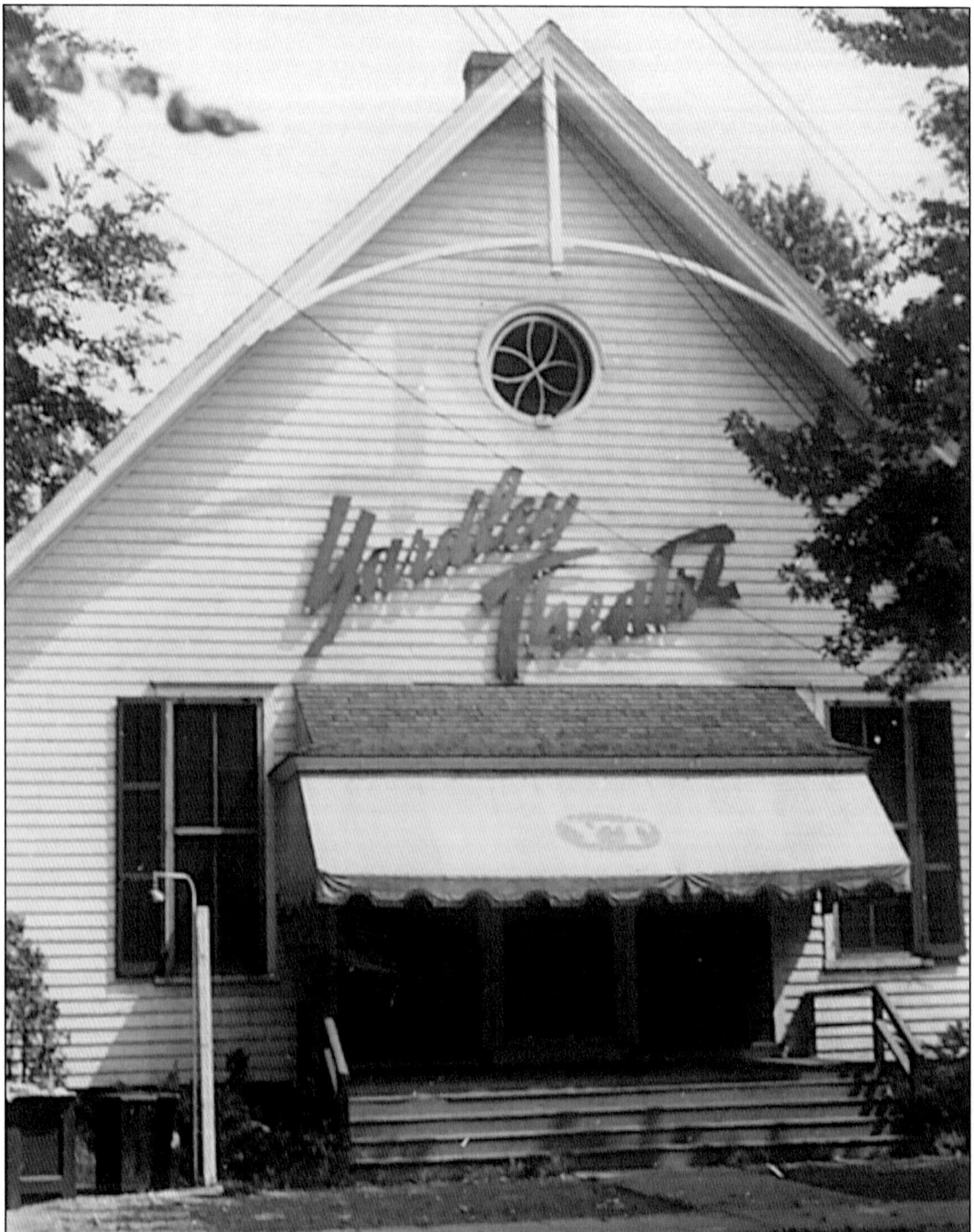

The Yardley Community Center has provided a meeting place for residents since 1851. The rear portion of the building was built for the Sons of Temperance and was used as a private school. The enlarged building, as seen from Main Street, was built by the Odd Fellows in 1878. The Odd Fellows Hall was used for classes when the Yardley School burned in 1917. It has been the venue for lectures, organizational meetings, dances, movies, and church services. In 1895 John Wanamaker, Philadelphia's "Merchant Prince," addressed the annual convention of the Bucks County Christian Endeavor in the Hall. Nat Burnes leased the Center in the early 1930s and created the "Cob-Web Theatre." In 1941, the Yardley Community Center Association purchased the building.

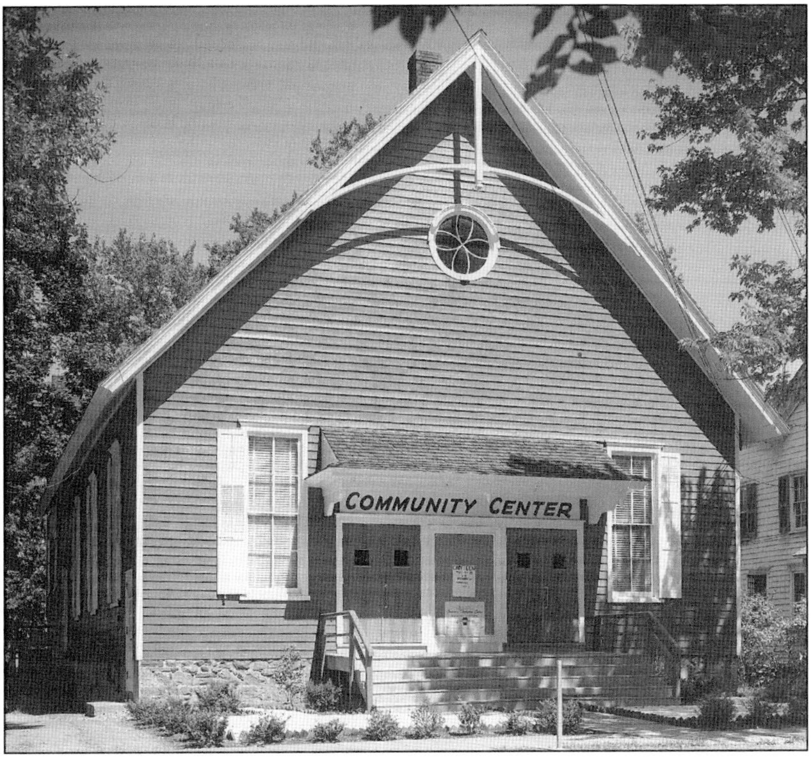

Since 1941 a board of directors has managed the Yardley Community Center. A variety of fund-raising activities has provided the money for maintenance and up-keep. Major renovations were made in 1958 when this photograph was taken.

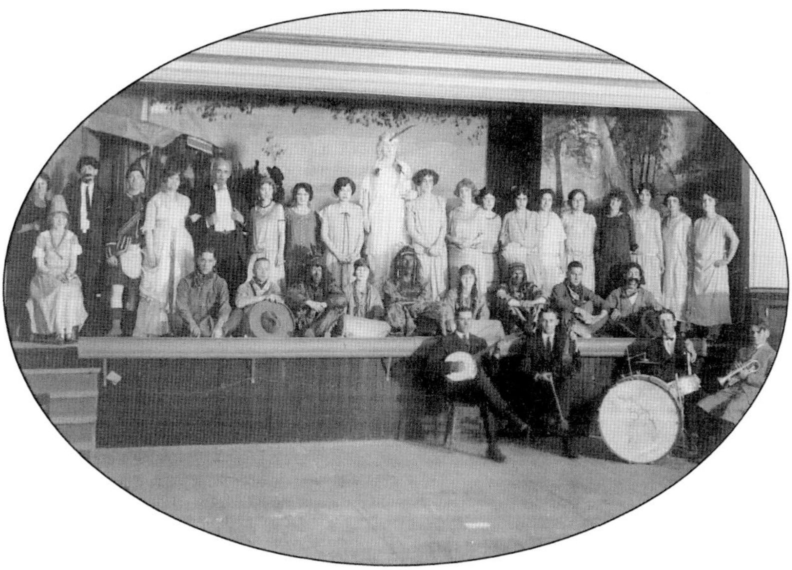

Local groups put on a variety of debates, plays, and minstrel shows in the Community Center. In the 1920s, the Chatauqua, a traveling show of lectures, concerts, and recitals took the stage. This photograph is of local actors in the play "Savage Land." Mrs. Elizabeth Kauffman (far left in the rear) directed the production.

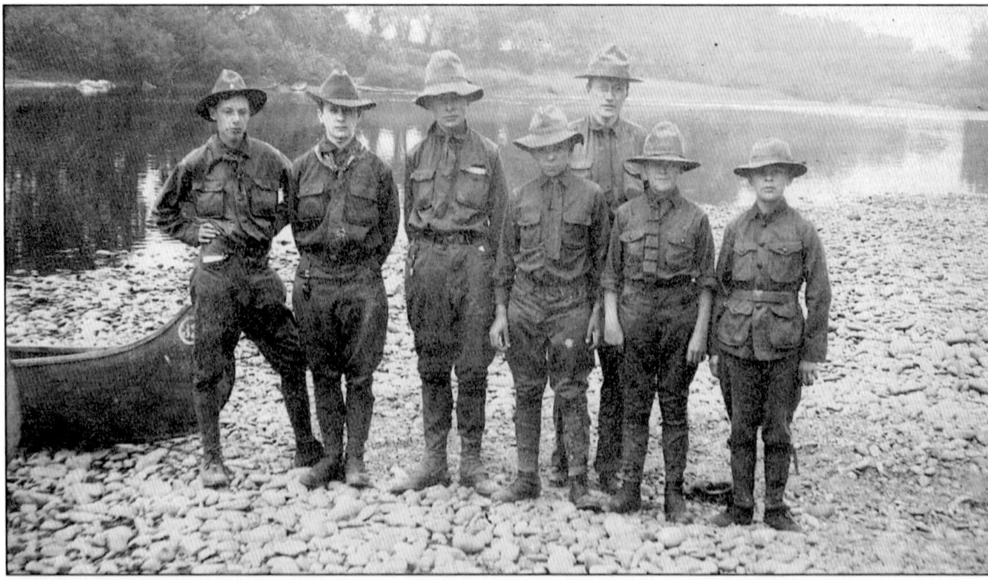

Boy Scout recruits returned from an expedition to New Hope and stopped (maybe camped) on White's Island at Scudders Falls, *c.* 1915.

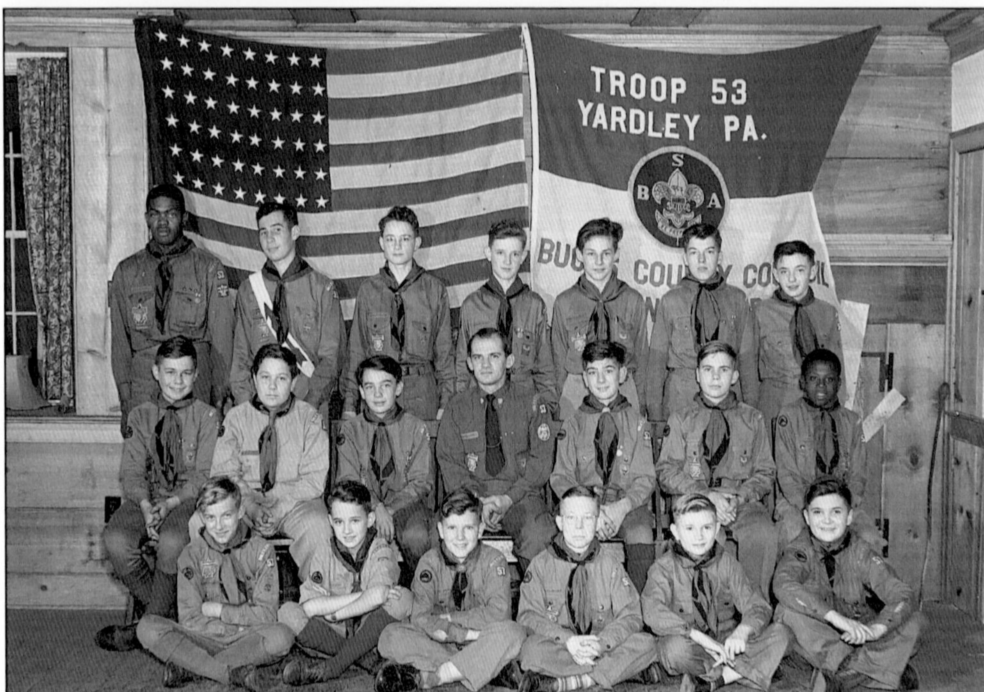

The Yardley Boy Scout Troop 53 had this formal portrait taken in 1946. Pictured from left to right are as follows: (front row) George McDonald, John Jones, Eddie Joe Miller, Jeffrey Bauhaus, William Felger, and Robert Penman; (middle row) Merle Sipler, Alan Ney, Peter Loel, John Ziaylek (Scout Master,) Fred Hallmark, Alan Dilliplane, and William Nicholson; (top row) Robert Galloway, Sharon Turner, George Jones, Donald Jones, Harry Glatz, Don Miller, and Edward Curley.

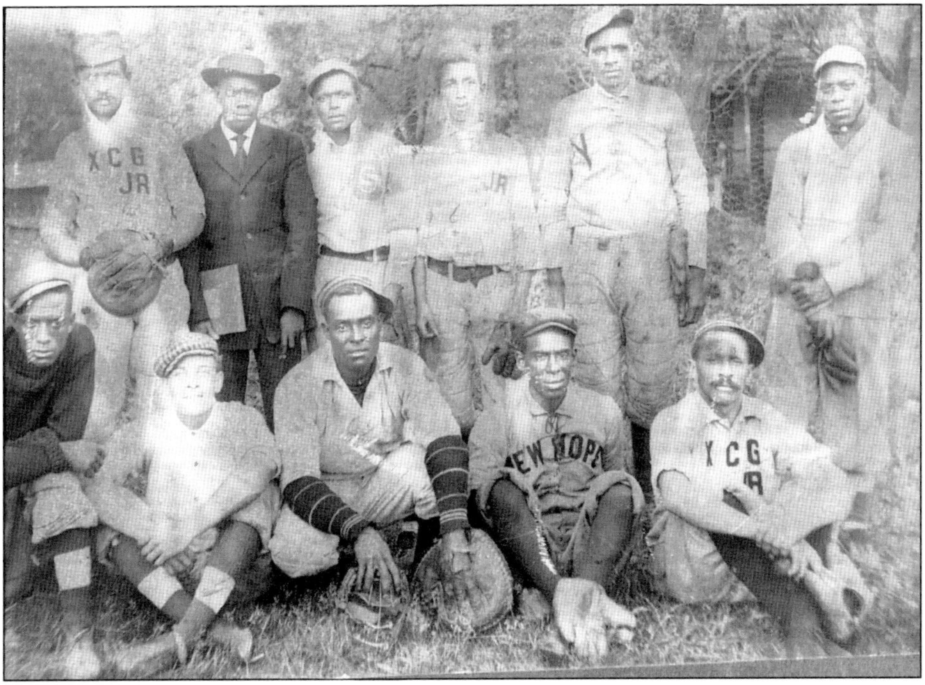

William Derry of Yardley led an African-American club team to victory in 1896. William is in a dark suit in the top row. To the left of William is John Derry. Morris Derry is seated on the far right.

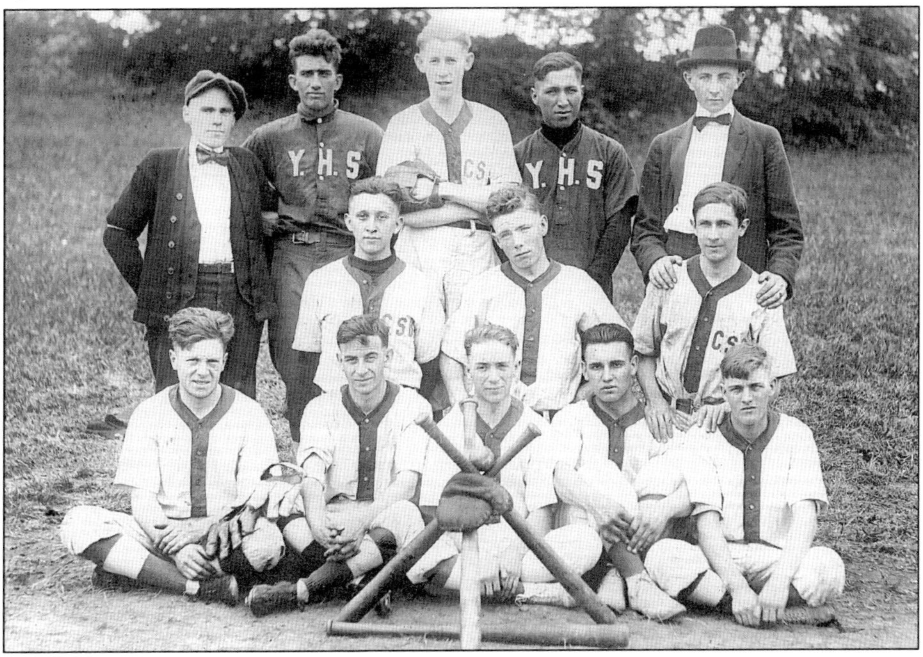

This c. 1915 photograph of the Yardley High School Baseball Team includes, from left to right, the following: (front row) Owen Neely, William Smith, Merrick Post, and R. Ruth; (middle row) Frank Gallagher, Morris Neely, and Lendrum South; (back row) Jimmy Marian, M. Miller, J. Van Artsdalen, M. Hoff, and E. Doyle.

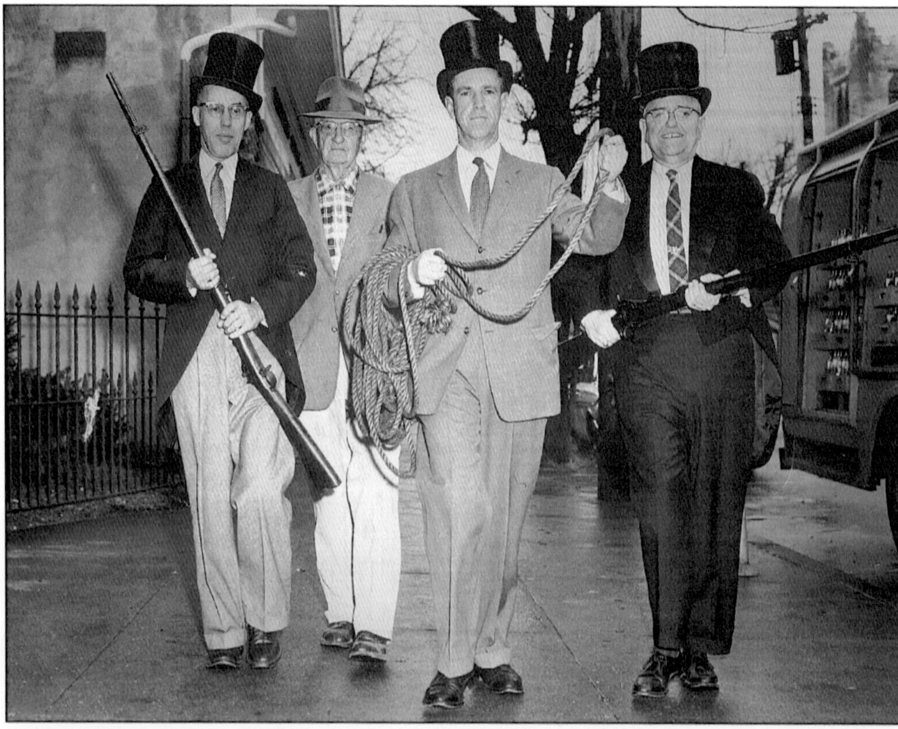

Searching for horse thieves and other town villains in the early 1950s are, from left to right, Ray Hampton, Louis Leedom, T. Sidney Cadwallader, and Ray Yantz. The Yardleyville Protective Company for the Apprehension of Horse Thieves and Other Villains was established 1868. The organization is now a social club.

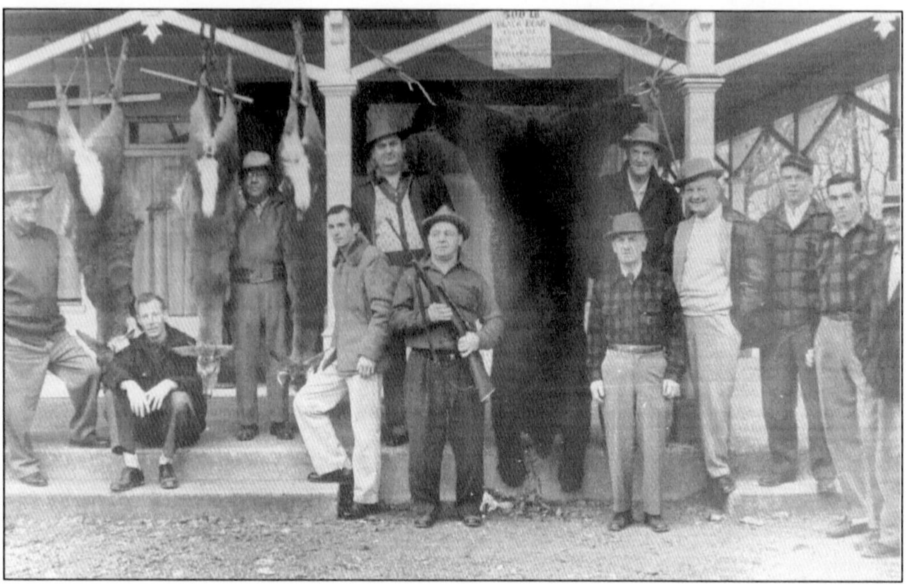

Members of the Yardley Rod and Gun Club gathered on the porch of the Yardley Inn in 1954. Pictured, from left to right, are: Leonard Frost, unidentified, Russel Willard, Jim Sheridan, Paul Messic, Edward Moffo (who shot the 500-pound bear,) Robert Lee, Edward Cryne, Herbert Melton, Arthur, Megin, Leroy Neeld, and Anthony Van House.

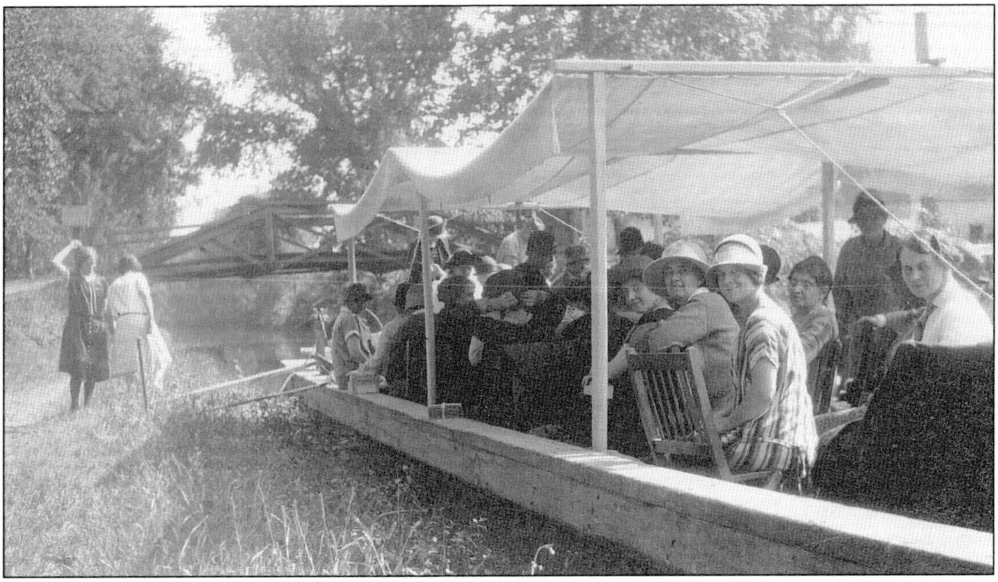

It was "Ladies Day Out" for the Yardley Civic Club on their annual canal boat ride to Brownsburg. This is a photograph taken of the Club's 1926 trip aboard the "Jennie Frank." The women's civic club was organized in 1915 and sponsored a variety of community events and town projects.

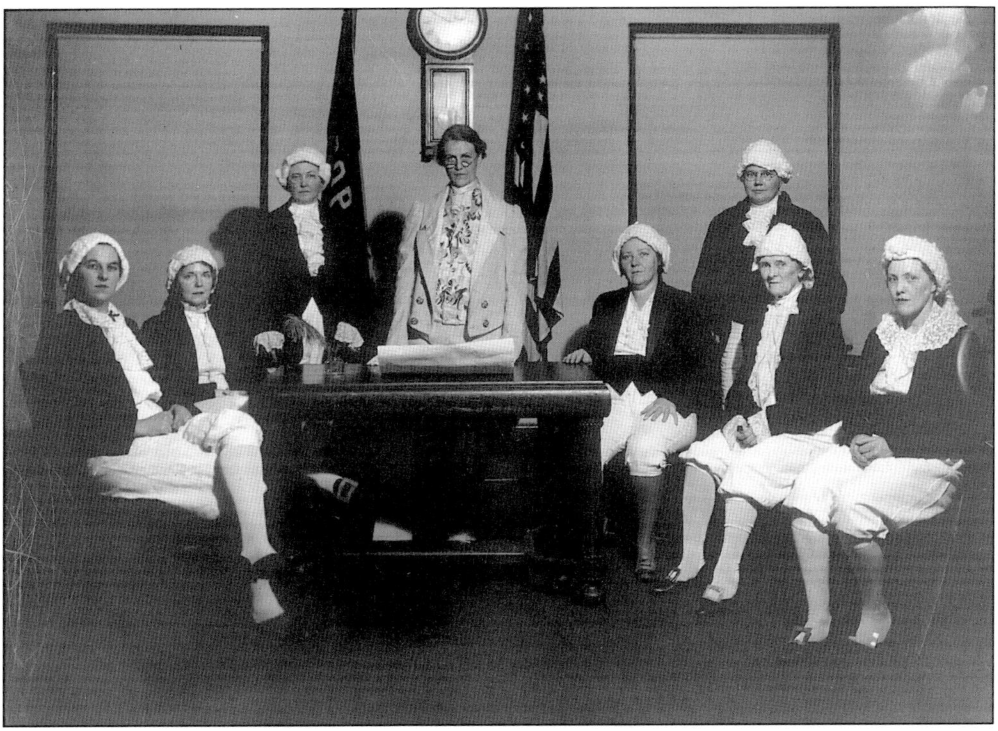

In September 1937, members of the Yardley Civic Club performed a small play about the signing of the United States Constitution. Assuming a patriotic pose are, from left to right, Mrs. Kinsey S. Dickel, Mrs. Vaughn S. Grundy, Mrs. Robert S. Johnson, Mrs. Robert Bellville, Miss Margaret Groome, Mrs. Norman Tallman, Mrs. Harvey J. Funk, and Miss Elizabeth Weeks.

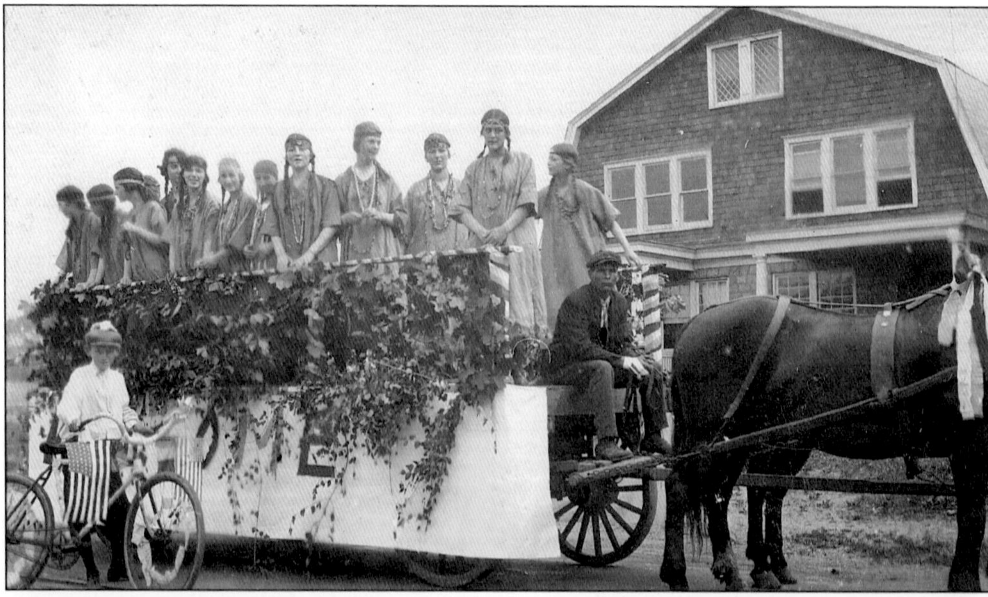

In 1921 the principal of the Yardley School advised the civic club that adults were needed to supervise children's play. The Lenni Lenape Camp Fire Girls was one of the many youth groups active in Yardley during the 1920s.

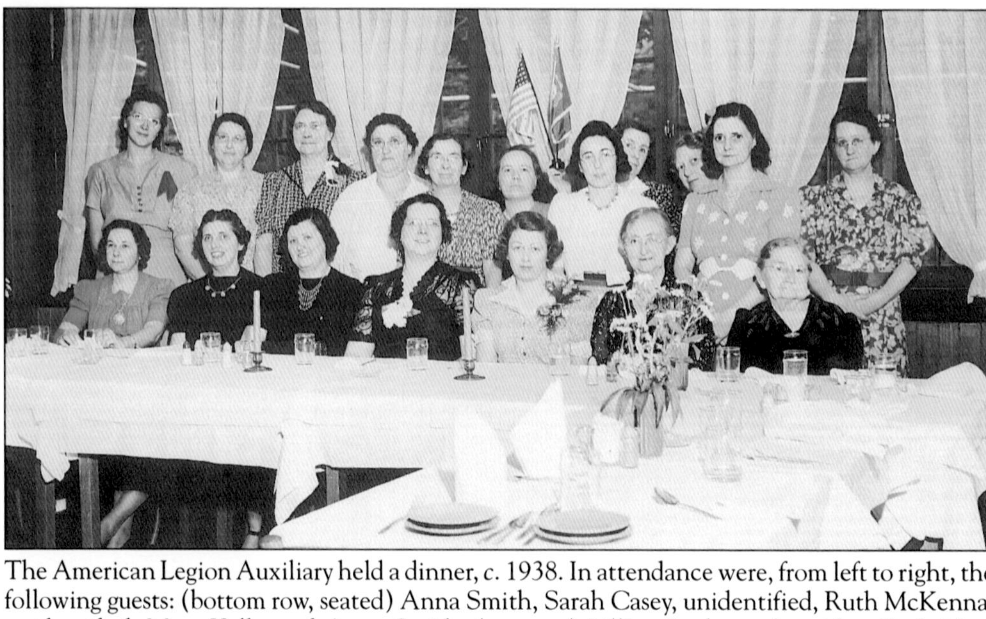

The American Legion Auxiliary held a dinner, c. 1938. In attendance were, from left to right, the following guests: (bottom row, seated) Anna Smith, Sarah Casey, unidentified, Ruth McKenna, unidentified, Mary Kelly, and Anne Smith; (top row) Lillian Rothermel, unidentified, Mary Doyle, Annie Kurfuss, unidentified, Margaret Dougherty, Marce Kelly, Katherine Smith, Edna Marion, Helen Doyle, and Mrs. Woolman.

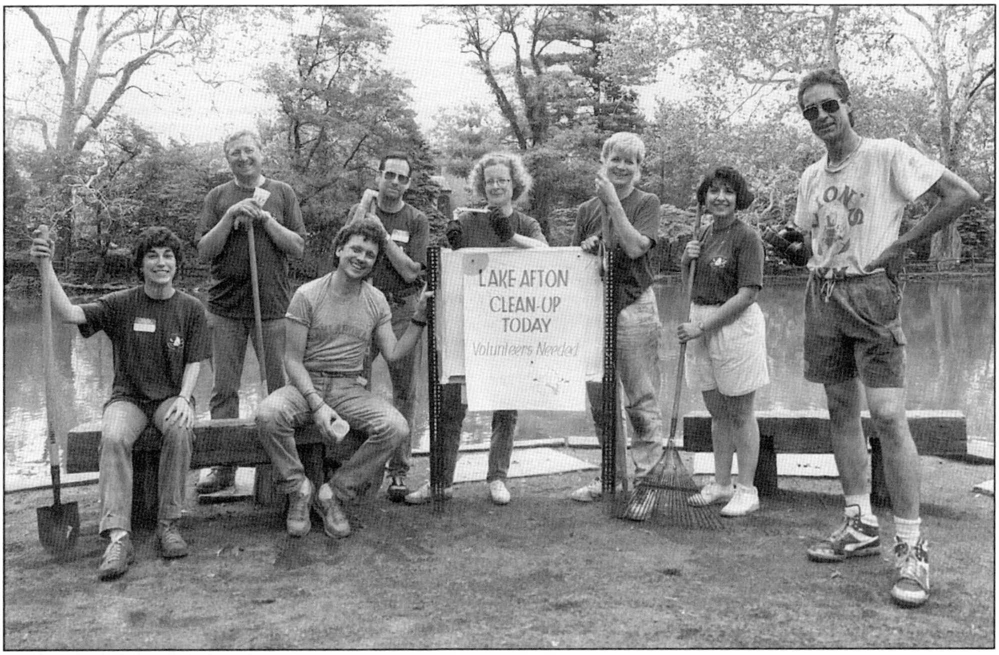

The Friends of Lake Afton was formed in 1970. Pictured here are, from left to right, as follows: Jean Bertolette, Heinz Graumann, Simon Titterley, unidentified, Susan Taylor, Lynn Gordon, Suzanne McHale, and Karl Gober, attempting to drum up volunteers for the annual Lake cleanup.

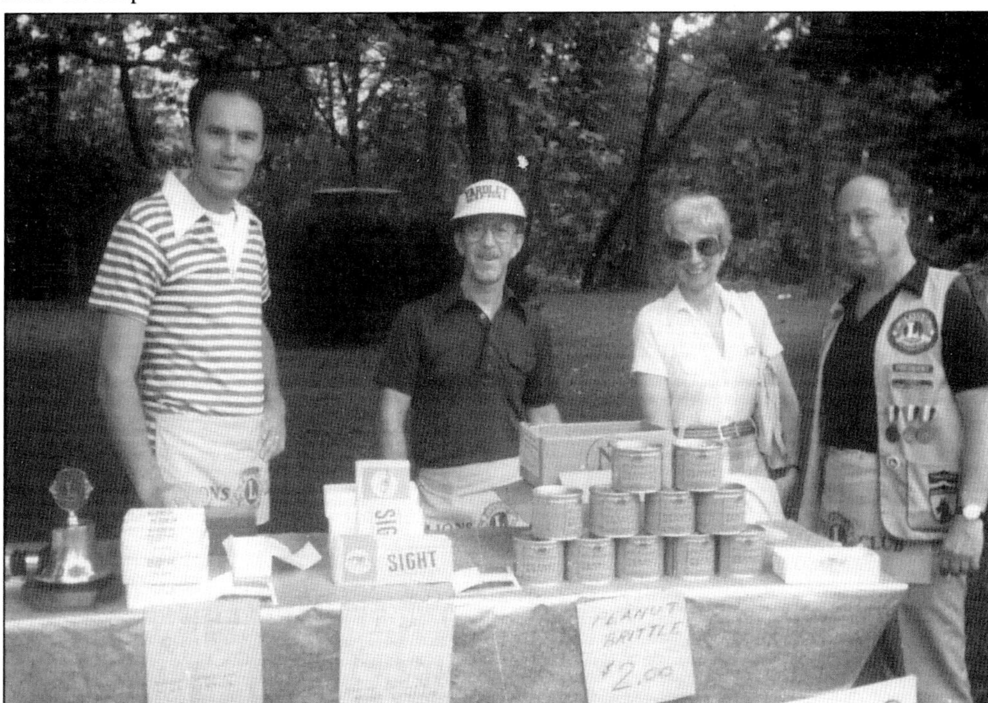

George and Joan Oppenheimer (right) staff a table for the Yardley Lions Club at the Tricentennial celebrations in 1982.

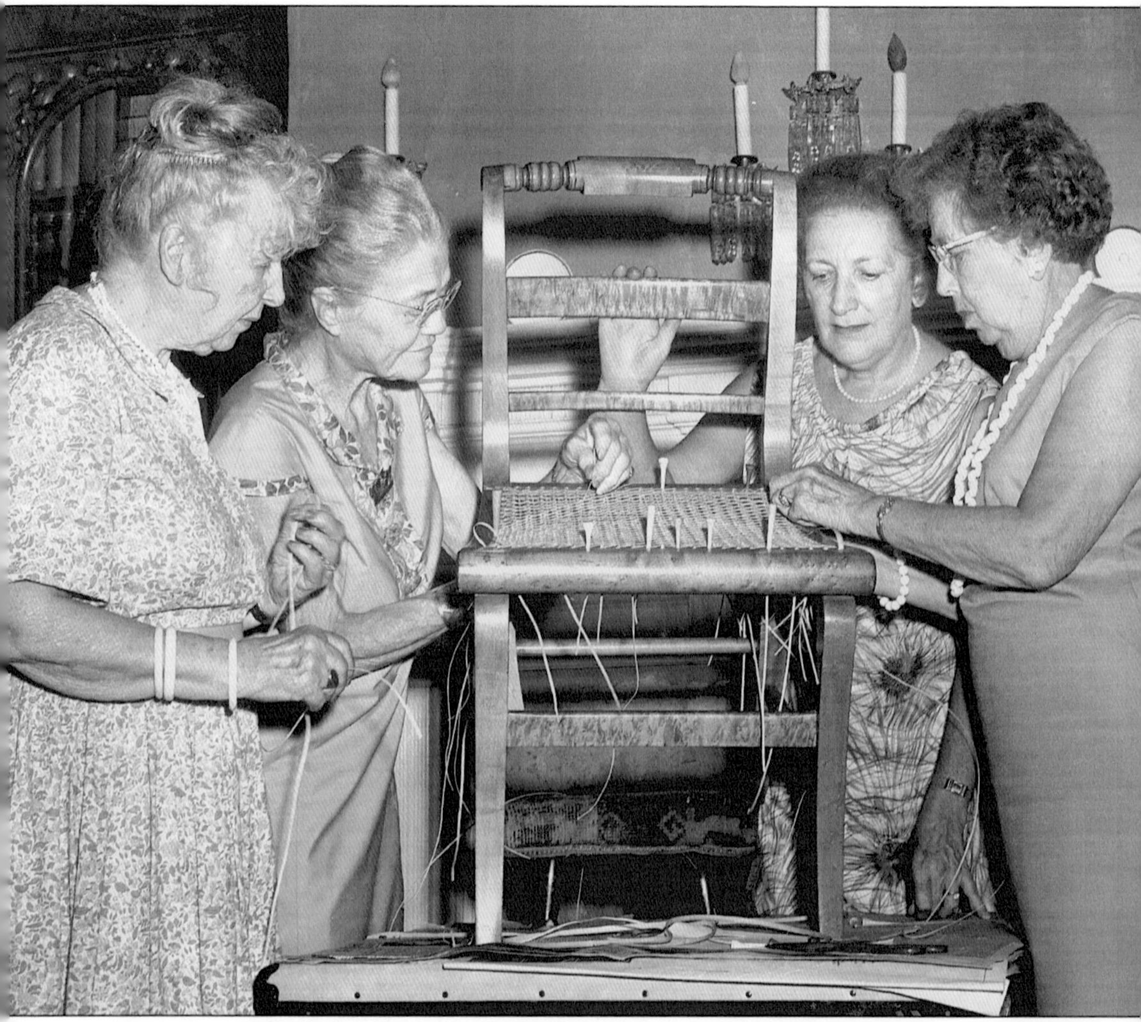

The Colonial Yardley Historic Association sponsored a street fair in the early 1960s. Pictured here, from left to right, are Mrs. Malcolm G. Newell, Miss Catherine Belville, Mrs. Isabel Brooks, and Mrs. Martha Paxson. The ladies are demonstrating their chair caning during an open house tour.

Four

Around Town

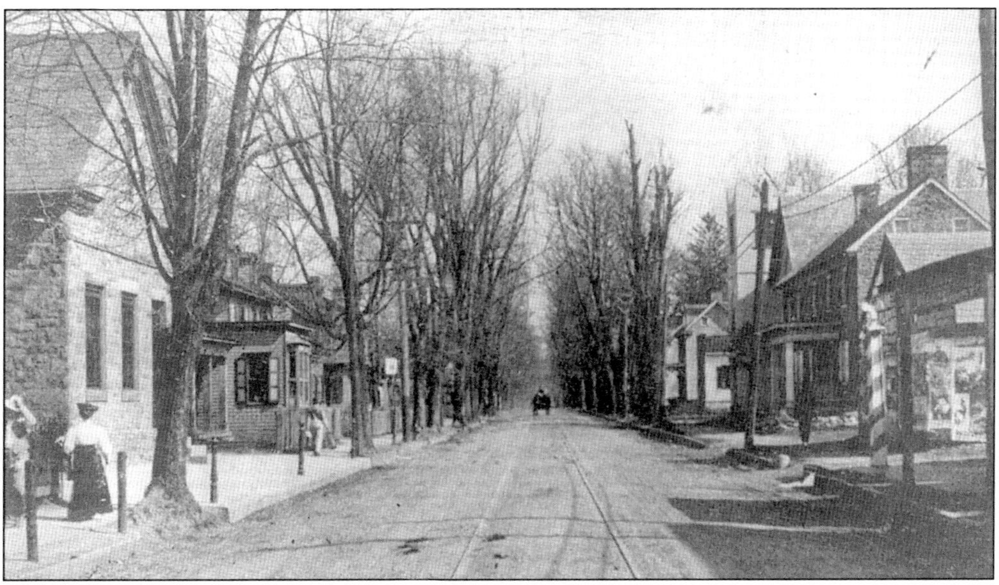

From 1700 to 1950, Yardley served as a small commercial district for rural Lower Makefield Township. For the most part, everyday day life was paced; some might say slowly. Residents' pleasures tended to be simple—walks down Main Street, a carriage ride, a visit to a friend. There was always swimming and fishing in the canal or river, and ice skating on the lake. In the late nineteenth and early twentieth centuries, local organizations sponsored dances, debates, lectures, and a variety of small-town celebrations.

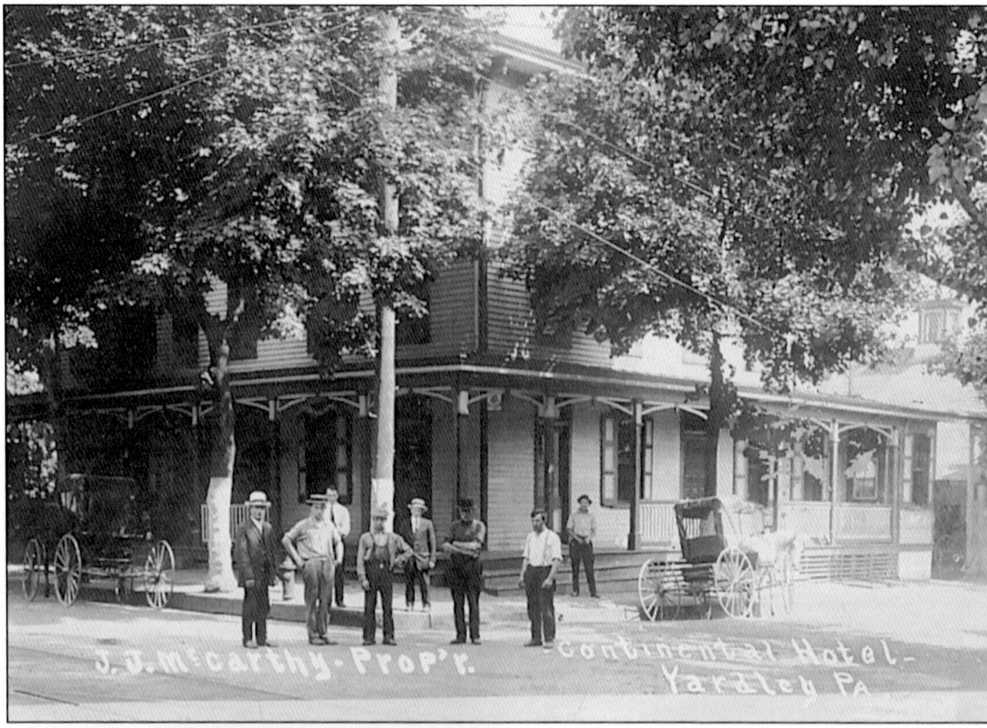

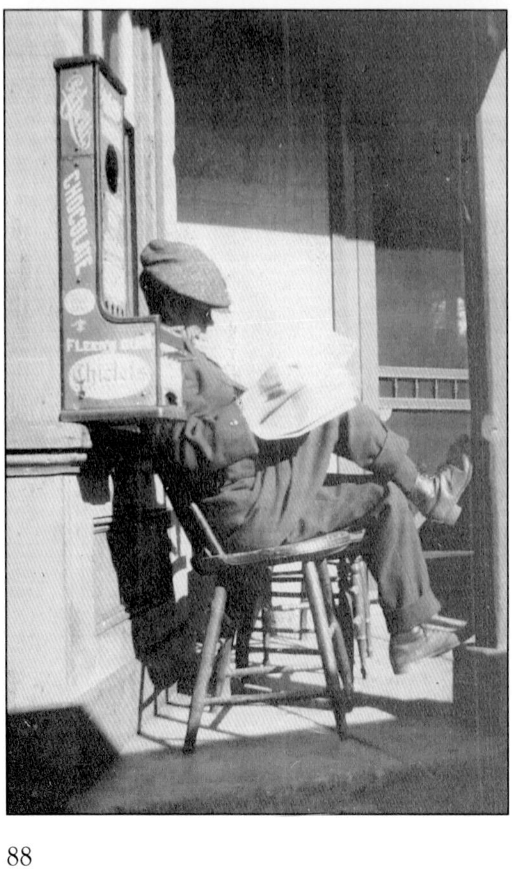

A group of men, some in straw hats, pose in front of the Continental Hotel, c. 1905. The Hotel was a popular hangout, as well as a summer resort destination. It was one of three public houses in Yardley that served alcohol; Lower Makefield, in contrast, was a "dry" municipality. Both borough and township had active temperance associations.

Across the street from the Continental at Wist's Corner you could get ice cream, soda, and sweets. John Shanahan had a good view of Main Street as he leaned back to read a newspaper on Wist's porch c. 1915.

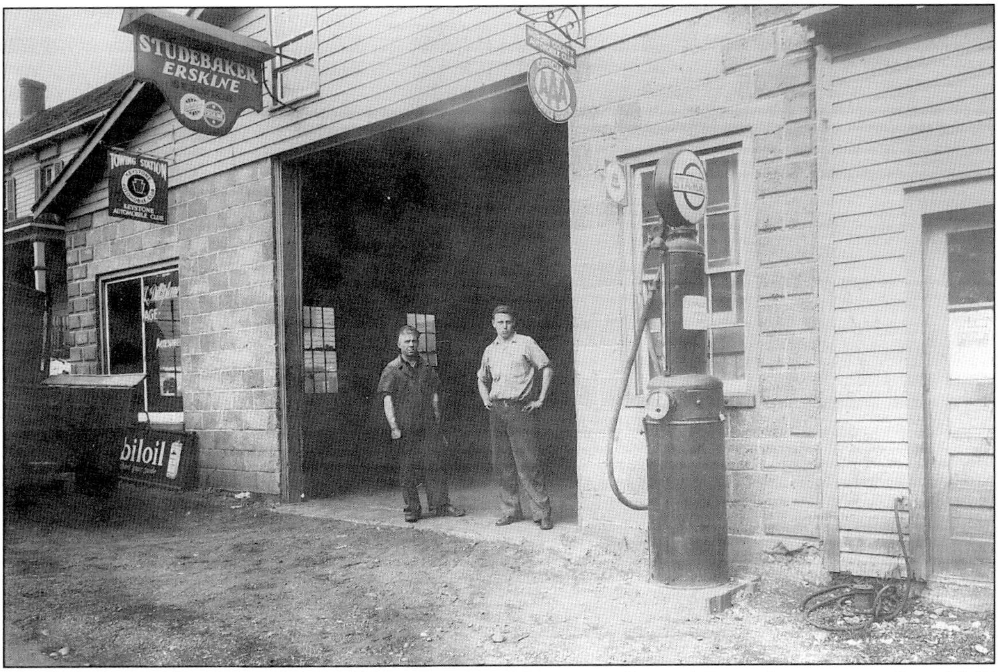

Walter Dilliplane (left) operated a service station on East Afton Avenue in this 1930 photograph.

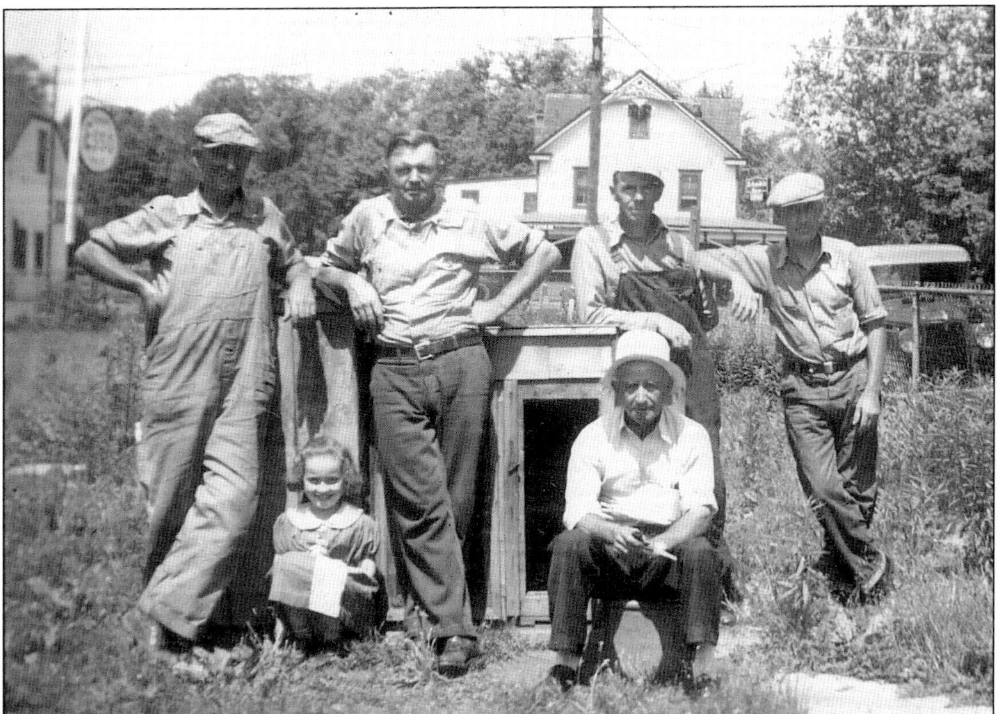

Thelma Wetzstein gets her picture taken in June 1937 with a crew of workers. Bob, Raymond, Stoutie, Roy, and Sam were in town to replace the old wooden planking on the bridge with steel grating.

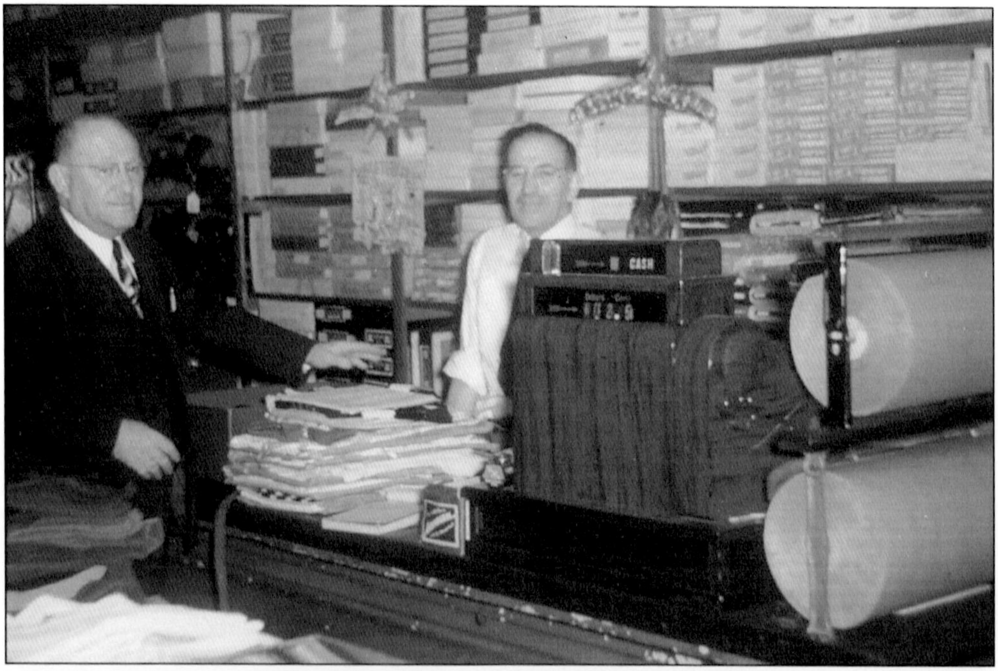

Mr. Louis Seplow stands behind the cash register in his Main Street department store, c. 1948. Seplow's was one of Yardley's many family-owned and operated businesses.

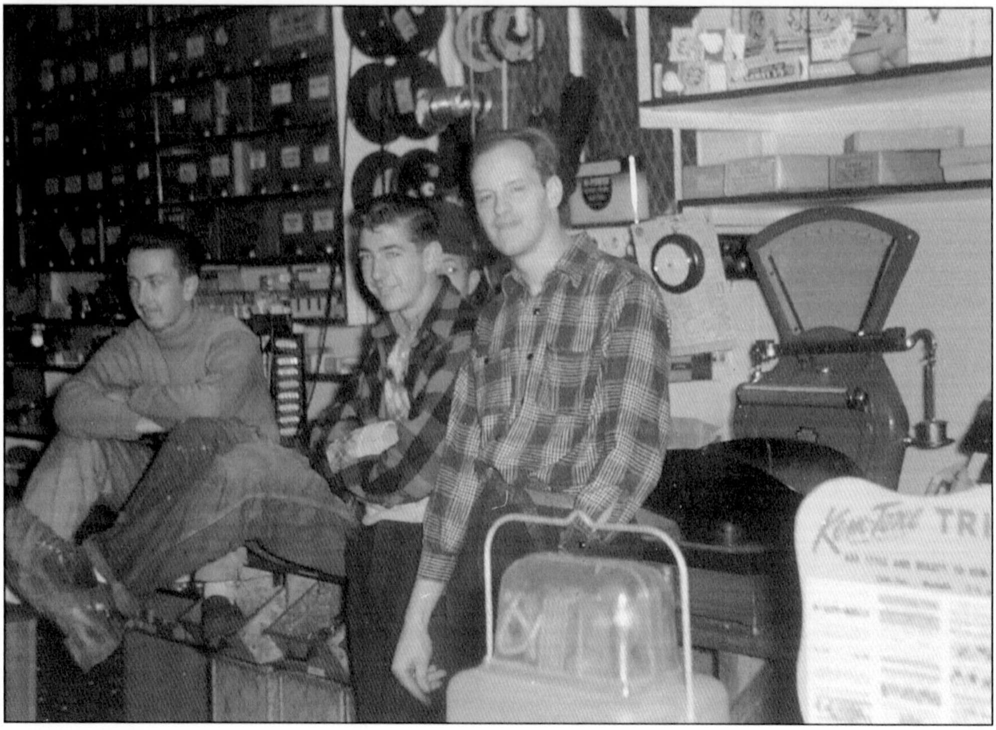

Bobbie Hackett, Freddie Hallmark, and Bill Beener hang out in Beener's Hardware Store, c. 1948. Beener's was a classic "mom and pop" hardware store. William and Molly Beener, and later their son Bill, were always ready to offer friendly advice.

Ruth McKenna was Yardley's postmistress in 1948 when this photograph was taken. The post office moved into borough hall in 1917. The trip to the post office was a daily ritual for most Yardley residents. Home delivery started in 1952.

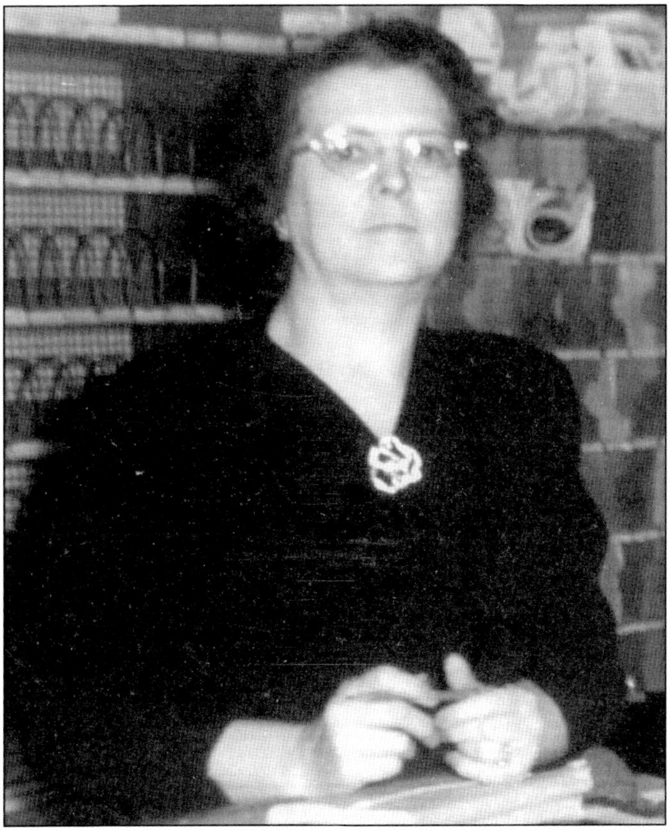

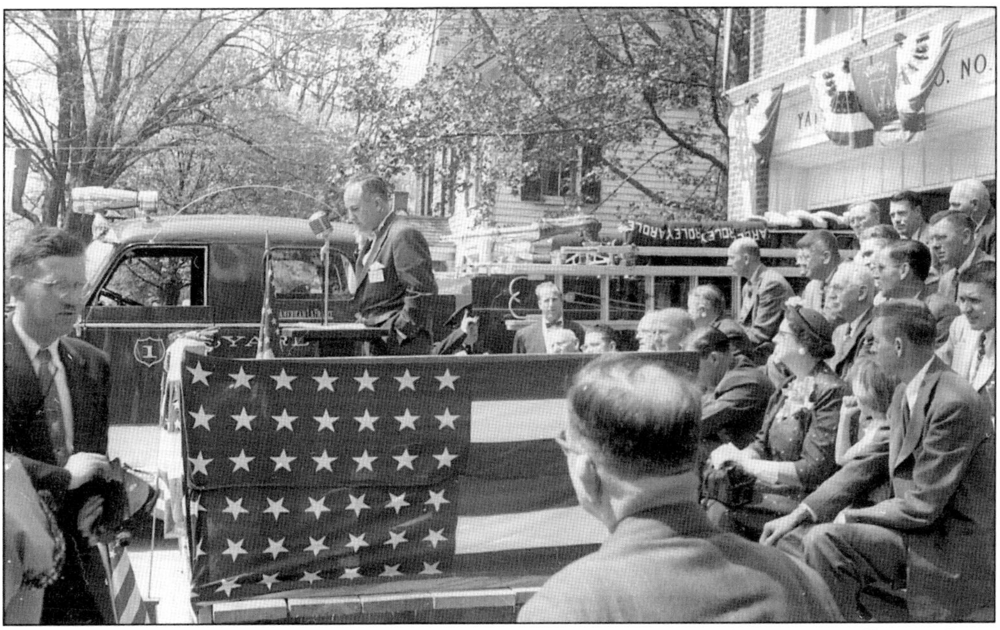

Myles Furey (at the podium) was mayor of Yardley during the 1950s. Like many Yardley residents who have been active in local government, Myles served in several positions—councilmember, president, and then mayor.

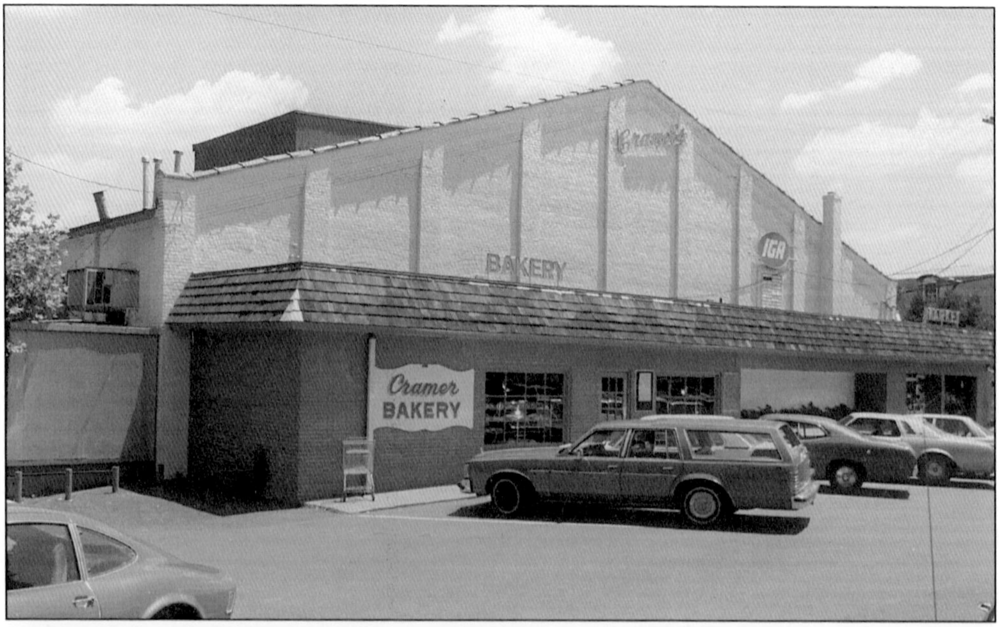

Cramer's Bakery has been a Yardley institution since the 1950s. John E. and Jane Cramer purchased the old power station building from the Leedom family in the 1970s. When the Valley Market closed in the early 1980s, the Cramer family opened the IGA, the last supermarket in downtown Yardley.

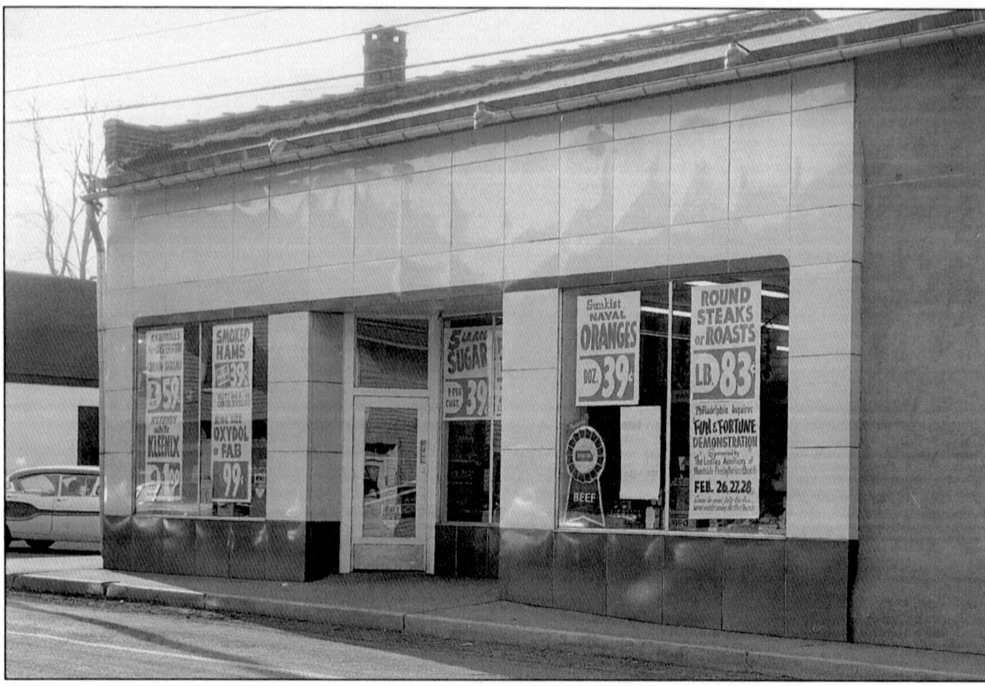

As competition with shopping centers increased after WWII, Yardley's business association encouraged new businesses to settle in town. In 1958, Irvin Honer from Northeast Philadelphia opened the Valley Market in the old power station. The building had previously been an ACME store.

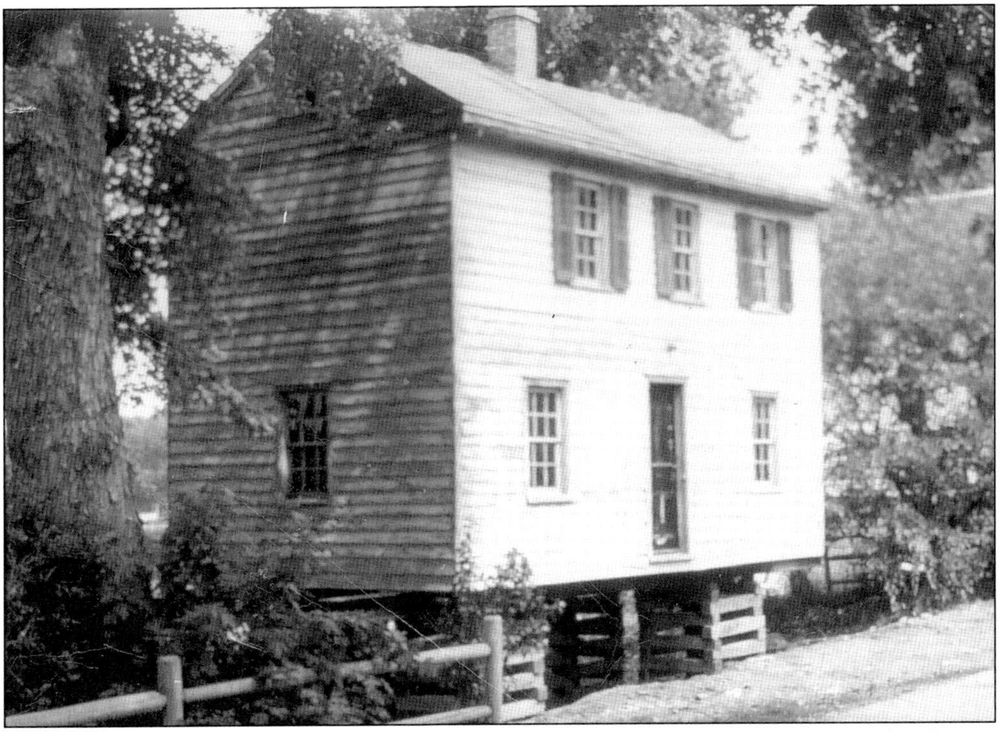

In the 1960s, several homes on Canal Street were moved canal-side to create parking behind Main Street businesses. When the house at 40 Canal Street was moved, a secret cellar was discovered lending support to a legend that the building was part of the Underground Railroad.

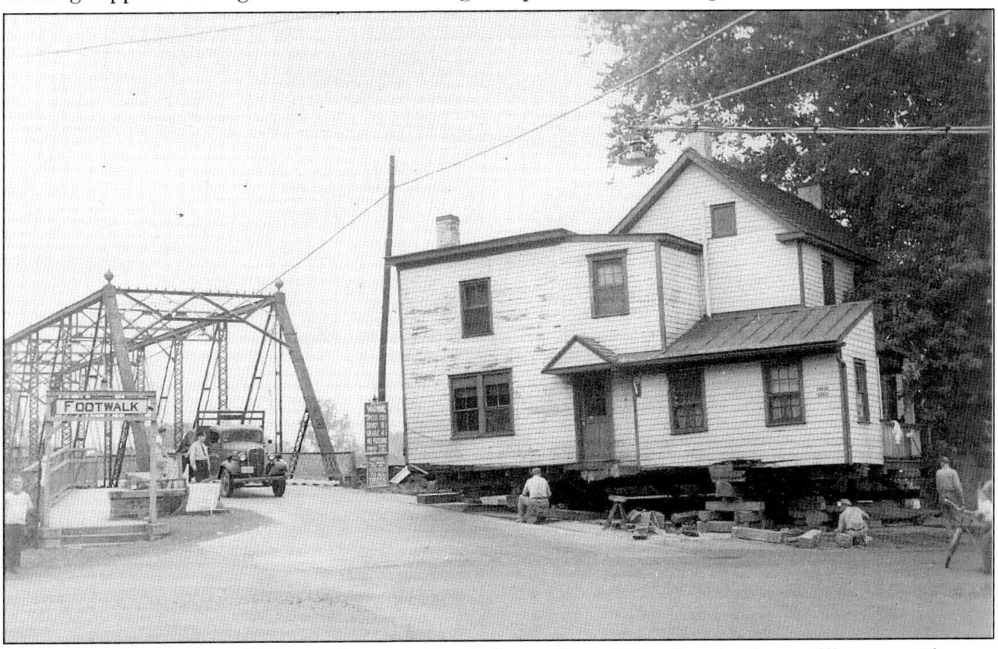

In 1947, the state of Pennsylvania decided to demolish the bridge tollhouse. Chester Wetzstein, the toll collector, purchased the house and moved it several hundred feet up East Afton Avenue.

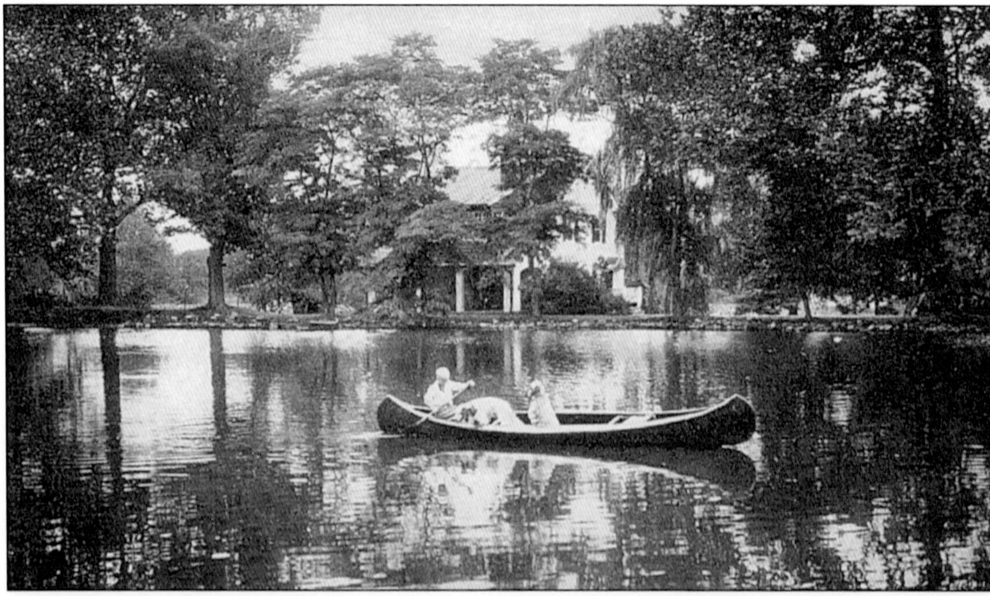

Lake Afton has been the subject of many postcards. In this *c.* 1930s view, a man and what seems to be a dog peacefully canoe on the lake. Afton has always been a private lake owned by surrounding property owners. The residence in the background, called "Bird Haven," was the home of Mr. and Mrs. Edmund Yarrington Barnes. It was the scene of many Civic Club activities.

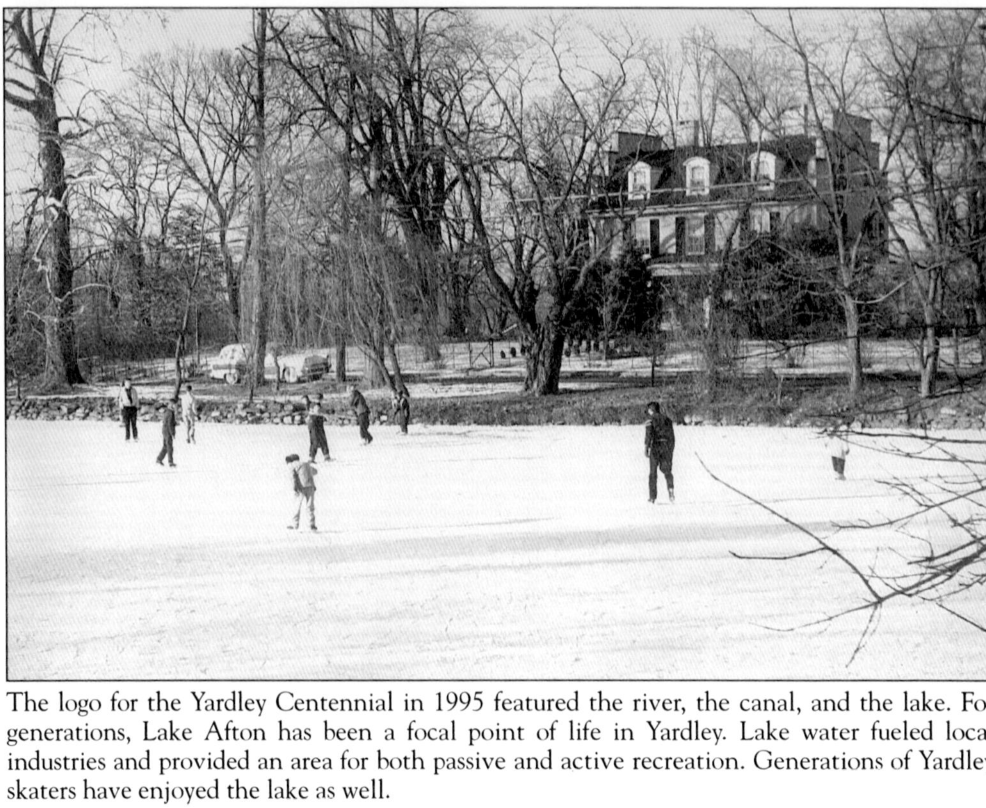

The logo for the Yardley Centennial in 1995 featured the river, the canal, and the lake. For generations, Lake Afton has been a focal point of life in Yardley. Lake water fueled local industries and provided an area for both passive and active recreation. Generations of Yardley skaters have enjoyed the lake as well.

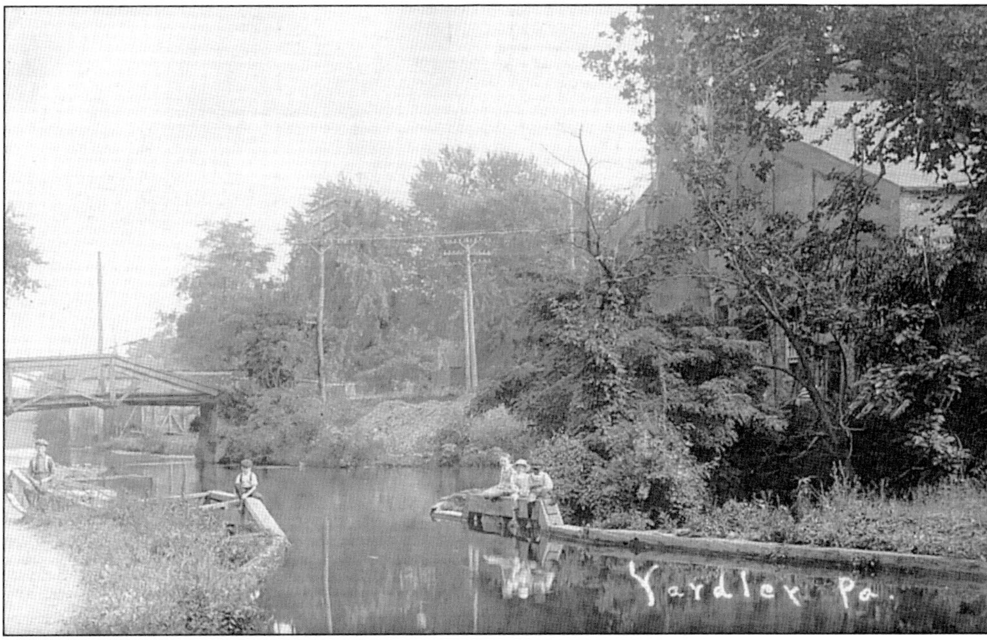

Yardley children loved swimming, skating, and fishing on the canal, and watching the mules and canal boats. Boat captains sometimes gave kids a ride on a canal boat. A group of boys gather at the Afton Avenue aqueduct in this photograph c. 1904.

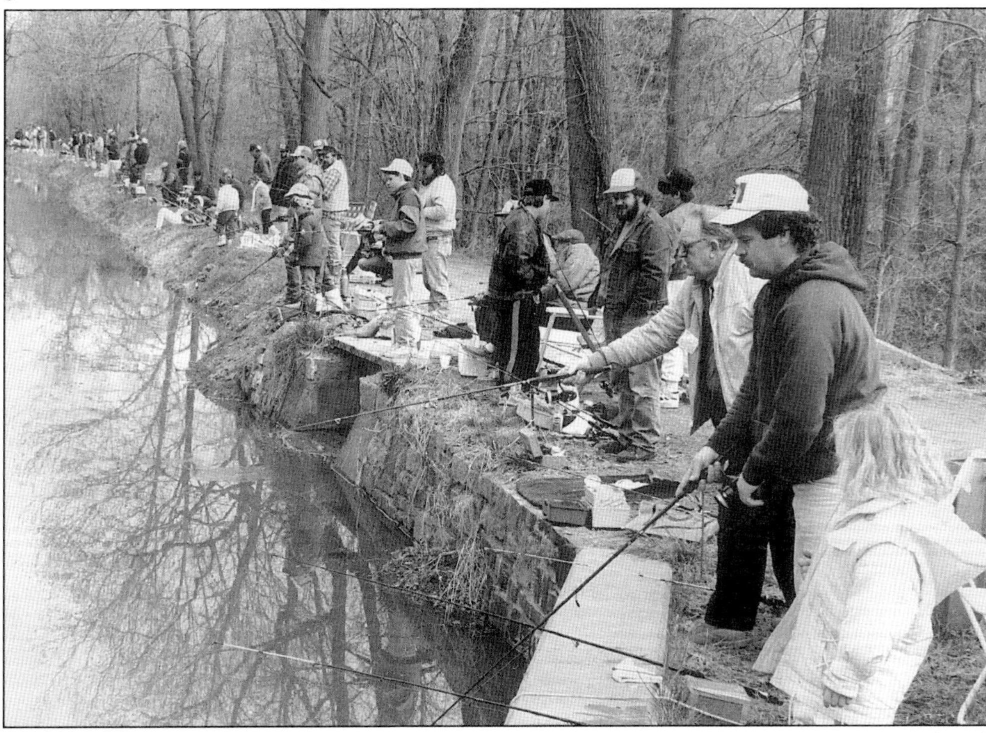

Through the years, the Commonwealth of Pennsylvania has stocked the Delaware Canal with fish. The first day of trout season always drew hundreds to the canal towpath in Yardley. In addition the towpath is ideal for riding a bicycle, jogging, or taking a walk.

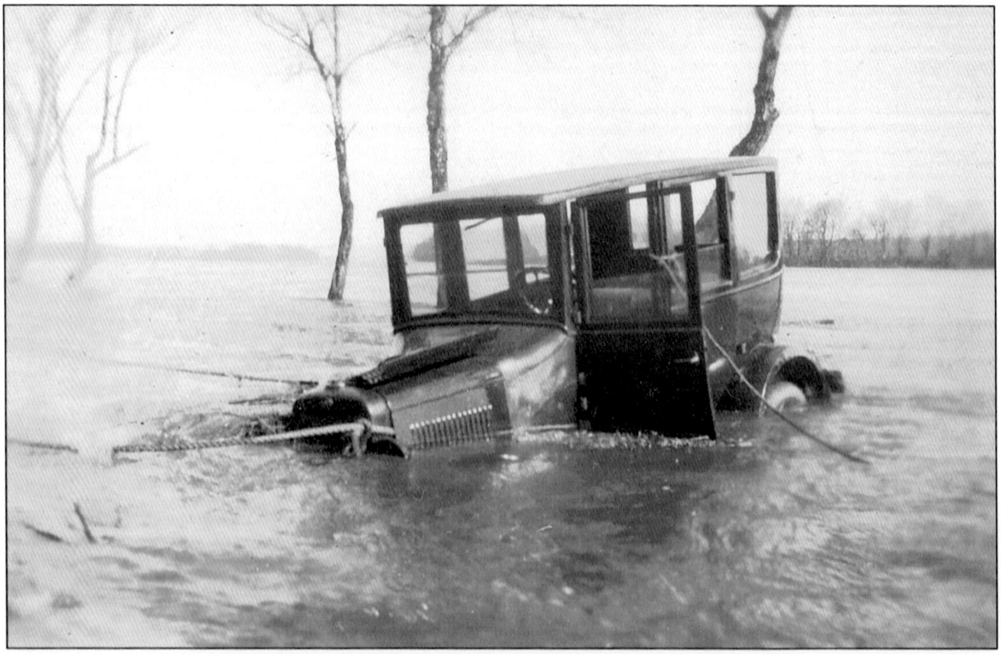

Major floods are mileposts in Yardley's history—1903, 1924, 1936, 1955, and 1996. Floods have destroyed bridges, homes, and cars. But they also bring the community together. In this photograph, a car washes away in the flood of 1924.

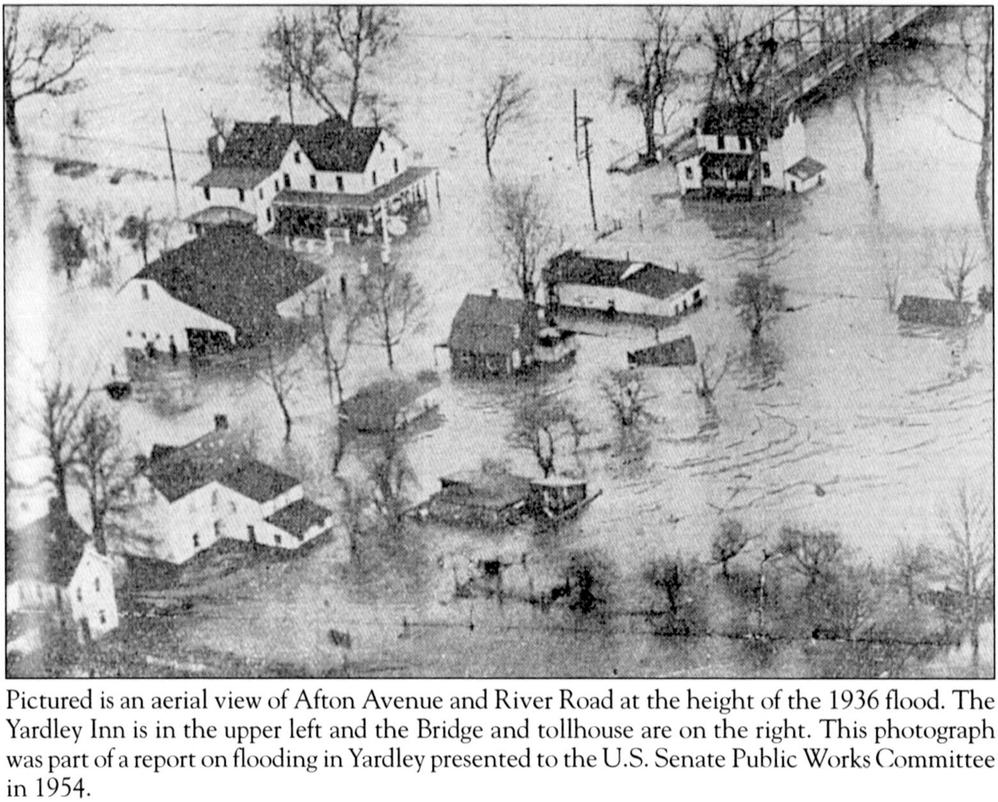

Pictured is an aerial view of Afton Avenue and River Road at the height of the 1936 flood. The Yardley Inn is in the upper left and the Bridge and tollhouse are on the right. This photograph was part of a report on flooding in Yardley presented to the U.S. Senate Public Works Committee in 1954.

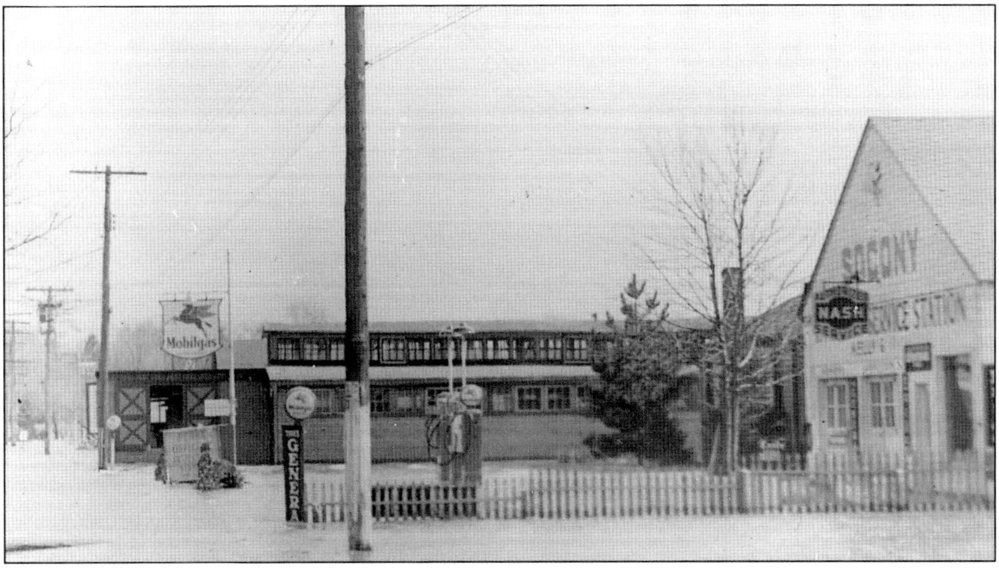

Looking down River Road toward Morrisville as commercial and industrial properties are inundated during the 1936 flood. In the center of the photograph is the Eagle Neckband Company; the Socony Service Station, which advertised Mobil gas, Nash cars, and Exide batteries, is on the right.

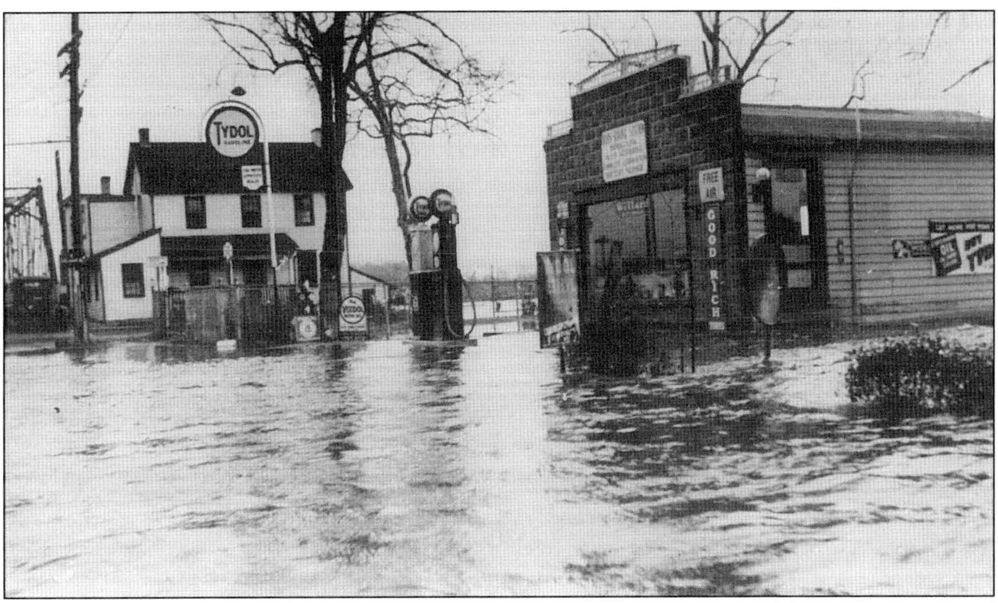

The Yardley Bridge, tollhouse, and Joe Yardley's Garage were photographed during one of several floods during the 1930s. Notice the signs for Goodrich tires, Tydol gasoline, and oil.

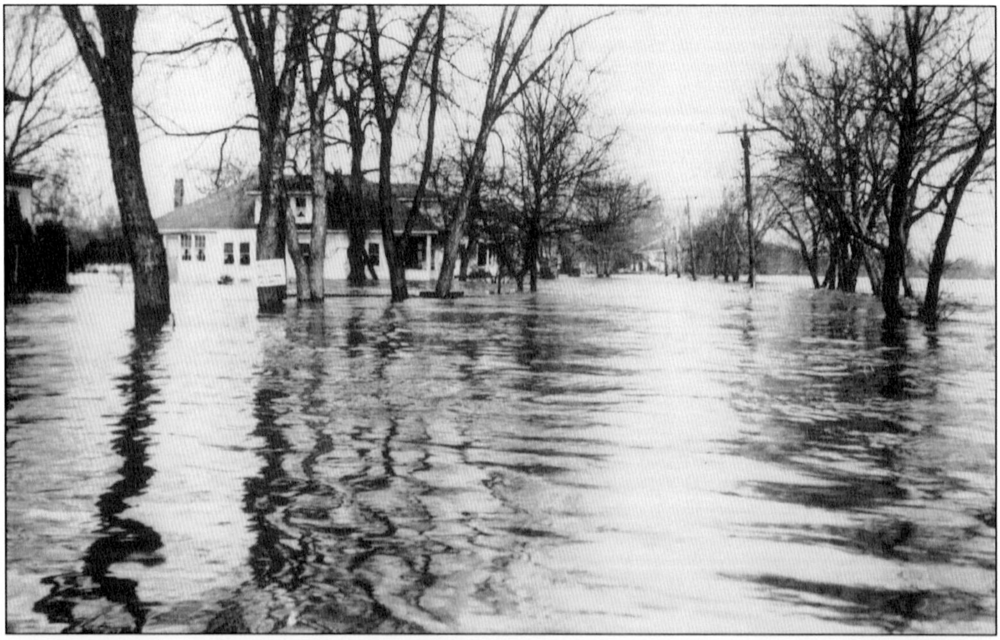

In August 1955, hurricanes Connie and Diane passed through the Delaware Valley. On the 18th and 19th, four inches of rain saturated the region. The river crested on the morning of August 20, flooding the area between the canal and river. This photograph was taken from the Yardley Inn looking up River Road toward New Hope.

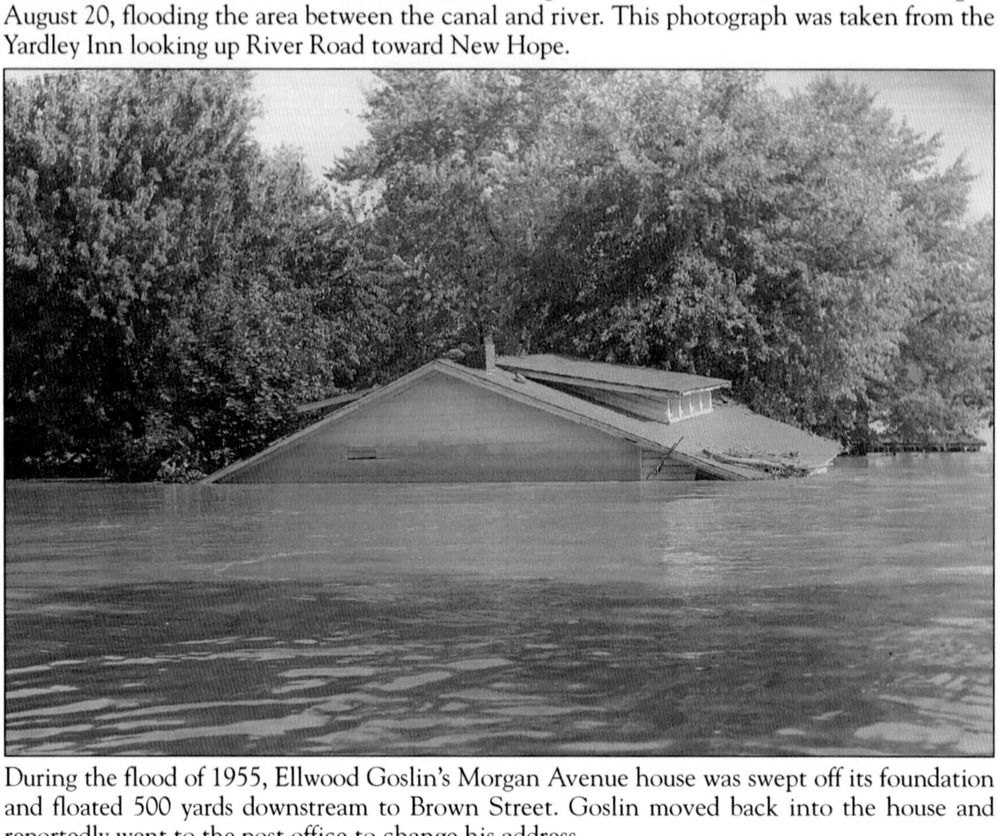

During the flood of 1955, Ellwood Goslin's Morgan Avenue house was swept off its foundation and floated 500 yards downstream to Brown Street. Goslin moved back into the house and reportedly went to the post office to change his address.

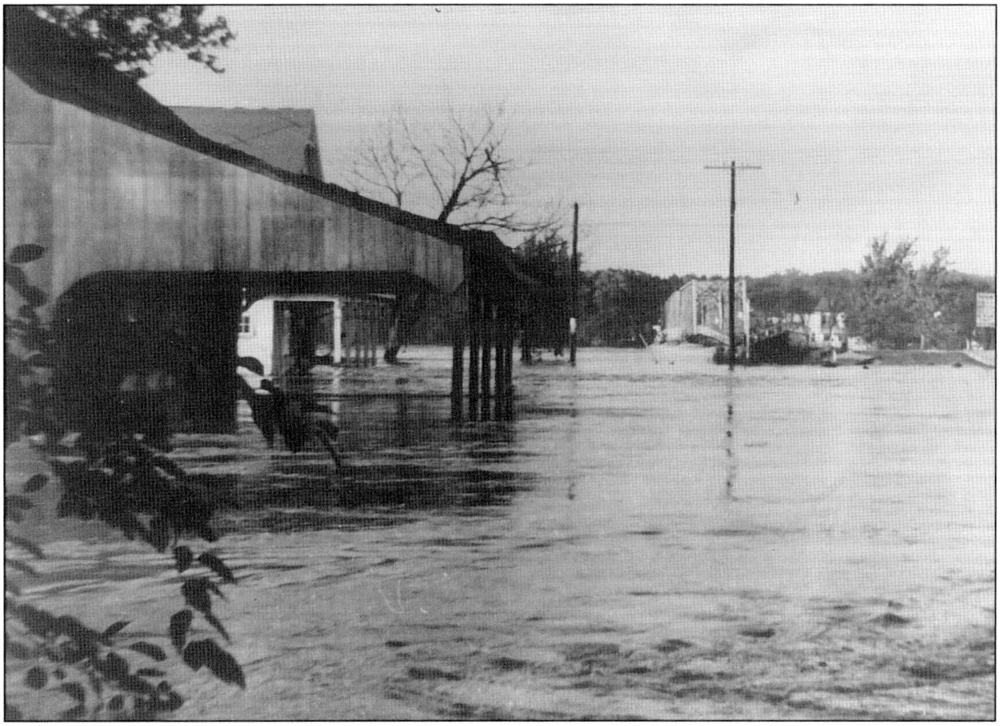

During the flood of 1955, the Delaware River crested over 20 feet above normal heights. In Yardley, several hundred families were evacuated. This photograph of Cryne's (the Yardley Inn) was taken on Saturday morning, August 20, before the Yardley Bridge washed away.

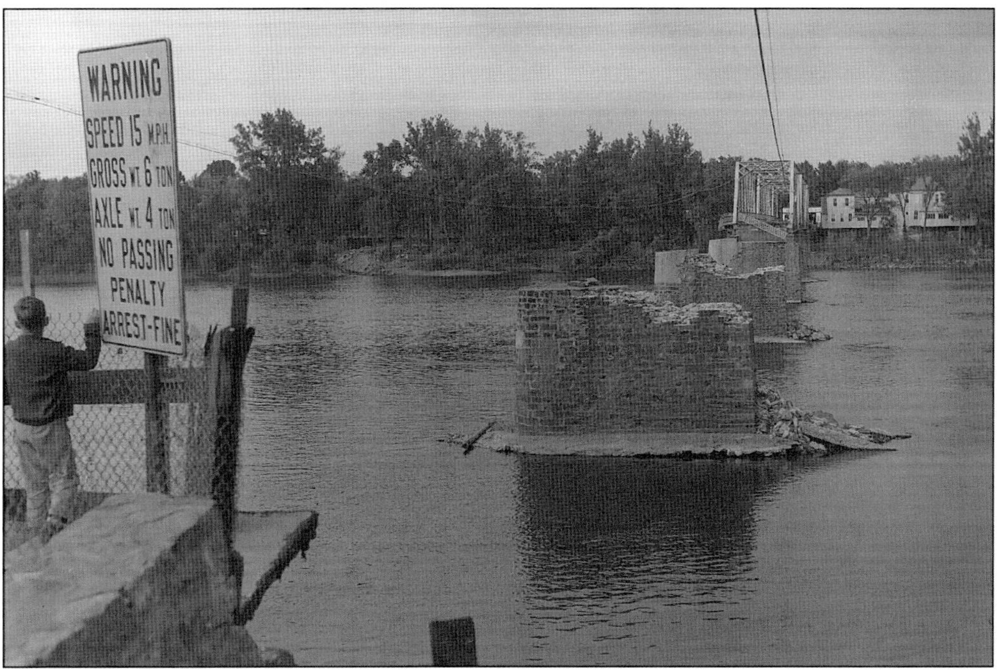

The Yardley Bridge broke up on August 20, 1955, when it was struck by a house. Three spans—roughly half of the 902-foot bridge—were knocked out.

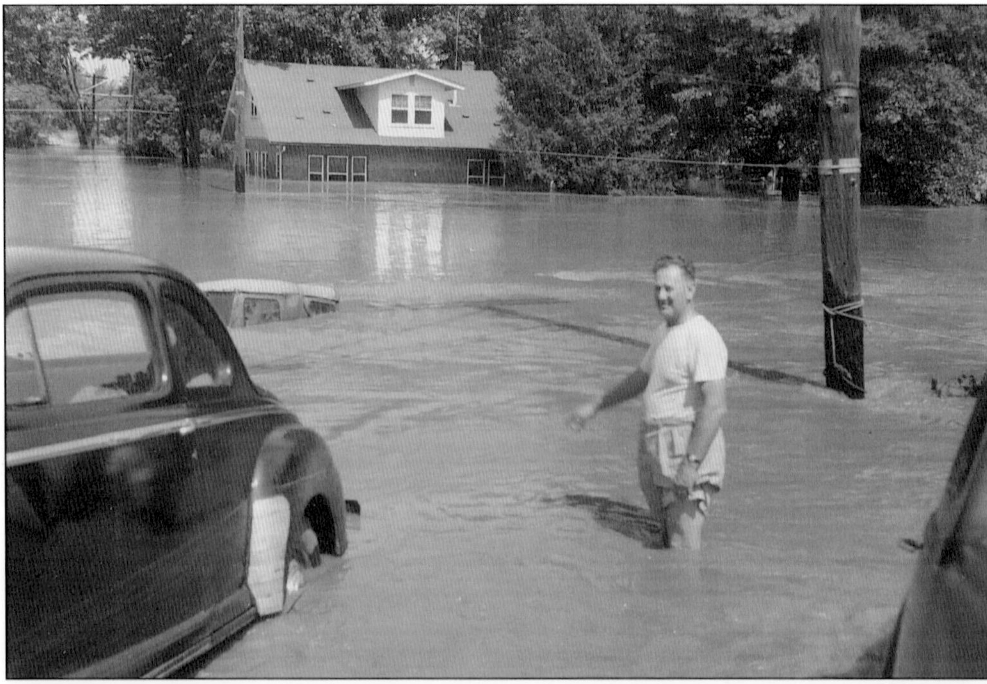

Thought to be "high and dry," cars left on the canal towpath were lost during the 1955 flood. This photograph was taken from the Mary Yardley footbridge at Fuld Avenue.

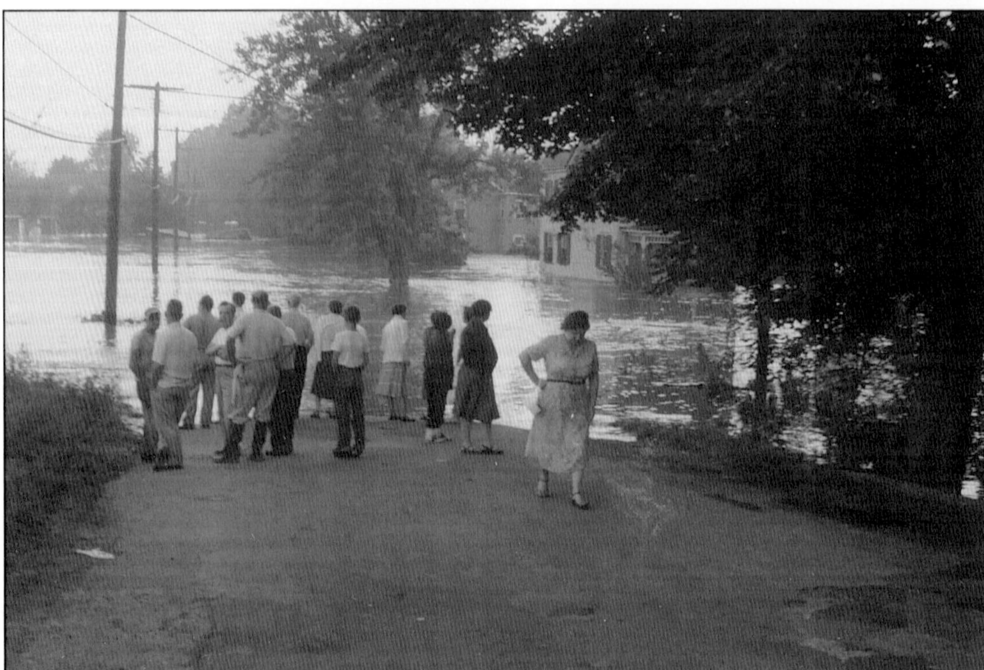

Residents and curiosity seekers gathered at College Avenue to view the devastating 1955 flood. In Yardley, the flood affected 274 families.

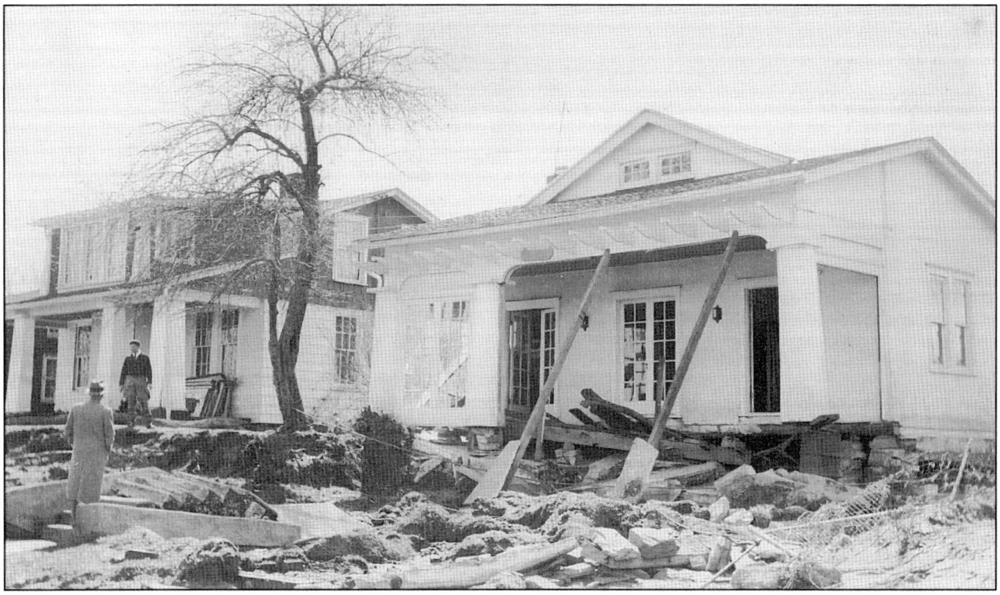

In 1936, over 80 homes were flooded. In some houses the muddy current flowed in the front door and out the rear. Residents surveyed damages after the flood—foundations had been washed away, furniture ruined, and wells contaminated.

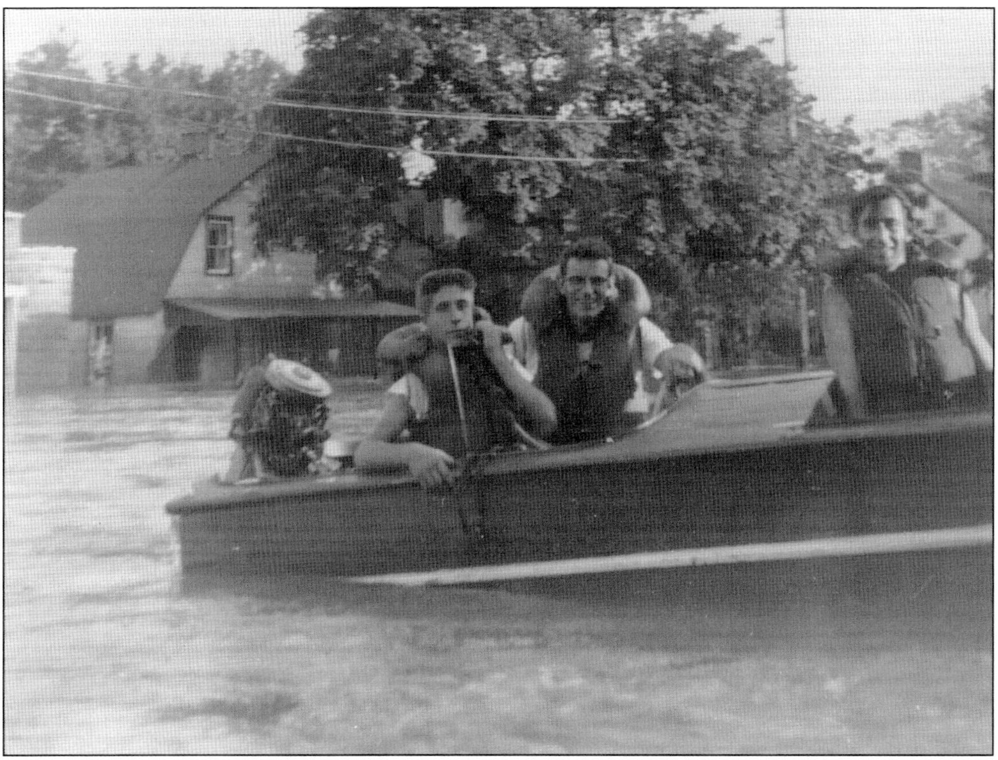

Don Elfen, Earl Wood, and Junior Coulton were among the many volunteers in private boats who rescued residents and patrolled neighborhoods during the 1955 flood.

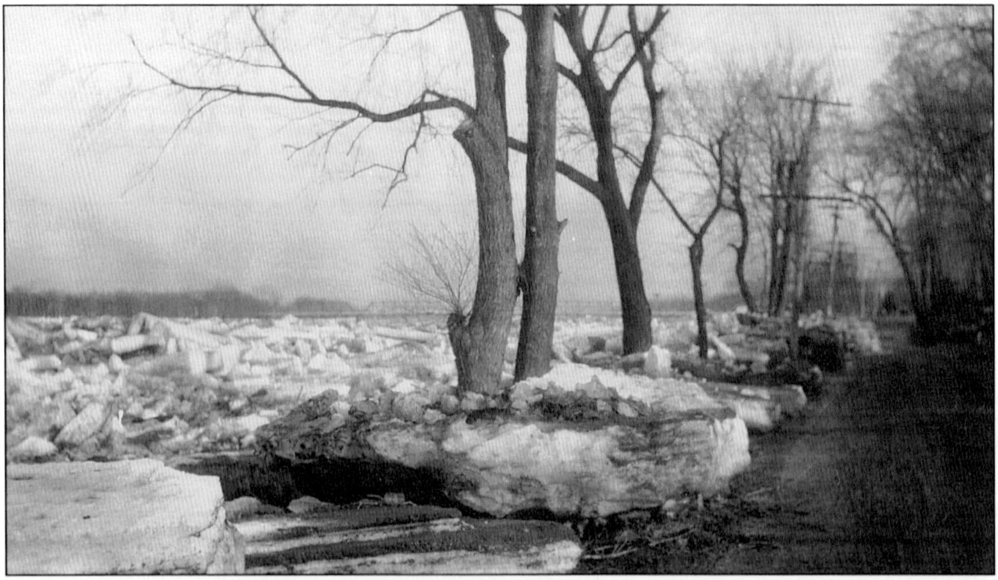

Fred Bebbington, a well-known local attorney and avid photographer, captured the break-up of the frozen Delaware River on March 5, 1934. Occasionally blocks of ice have closed River Road. An ice jam caused major flooding in January 1996.

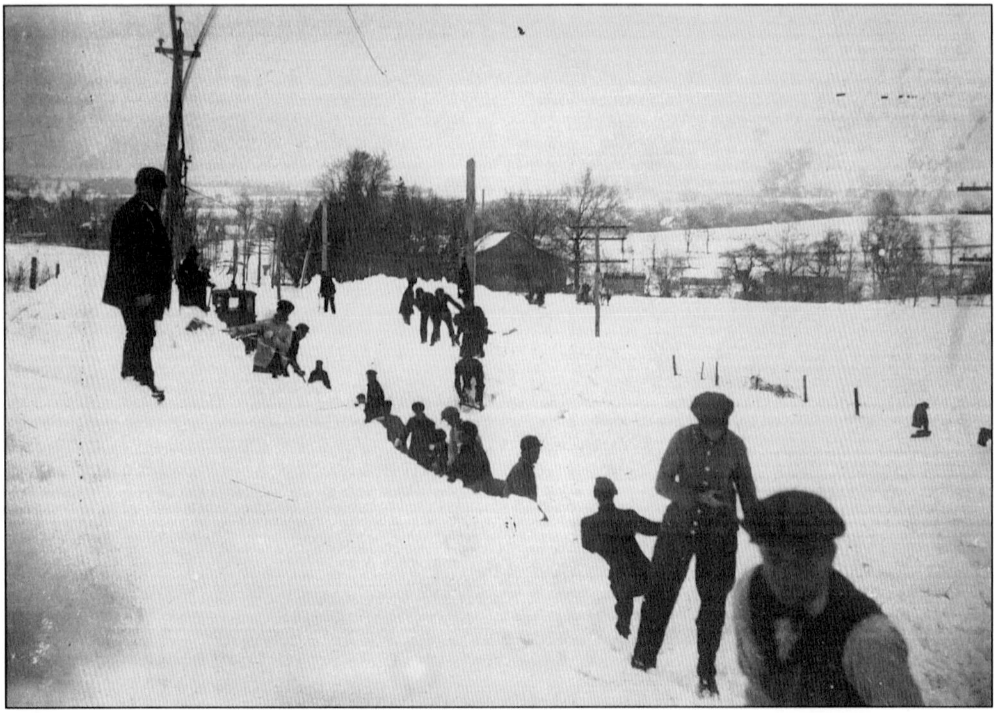

Workers on the Yardley-Newtown Road dug out after a major snowstorm, c. 1902-1903. The view is from Scammell's Corner looking toward Yardley. The Streetcar Company may have hired the crew.

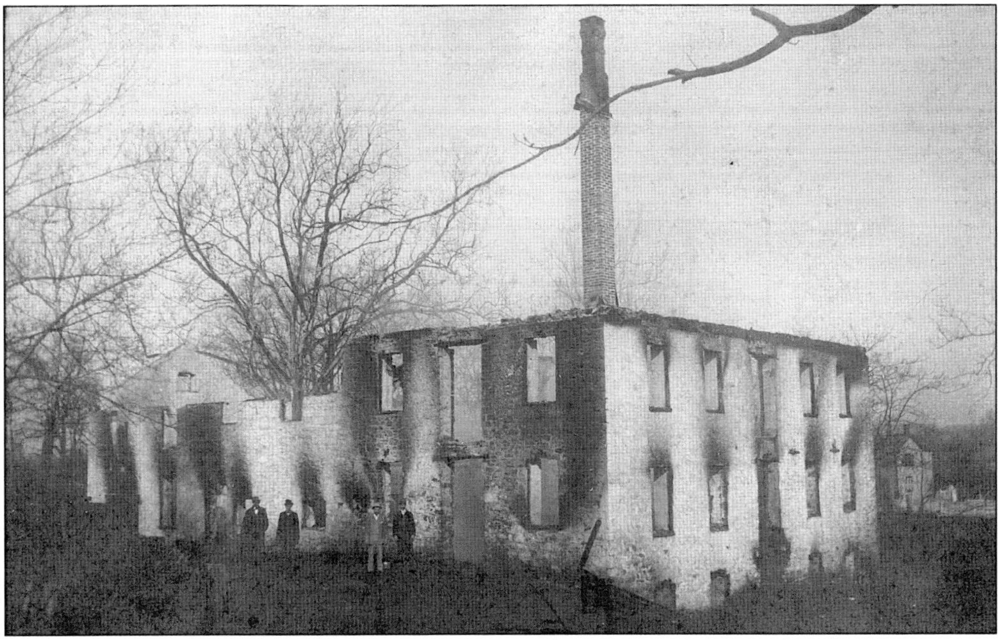

In January 1901, a fire destroyed the buildings and contents of the Yardley Mills Company. It was the first major fire fought by the Yardley Fire Company, which had been established in 1897. Later, A.J. Cadwallader, the mill owner, donated $100 to the fire company coffers.

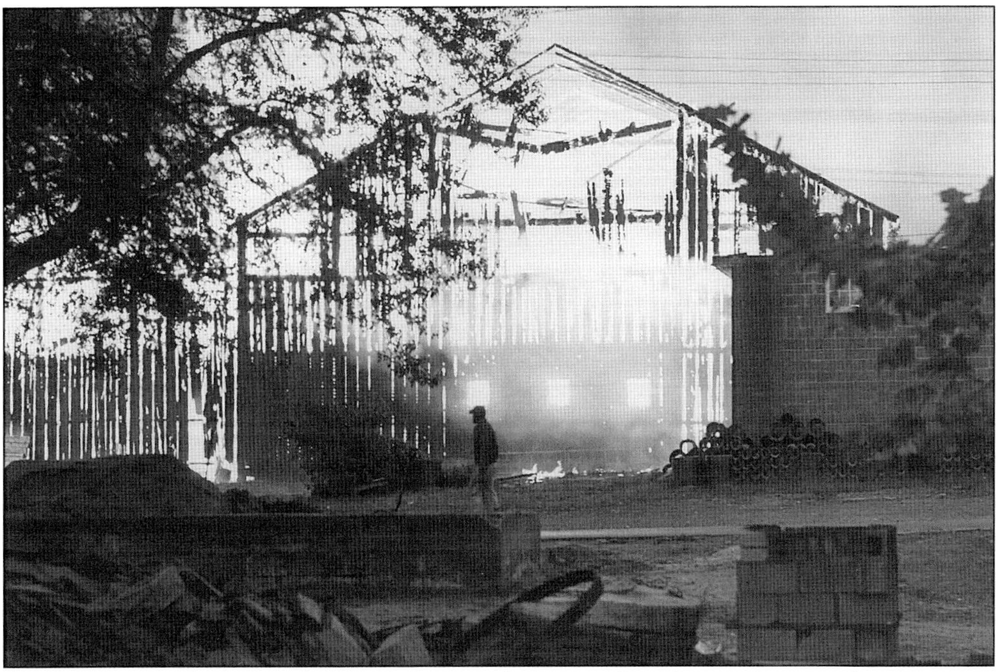

Early in the morning of October 10, 1957, a fire erupted in the Leedom Lumber Company yard. The fire threatened the old wooden buildings in downtown Yardley. Local photographers Frederick and Lucille Eiffert documented the blaze. Owner Lewis Leedom often recalled how water from the Delaware Canal was used to fight the blaze. The yard was turned into a parking lot.

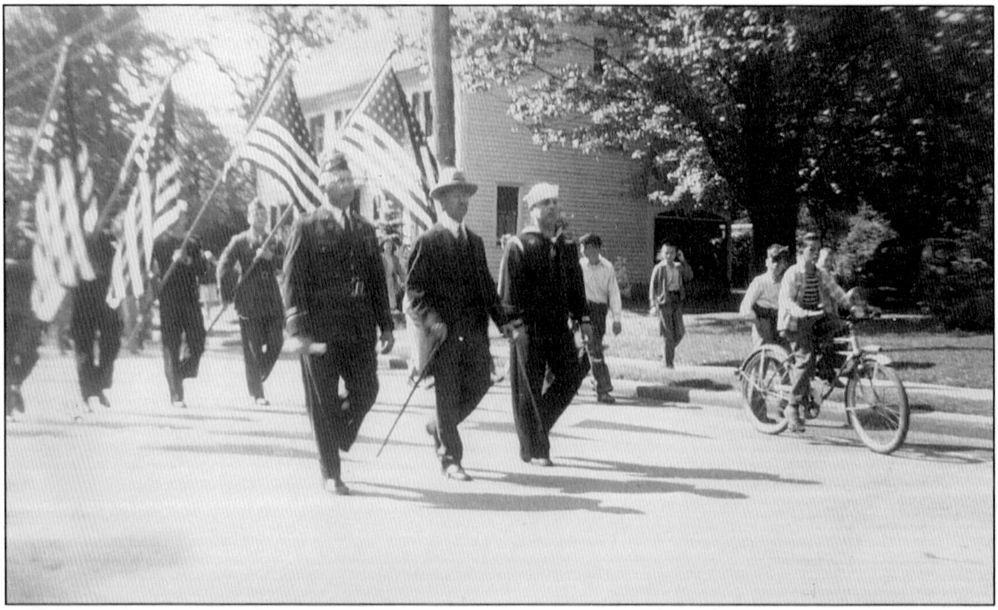

Algernon S. Cadwallader led the Memorial Day parade, *c.* 1947. Mr. Cadwallader (1886–1962) served as burgess, and was the grandson and namesake of Yardley's first burgess. Everyone knew his signature hat and cane.

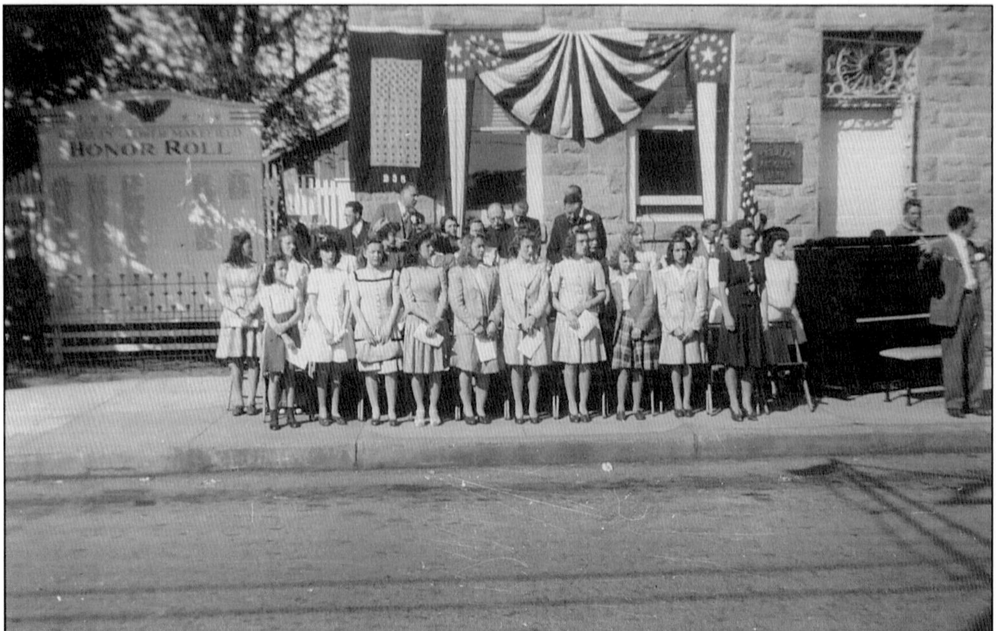

The Lower Makefield Chorus and Band performed during an Honor Roll dedication in May 1943.

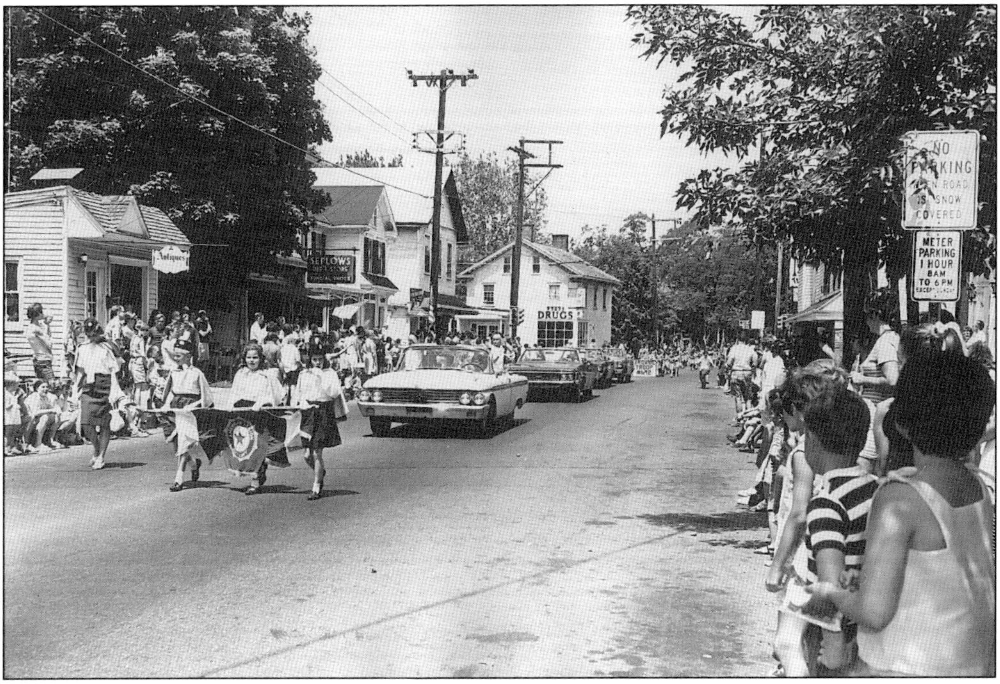

Memorial Day parades, organized by the Knowles-Doyle American Legion and the Veterans of Foreign Wars Post 639, have been a Yardley tradition for decades. Most parades start in the Maplevale development outside of town and proceed up Main Street to the American Legion building. Borough and township officials, the Pennsbury High School band, police and fire departments, and a variety of community groups join local veterans in the annual celebration.

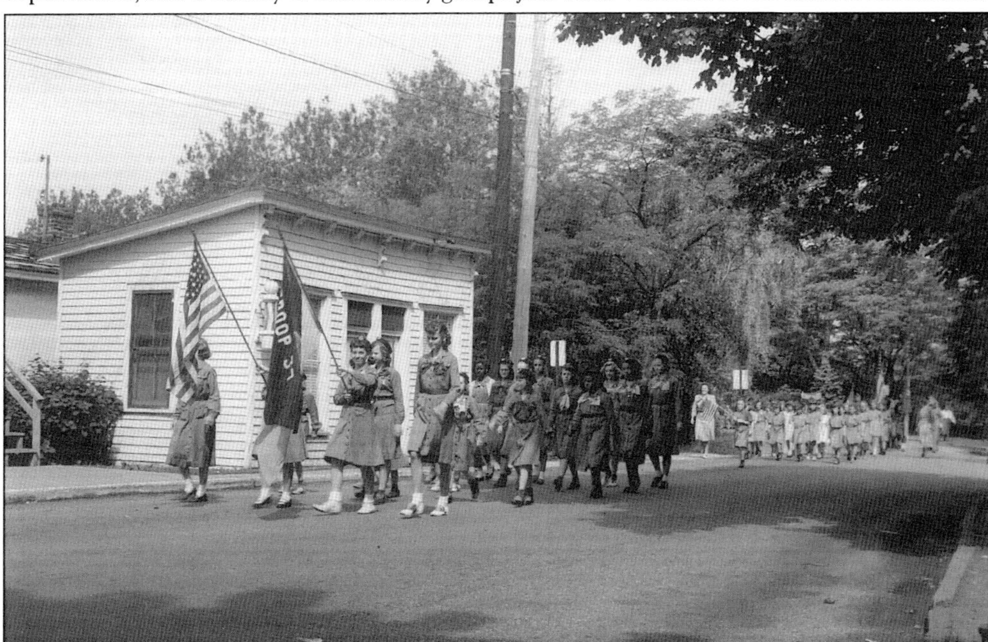

A troop of Girl Scouts marches past Archie Gallagher's barbershop in the 1951 Memorial Day Parade.

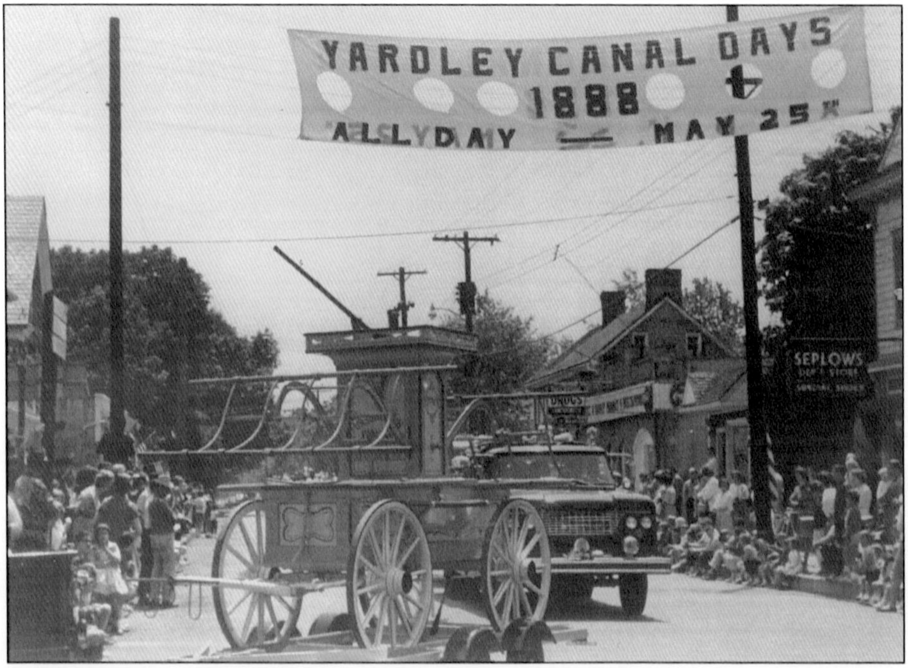

The roots of Yardley's present "Harvest Day" date to 1963 when the Carl F. Norberg Research Center, a subsidiary of the Electric Storage Battery Company, planned the "Canal Days" event. On May 25, Parade Marshall J. H. Chrismer led floats, bands, horseback riders, and antique cars down Main Street to McDonald's field on College Avenue. The success of Canal Days led to the organization of the Colonial Yardley Historical Association.

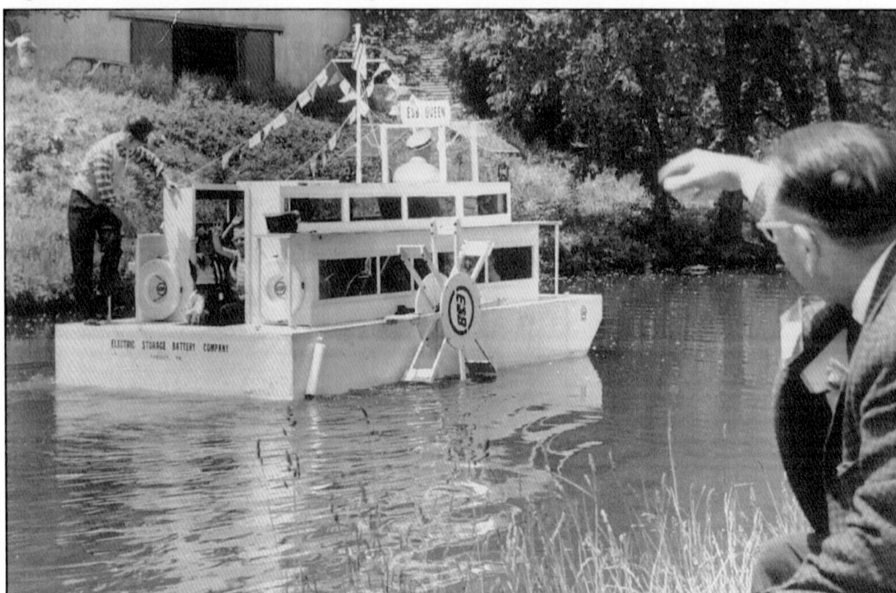

The showpiece of "Canal Days" was the "ESB," a small battery-powered paddle wheel boat. Parents as well as children swarmed all over the boat from the early morning until dark. E.J. Dwyer looks on as Skipper Leroy Solomon and Tom Prall take the boat on its maiden cruise on the canal.

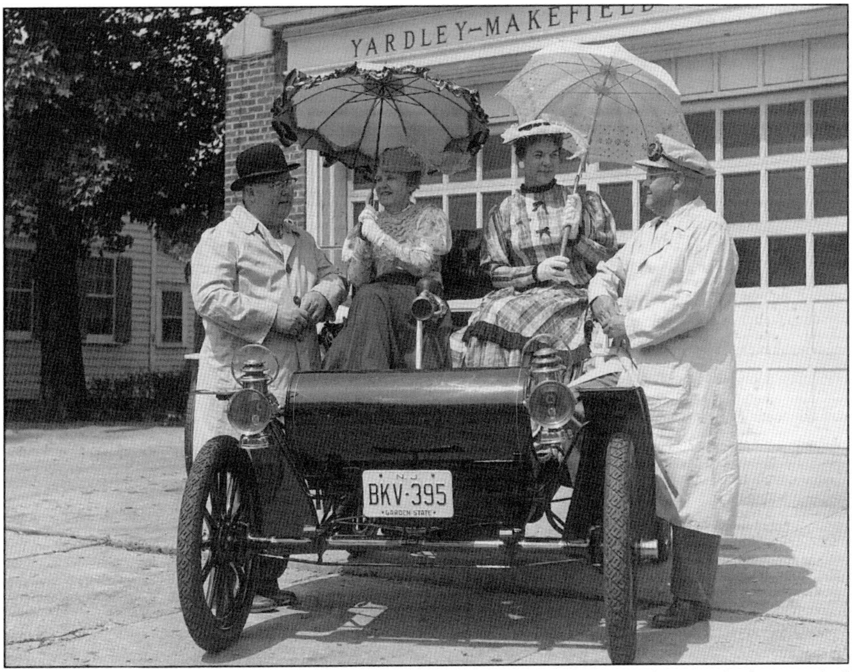

Costumed employees of the Carl F. Norberg Research Center posed outside borough hall in a battery-operated car during Canal Days. A gaslight era theme was chosen in honor of the company's 75th anniversary.

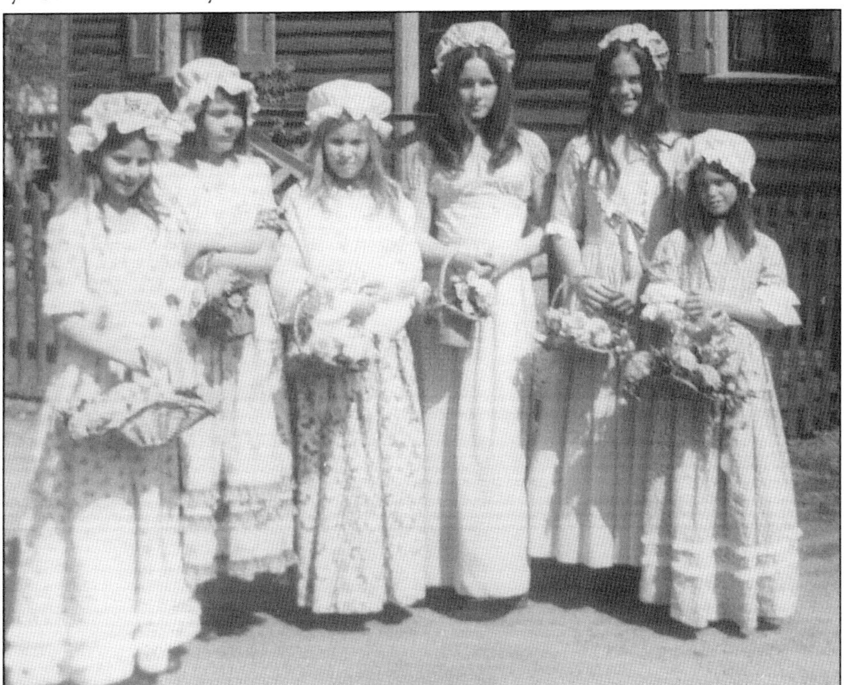

Dressed in Colonial costume during one of several Colonial-era street festivals held in Yardley during the 1960s, from left to right, are Linda Chamberlain, Nadine O'Gorman, Katy Roches, Renee Roches, Lynn De Coursey, and Sue Hensler.

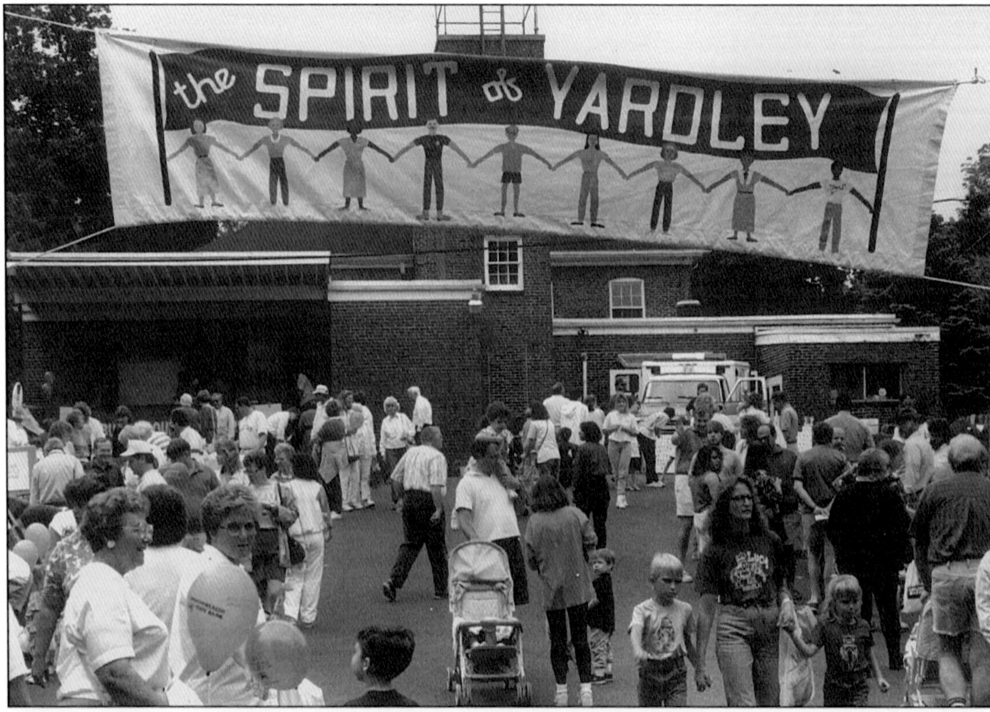

On September 10, 1970, Mayor John B. Cole proclaimed September 19 as Harvest Day. Activities during the day included various competitions, a flea market, craft demonstrations, silent movies, carriage rides, and an old-fashioned country-dance.

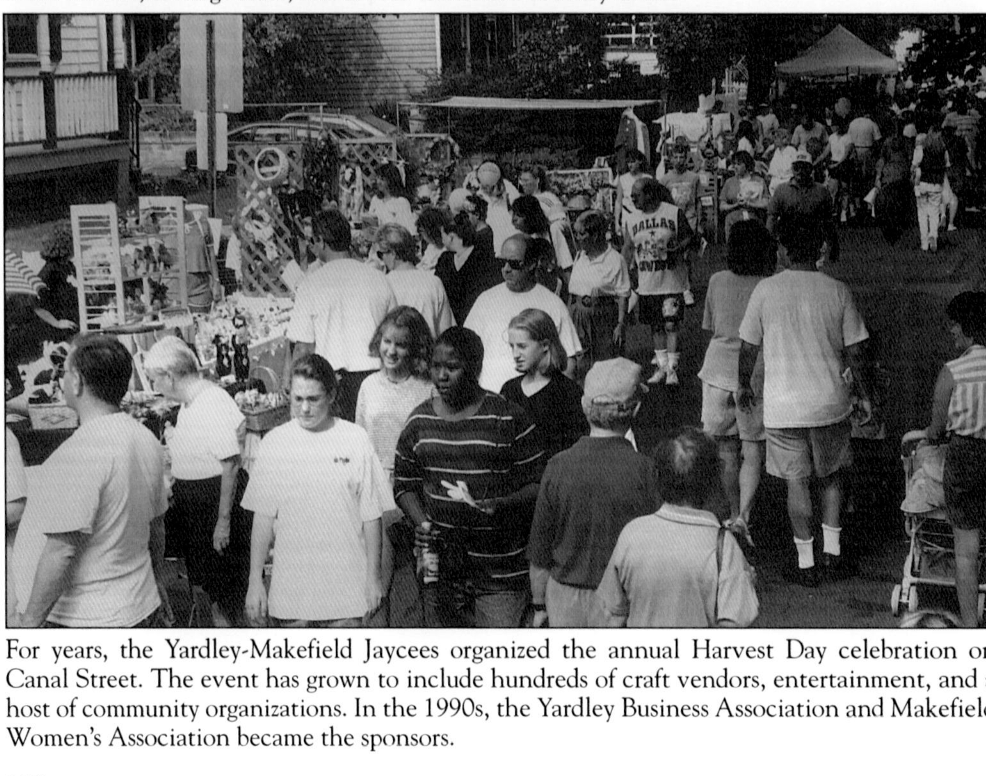

For years, the Yardley-Makefield Jaycees organized the annual Harvest Day celebration on Canal Street. The event has grown to include hundreds of craft vendors, entertainment, and a host of community organizations. In the 1990s, the Yardley Business Association and Makefield Women's Association became the sponsors.

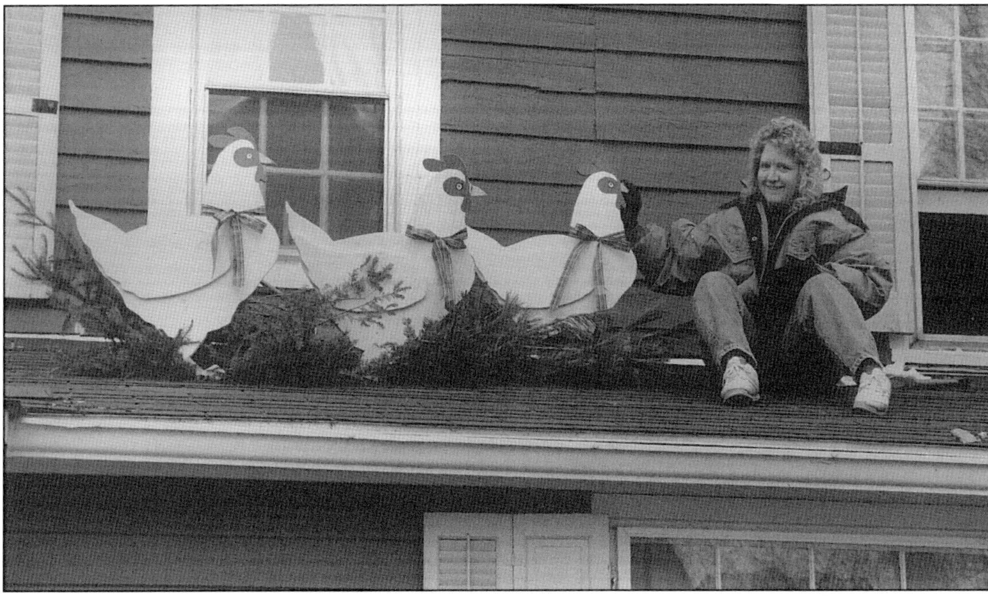

Since at least the 1960s, Canal Street has been a symbol of Yardley's history and community spirit. Residents host the annual Harvest Day, hold neighborhood yard sales, and annually display the "Twelve Days of Christmas." Beth Thompson places "three French hens" on the roof of her Canal Street home.

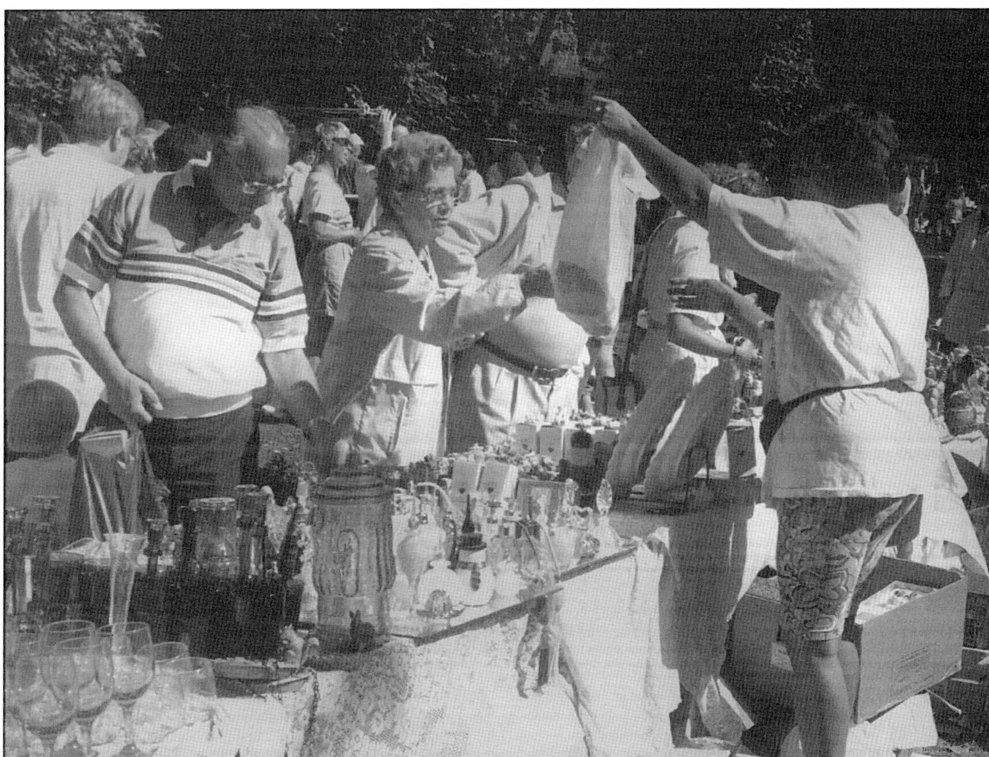

Bargains abound at the Yardley Friends Flea Market, a traditional September event held on the meeting house grounds on North Main Street.

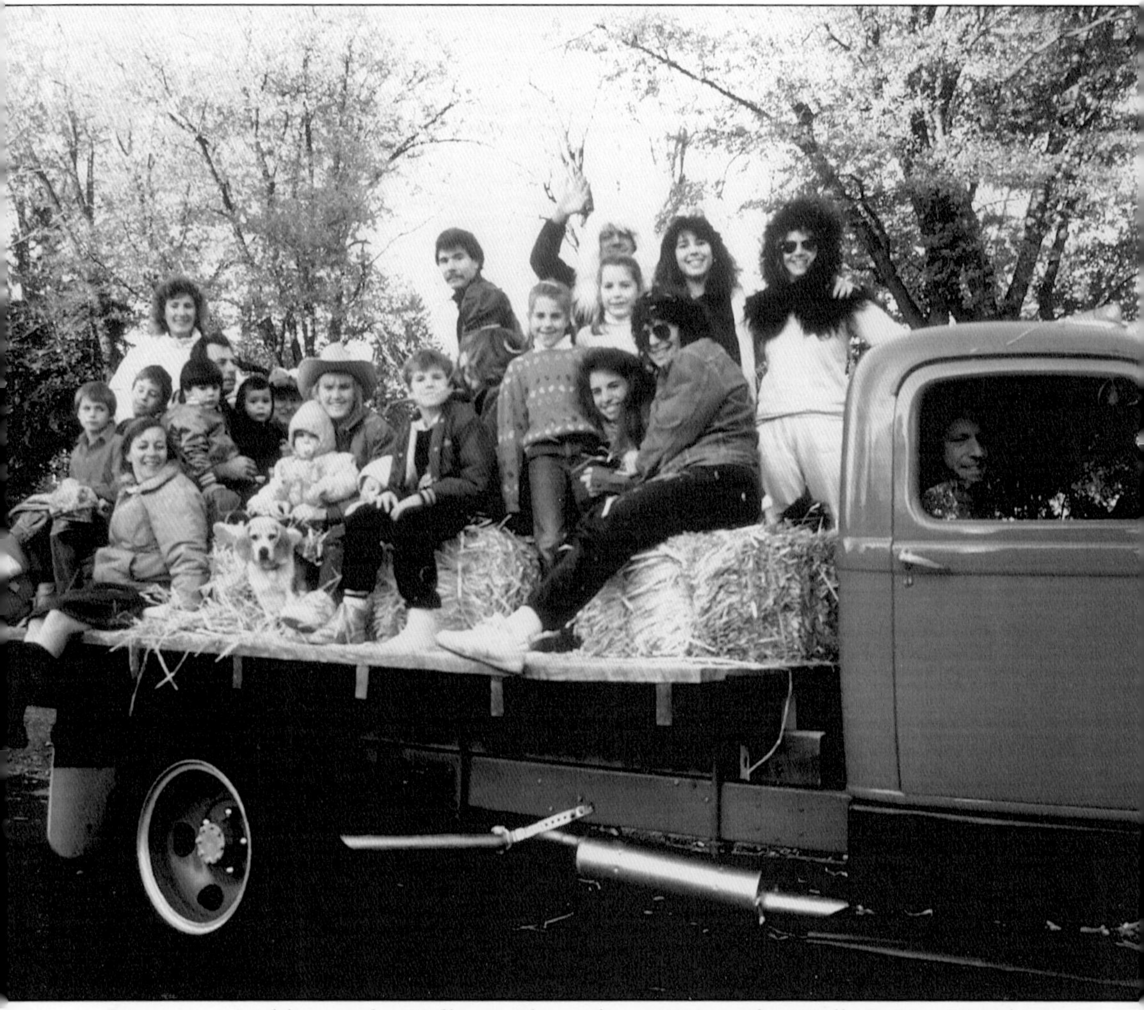

Rivermawr neighbors took a Halloween hay ride in 1988 on the "Will 'O Wisp." Brad Varney purchased the 1937 red Dodge truck from Sam Yardley in 1974. The truck, which had been used to haul grain, can usually be seen in Yardley's Memorial Day parade.

Five

PEOPLE

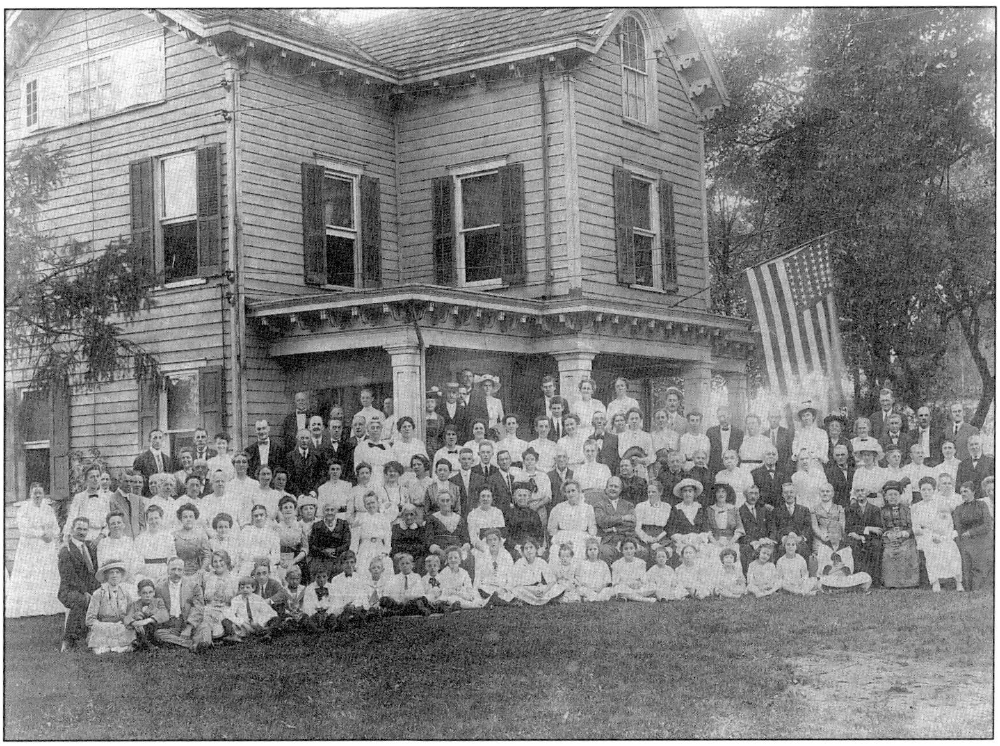

A community's history is more than organizations, buildings, and events. History is the story of people. Yardley's history is the story of thousands of individuals and hundreds of families. Some left a photographic record; others are only a memory. In 1909, Edward W. Twining's only son, Stephen B. Twining, organized a family reunion—an event that continued annually into the 1930s. Over one hundred family members gathered in front of the Twining home on West Afton Avenue for this family portrait.

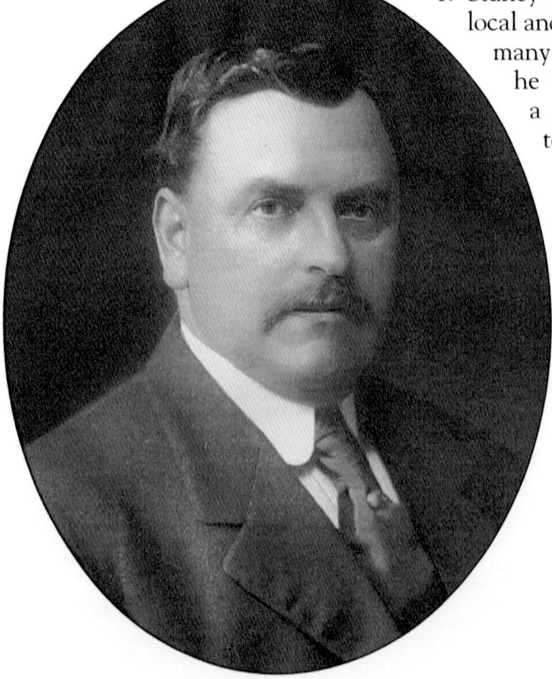

T. Sidney Cadwallader (1861–1950) was active in local and county politics. He was also a member of many community organizations. As a young man he managed a local creamery and operated a general store in Yardley. Eventually he took over the family business, the Yardley Mills Company, and moved into Lakeside. His parents were Algernon and Susan Yardley Cadwallader.

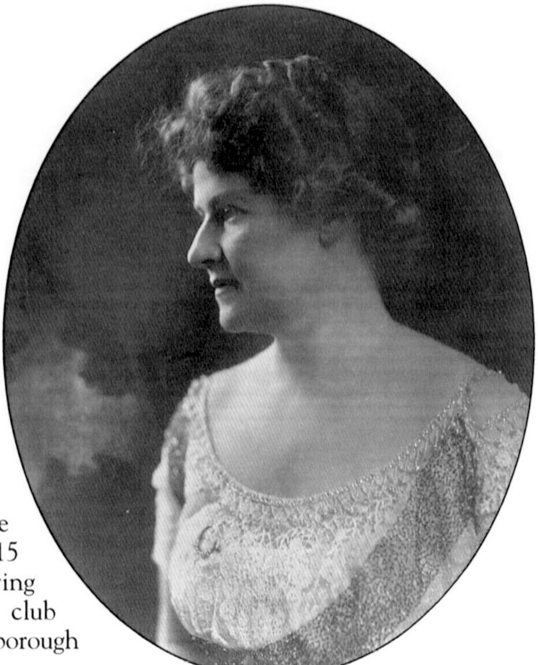

Mrs. A. J. Cadwallader was president of the Yardley Civic Club from its founding in 1915 to 1919. The club was dedicated to improving the conditions of the community. Many club members were the wives and daughters of borough officials and local businessmen.

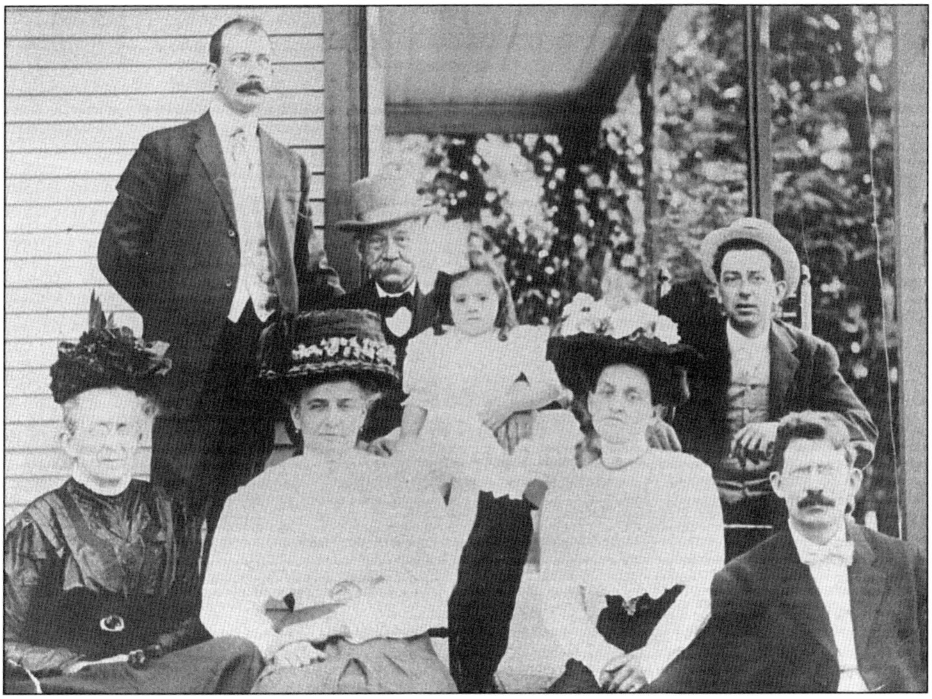

Watson W. Cadwallader and members of his family gathered for a photograph on the front porch of their West Afton home. Pictured in this *c.* 1900 photograph, from left to right, are as follows: (bottom row) Mary (nee Slack,) Mary, Laura, and George; (top row) Gilbert, W. Watson, Catherine, and Agnew Cadwallader.

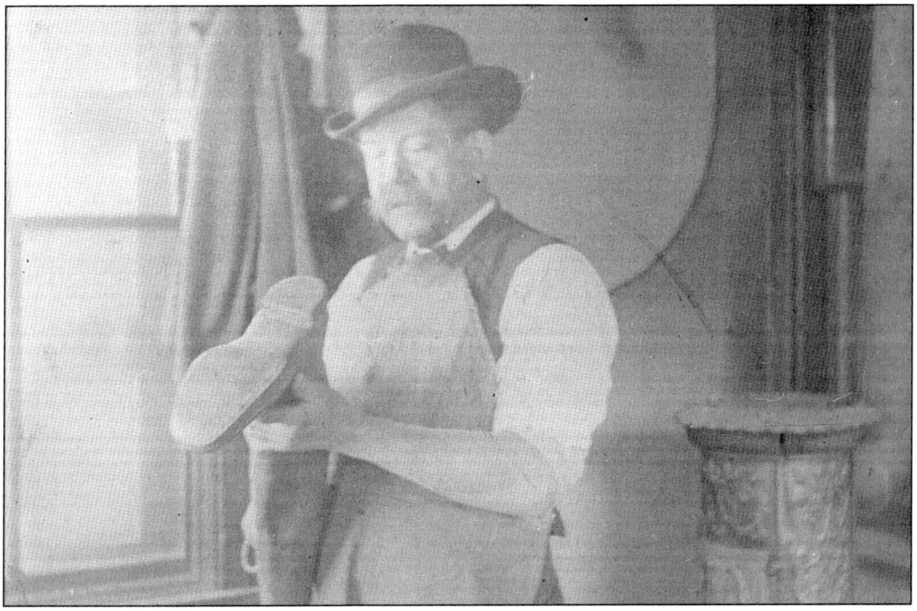

Watson W. Cadwallader (1844–1911) operated a shoemaking shop at 17 East Afton Avenue. Against the pacifist tradition of his Quaker upbringing, he enlisted in the Civil War. Watson and his wife Mary Ellen Slack had six children. For many years, their son Charles G. operated the Yardley Florist on South Main Street.

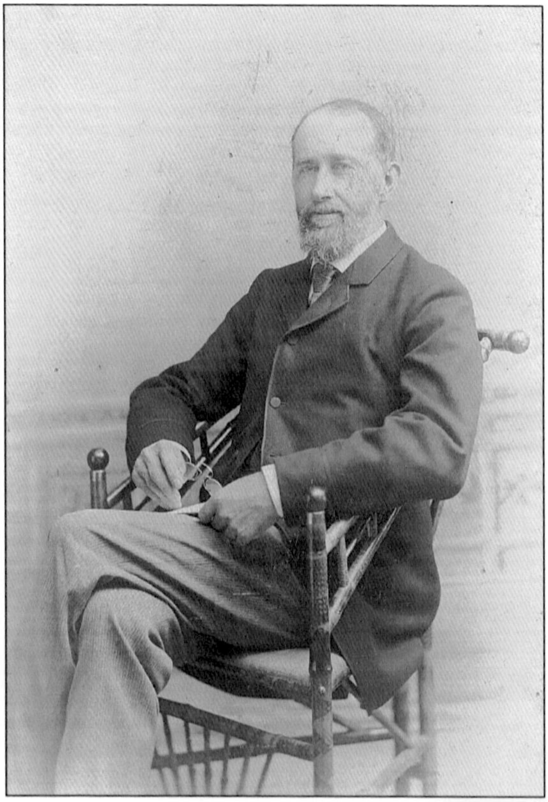

Stephen B. Twining was the son of Edward Twining, the first president of Yardley Borough Council. His family operated a farm and quarry on the hill between Afton and Reading Avenues. Stephen B. served on The Yardley Borough council when this portrait was taken, *c.* 1910.

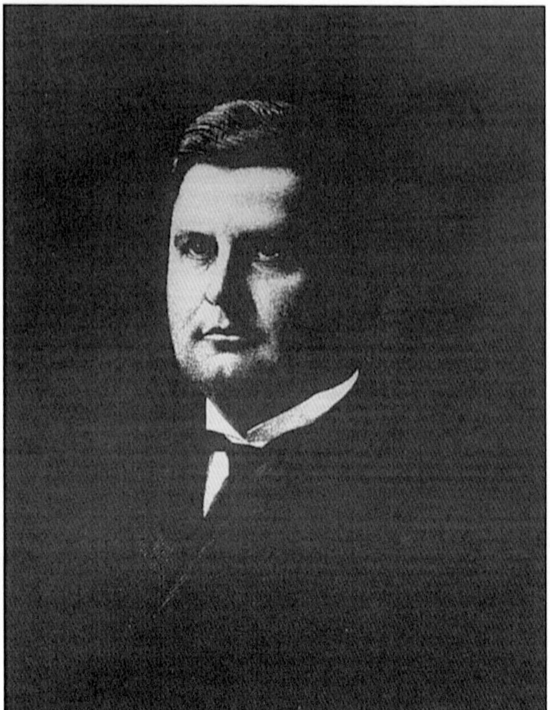

Charles Twining Eastburn was born in 1873. He was described as one of the most active and successful businessmen in Bucks County. In 1894, he assumed responsibility for the Twining quarries and became the largest stone dealer in Eastern Pennsylvania. In 1903, he married Margaret B. Phillips. He was active in the community, serving on borough council, the board of health, and as a member of the Fire Company.

Dr. Abraham Livezy (1821–1896) was born in Solebury. He attended Jefferson Medical College, and in 1872 moved to Yardley. He established a medical practice, opened a drug store, and built a home on South Main Street. Dr. Livezy taught at the Female Medical College in Philadelphia, contributed to medical journals, and wrote an advice column for *Peterson's Ladies' Magazine*.

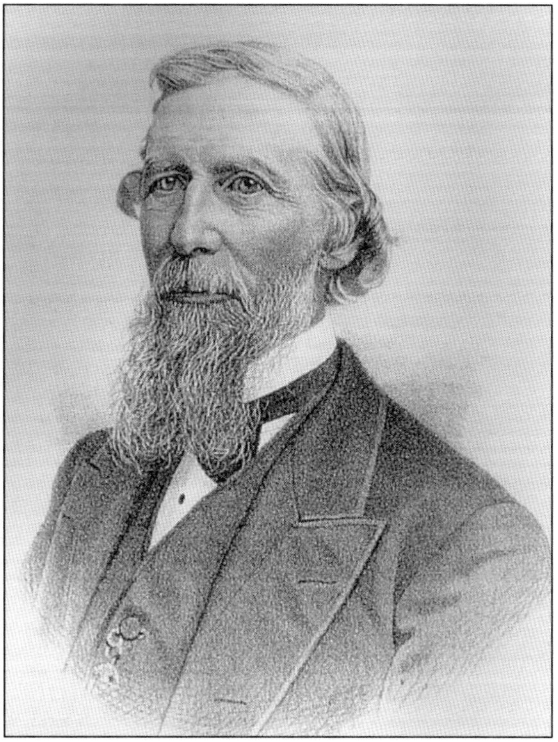

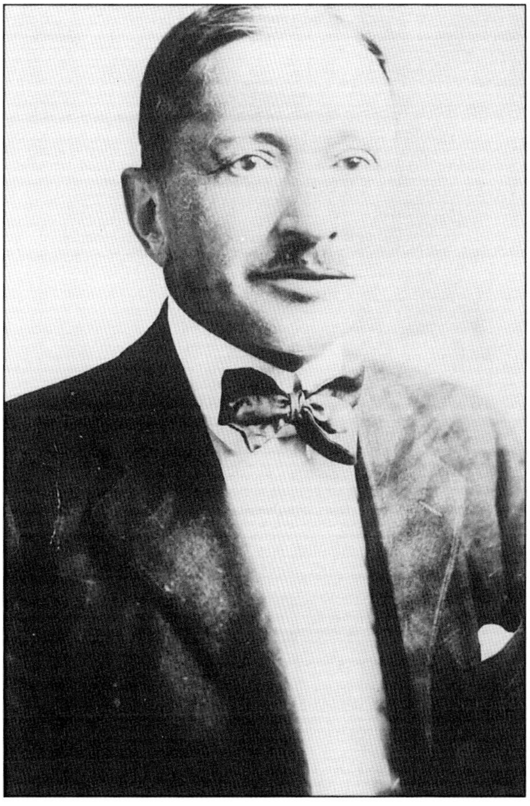

Yardley has been home to a number of small-town, "country" doctors. One of the better-known, Dr. Henry Linn Bassett, established a home and office at 70 South Main Street. Dr. Basset served on borough council, for many years was a member of the board of health, and delivered generations of Yardley babies.

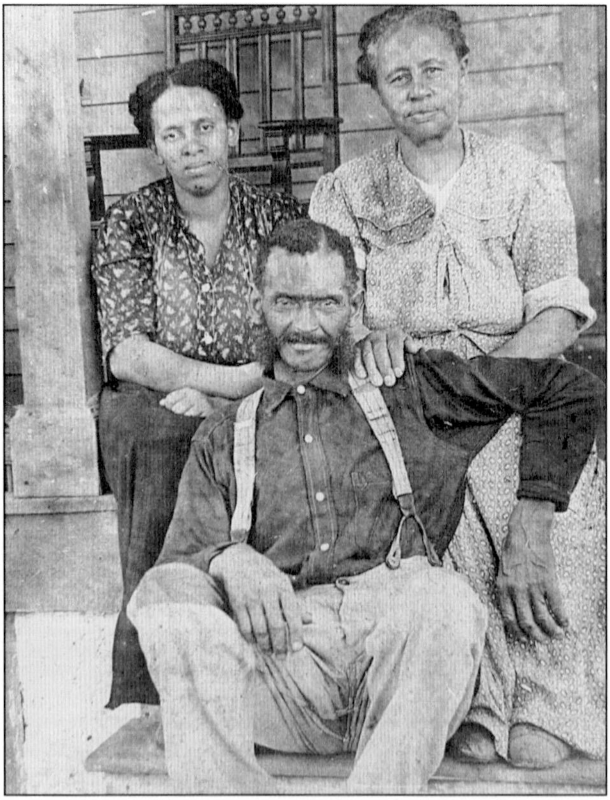

African Americans came to Yardley as slaves and freemen. The Derry family is one of the oldest African-American families in the community. Mary Derry, born in 1790, is listed in the 1850 Lower Makefield census. This undated photograph is of James and Julia Derry and their daughter Della (left) in front of their home.

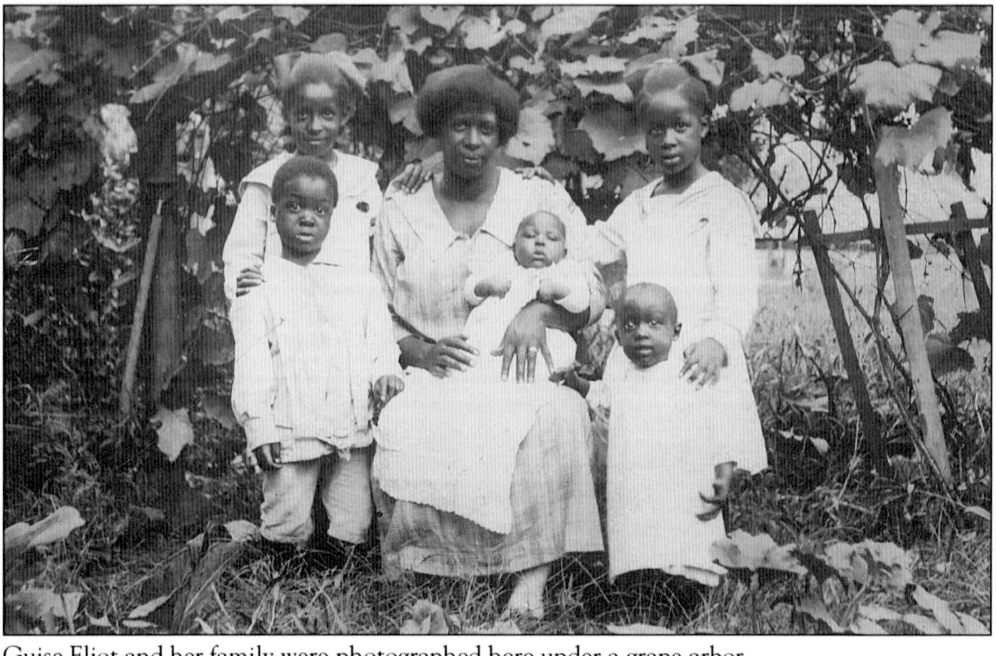

Guise Eliot and her family were photographed here under a grape arbor.

In 1899, Albert Johnson left Yardley and went to Boston in search of work. The letters he sent to his mother in Yardley described meetings in Boston to protest lynching in the South.

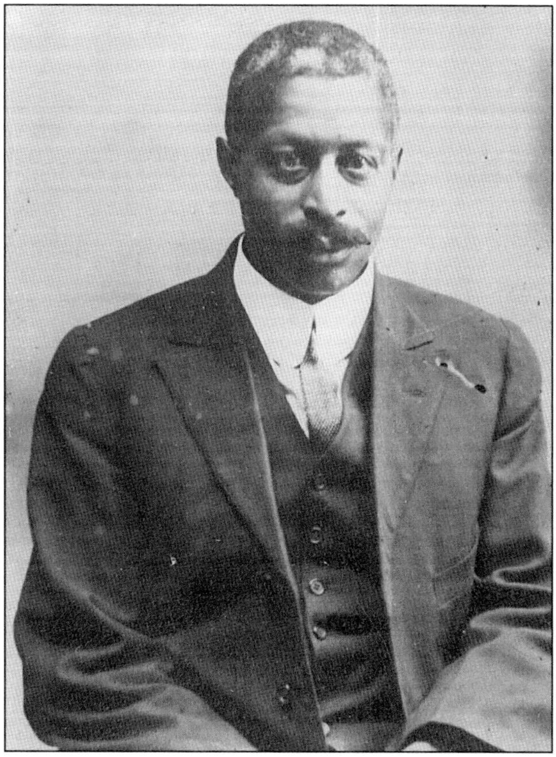

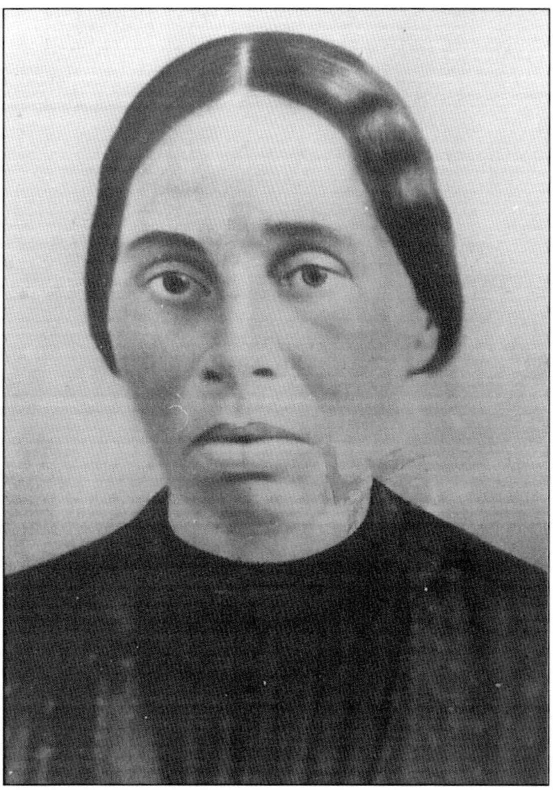

Julia B. Miller, who was part Cherokee, was born in the South in 1855, moved to Yardley and married John Derry.

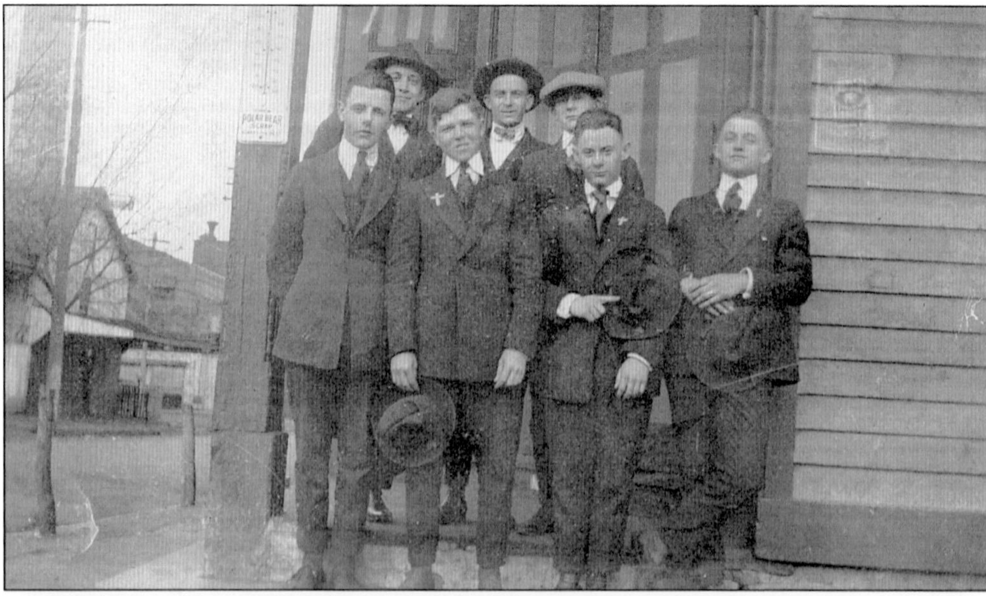

It was Palm Sunday, *c.* 1920, when this group of young men gathered on Pursell's corner for a photograph. Pictured from left to right are the following: (front row) Cliff Doyle, Ned Baird, Buck Smith, and Henry Bergen; (back row) Bill Gallagher, Bill Smith, and Mr. Baird.

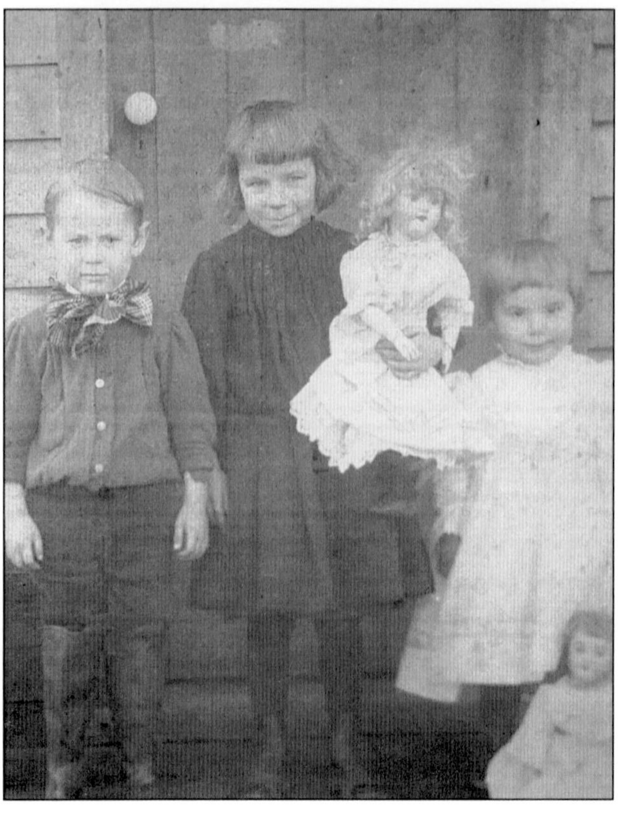

Some Irish Catholic workers settled in Yardley after the construction of the Delaware Canal in the 1830s. Their numbers increased around 1900 when several industries were established in the borough. William and Annie Smith settled on Pennsylvania Avenue. The Smith children, Buck, Anna, and Alice, and some friends are pictured in this photograph, *c.* 1907.

T. Galvin, Earl Denahan, and a friend dressed up for this studio photograph. When the photograph was taken around 1915, there wasn't a photography studio in Yardley. Residents had photographs taken in Trenton or on the Boardwalk in Atlantic City.

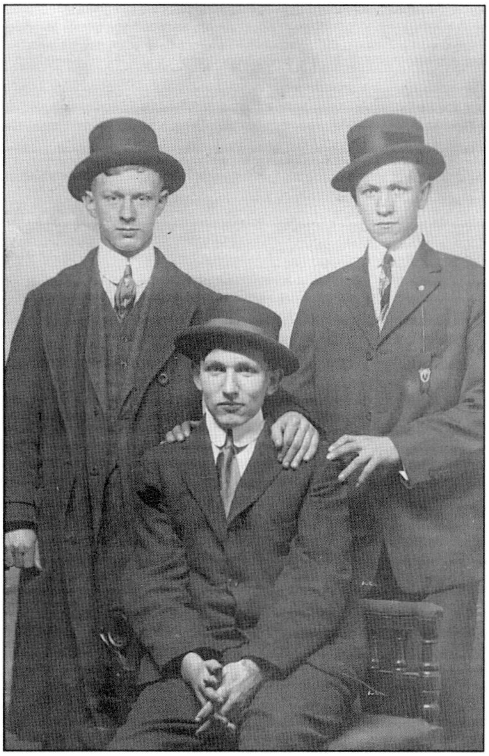

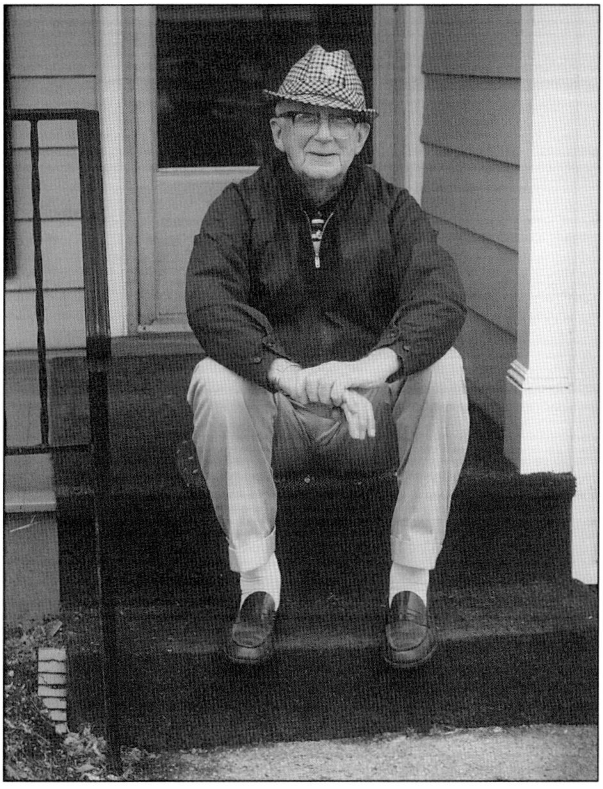

Vince Casey was photographed in 1984 in front of his home at 7 South Main Street. The family once ran an ice cream parlor in the front room. Vince was an active member of the Fire Company and one of Yardley's classic storytellers.

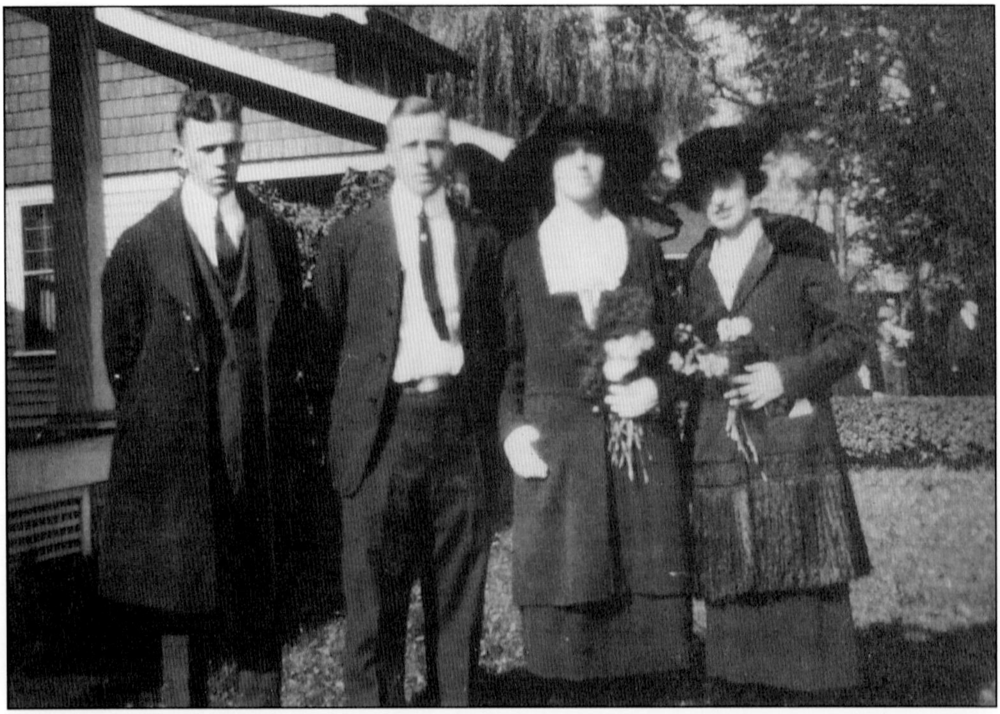

Joseph and Inez Yardley moved into the family home at 73 North Delaware Avenue, *c.* 1915. Joseph operated a service station on East Afton Avenue; his son Harvey operated the station through the 1980s. Joseph's brother Sam lived on the "Will of the Wisp" farm outside of town.

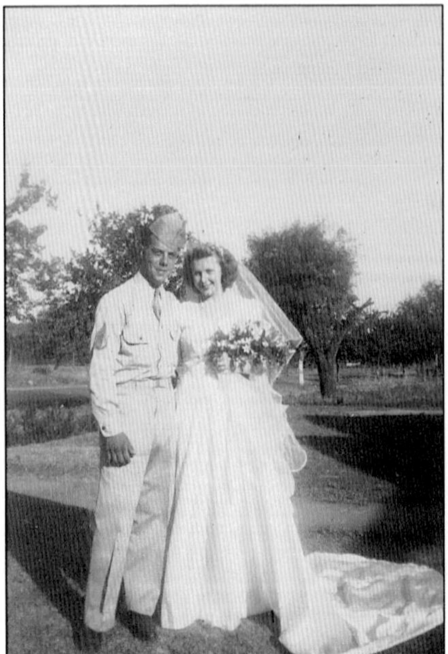

John and Dolly Giambattisto were married August 5, 1943. A year later, Mrs. Giambattisto received notice that John was seriously wounded during WWII combat in France. Several days later she was notified that he had died. Sergeant Giambattisto had never seen his three-month old son, John.

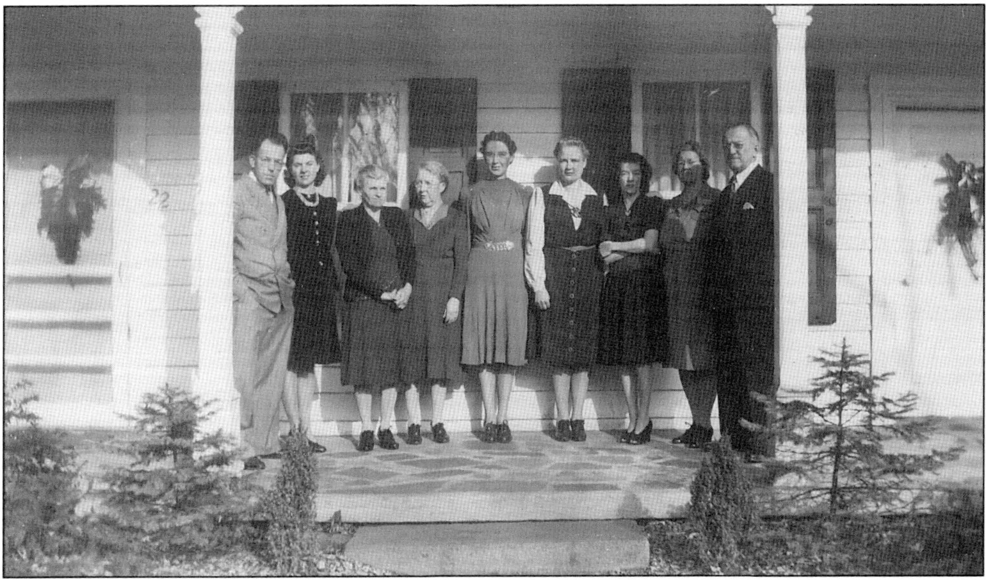

Gathered on the porch of the Blaker home on South Main Street in 1942, from left to right, are: Alvin & Gertrude Blaker, Estella Blaker, Annie Flowers, Anna Wright, Helen Blaker, Ida Blaker, and Edna and John Kidder.

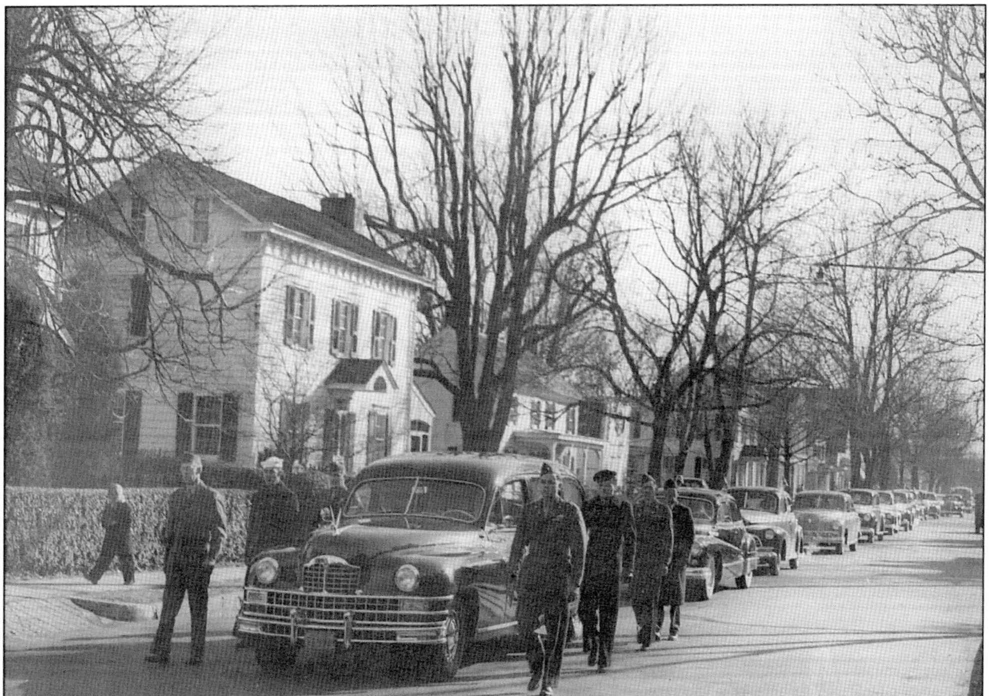

A military Honor Guard headed by Lieutenant Colonel Robert C. Belville and Funeral Cortege for Sergeant Thomas E. Neely passed down Main Street on December 20, 1947. Sgt. Neely, a ranger with the 38th Infantry, Second Division, was killed in Normandy on June 17, 1944. He was buried in the Catholic cemetery on River Road. Art Megin is on the left.

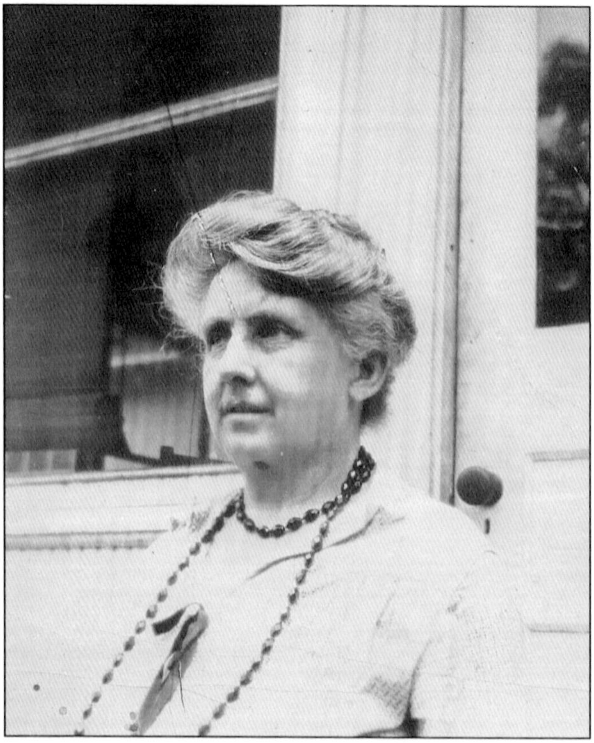

Mattie Wist (shown here *c.* 1920) and her husband, Frank, operated a store on the northwest corner of Main and Afton. For decades this intersection was known as Wist's Corner, and was a hub of activity in downtown Yardley.

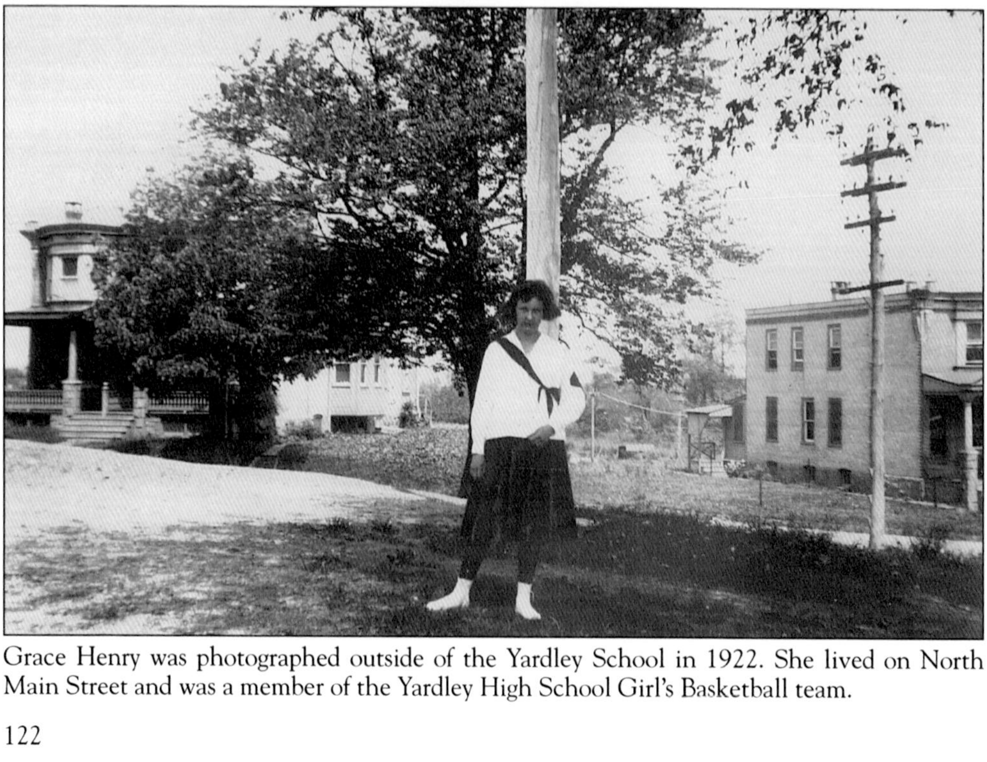

Grace Henry was photographed outside of the Yardley School in 1922. She lived on North Main Street and was a member of the Yardley High School Girl's Basketball team.

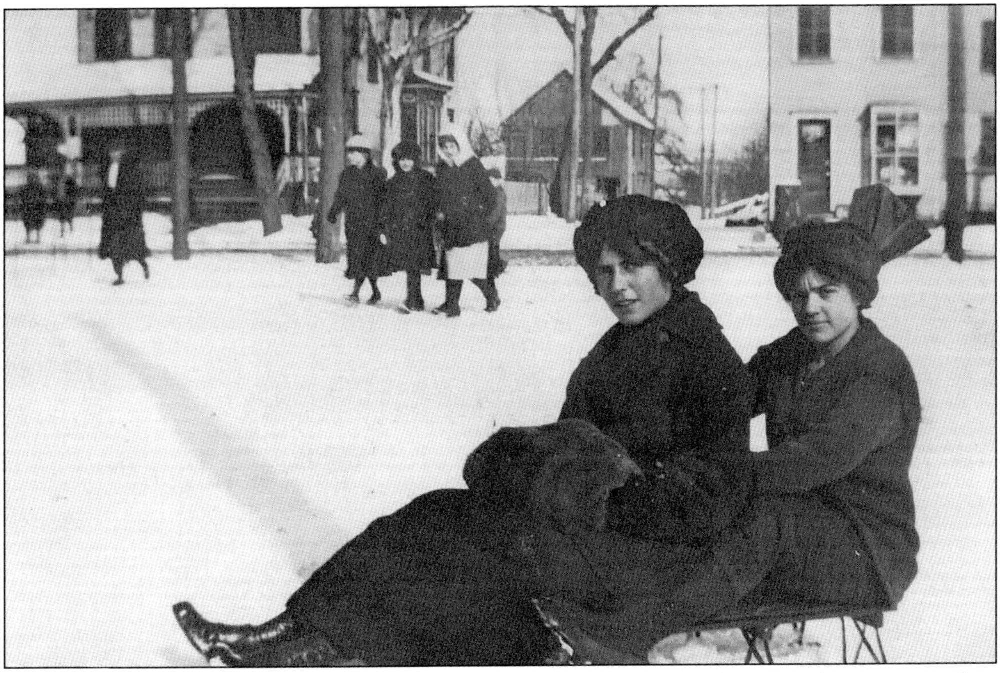

Many Yardley residents recall sledding on College Avenue. One local story is about a young boy who sledded under a streetcar and he lived to tell the tale. Inez Yardley and a friend stopped for a picture at the bottom of the hill, c. 1915.

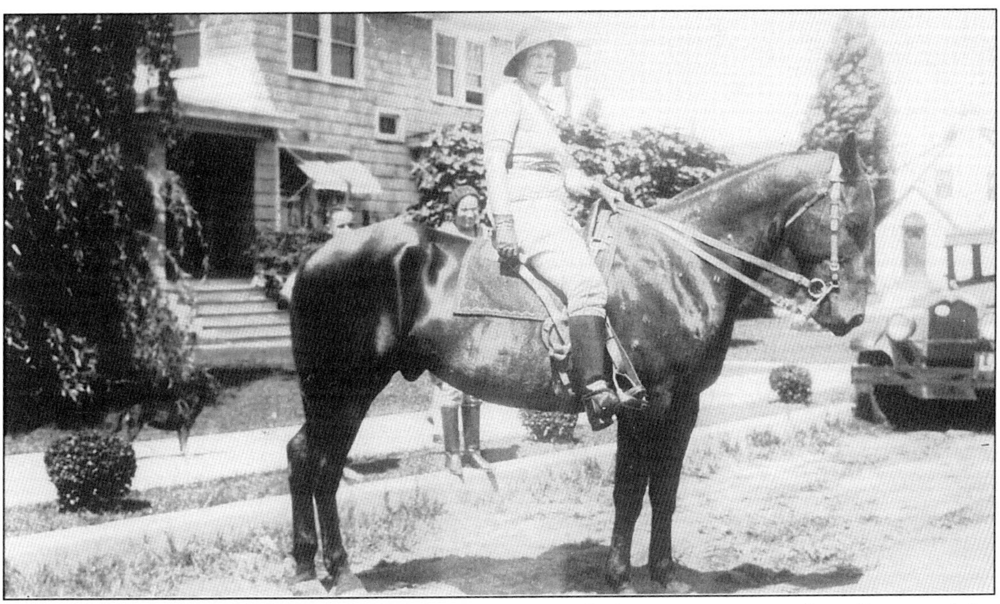

Helen Mackey and her horse were ready to compete with the increasing number of automobiles on local streets, c. 1920.

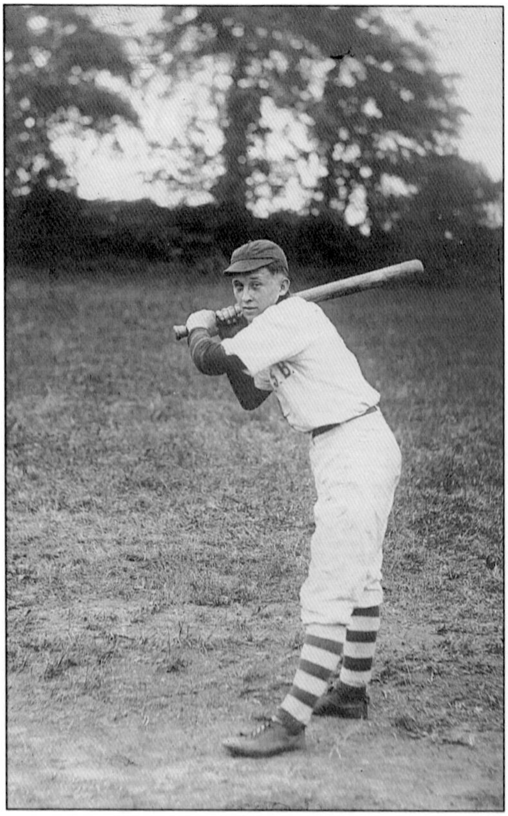

Frank Gallagher was a member of the Yardley baseball team. This portrait, c. 1915, was found in a scrapbook with the caption, "Some Pose, huh!" The son of Columbus "Lum" Gallagher and Alice Powers Gallagher, Frank later married Ada Smith. Frank's father Lum, whose family lived at 65 East Afton, operated a blacksmith shop on South Main Street.

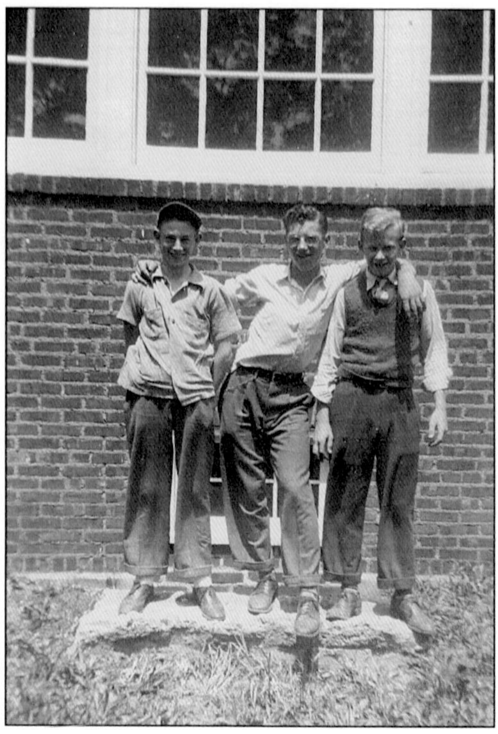

Three friends, Junior Coulton, Bob Sands, and Bud Smith are photographed together in front of the Yardley School in 1941. Bud became the Mayor of Newtown Borough.

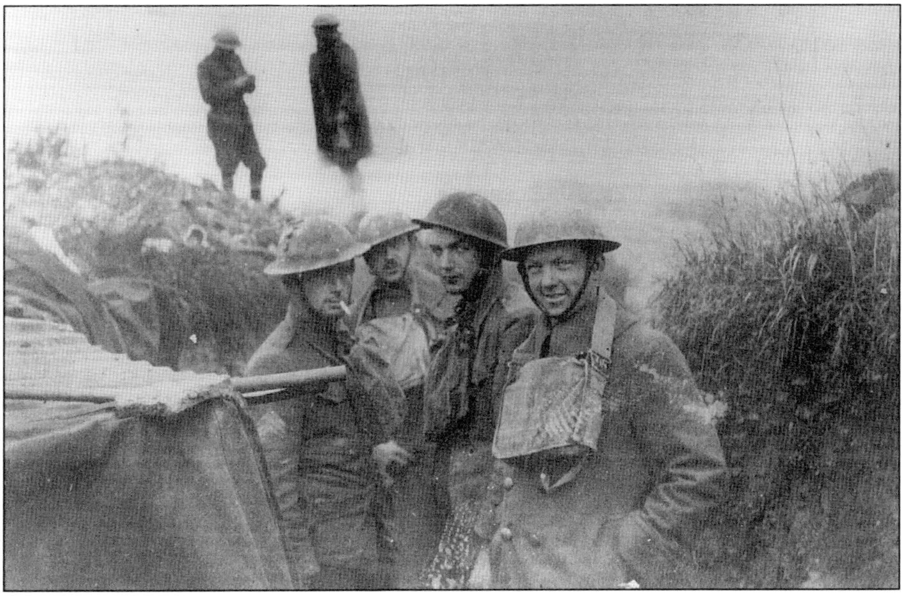

Virgil Kauffman (right) was one of 81 sons and daughters of Yardley and Lower Makefield who served in WWI. Virgil came from a large family that grew up on South Main Street. During the war he served as a photographer in the Army Air Corps. He was a pioneer in aerial photography and founded the Aero Service Corporation.

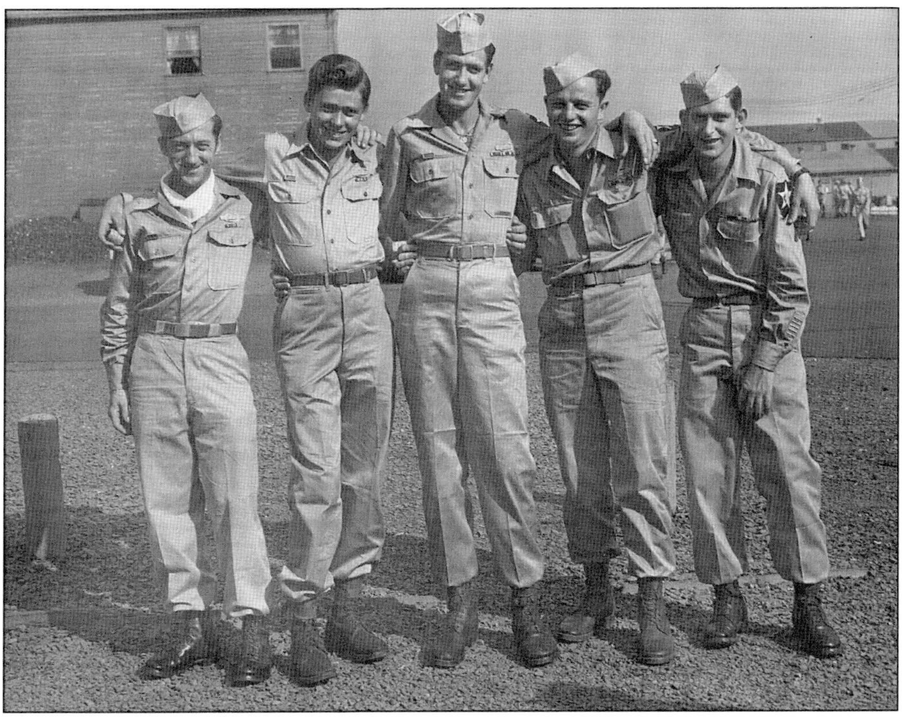

Wesley "Bing" Francis (left) was one of the many men and women of Yardley who served during WWII. He was the son of George and Minnie Francis, attended the Yardley School, and served in the Second Division, 38th Infantry Regiment, United States Army. The family lived on Brown Street

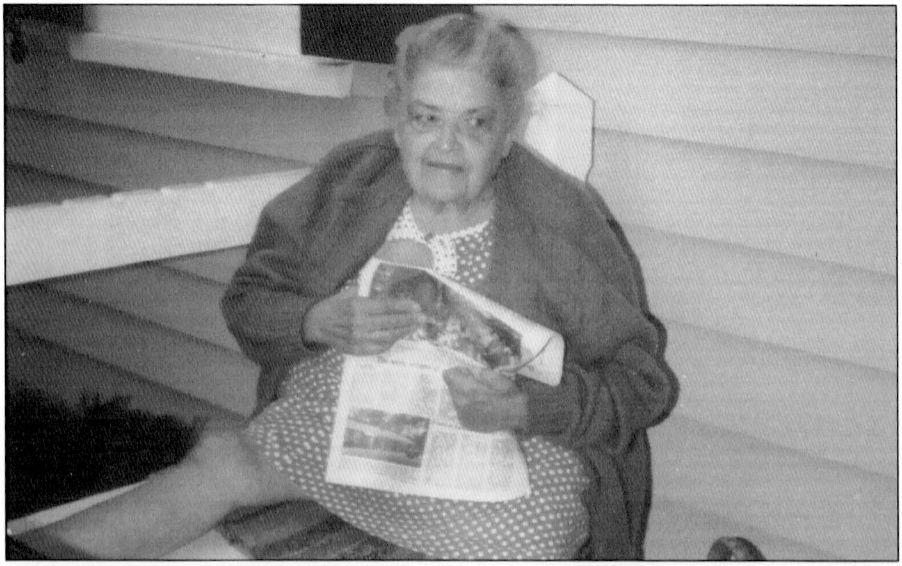

Everyone in Yardley knew Helen Leedom. Residents remember her sitting on the porch of her Main Street home or behind the counter at the Leedom Lumber Company. Born in 1903, Helen's parents moved to Yardley in 1909 when her father, Lewis C. Leedom, became a partner in a local lumber business. In 1925, the Canal Side Coal and Lumber Yard became the Leedom Lumber Company.

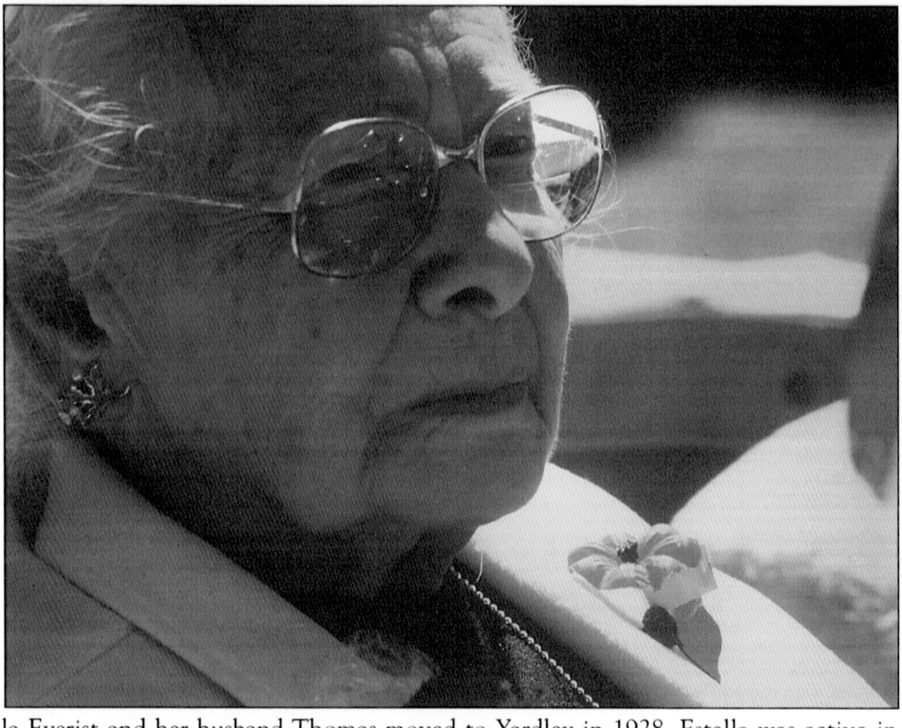

Estella Everist and her husband Thomas moved to Yardley in 1928. Estella was active in the Yardley Civic Club and the Martha Washington Garden Club. For 30 years she described herself as "maid of all work" at the Yardley Community Center. A chief Navy yeoman during WWI, Estella rode proudly in Yardley Memorial Day parades.

Catherine Belville lived at Lanrick Manor, a beautiful Federal-style mansion on River Road built about 1805. Her interest in history led to her involvement in the promotion and preservation of Yardley's history. She was the inspiration and one of the founding members of the Colonial Yardley Historic Association. In 1970 the word "colonial" was dropped and the Yardley Historical Association was formed.

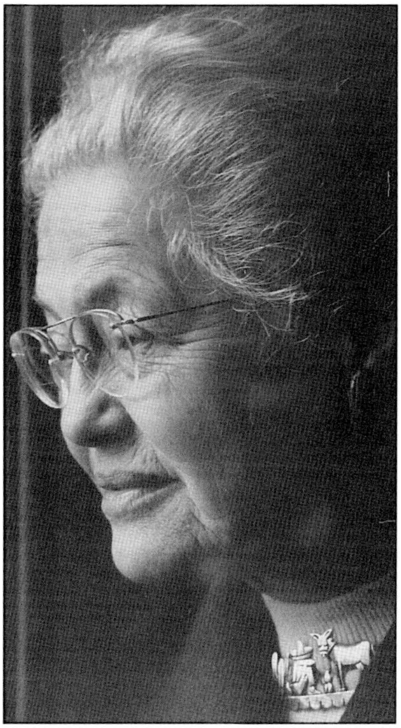

Annamae Bakun participated in Lakeside Strawberry Festivals sponsored by the Yardley Historical Association, c. 1972. She moved to Yardley in 1959. Her interest in old homes, antiques, and colonial life led to her involvement in the Colonial Yardley Historic Association. Annamae has served as President of the Yardley Historic Association for several decades.

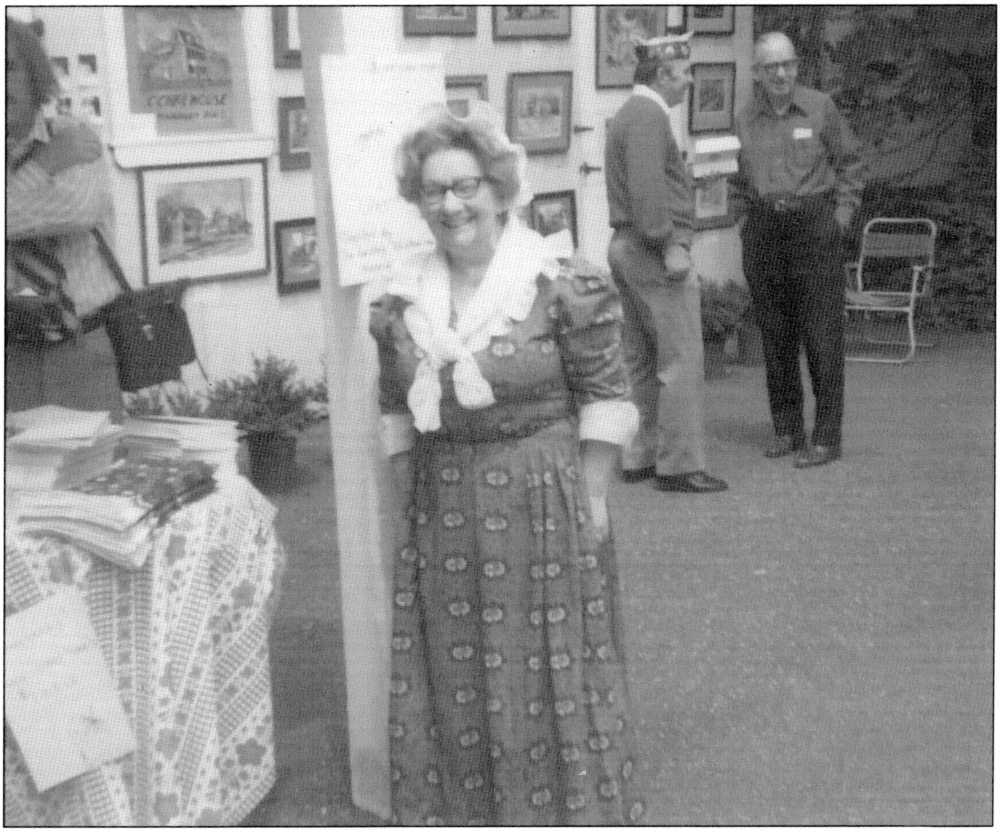

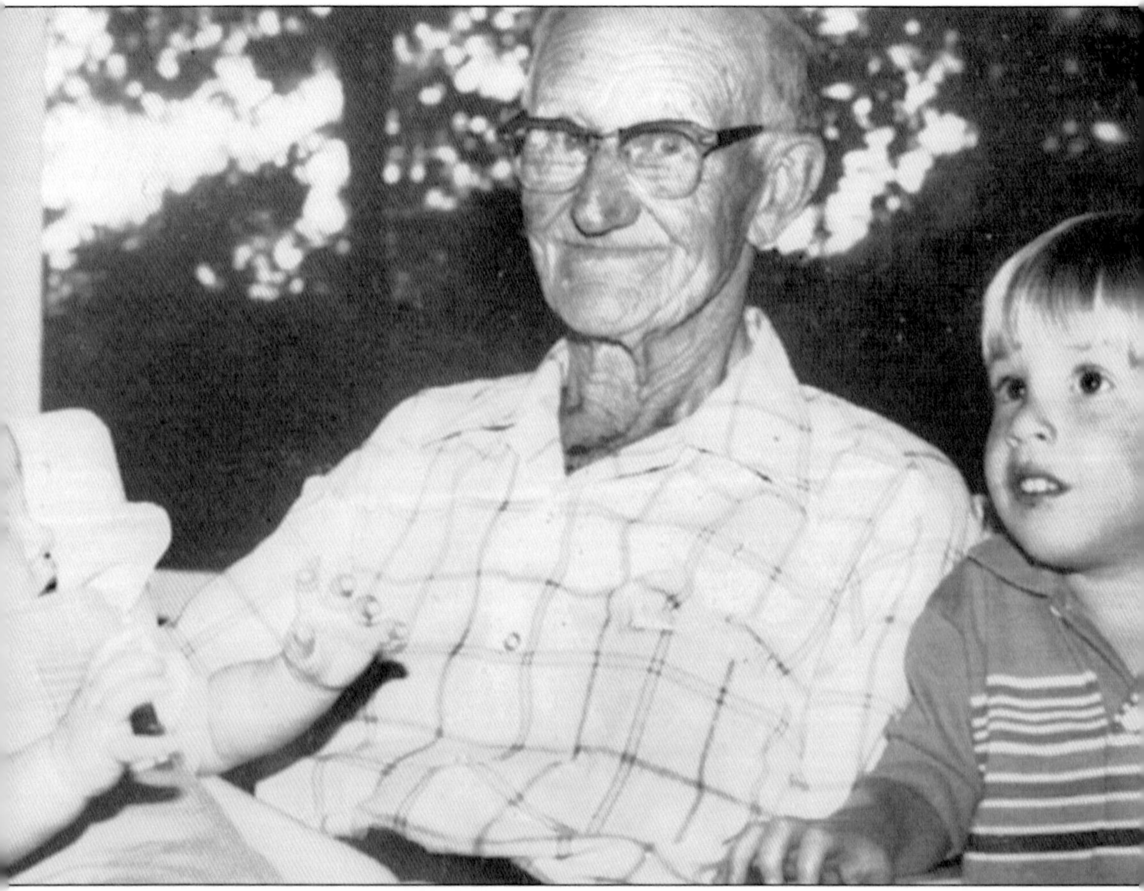

Chester Lear was born in Riegelsville, PA, in 1894. Two years later, his father became a canal locktender, and the family moved to Lock House Number Six above Woodside Road. Chester frequently entertained young and old with his tales of the past and memories of life along the canal. "When I was a little shaver, boats would come in bunches, anywhere from 40 to 50 boats would go through Yardley from four to ten (p.m.) . . . (the canal) was the only transportation in this village . . . your groceries come in by boat . . . anything you could think of . . . cloth, muslin, gingham and stuff . . . they had a young fellow called a runner . . . I'd run up to the store and tell them . . . old person Cadwallader and them . . . they would go down and buy what they wanted . . ." Chester experienced the end of an era.